The Scalping of the Great Sioux Nation

A Review of My Life on the Rosebud and Pine Ridge Reservations

Philip E. Davis

Hamilton Books
A member of
The Rowman & Littlefield Publishing Group
Lanham • Boulder • New York • Toronto • Plymouth, UK

Hamilton Books
4501 Forbes Boulevard
Suite 200
Lanham, Maryland 20706
Hamilton Books Acquisitions Department (301) 459-3366

Estover Road
Plymouth PL6 7PY
United Kingdom

Printed in the United States of America
British Library Cataloging in Publication Information Available

Library of Congress Control Number: 2009932290
ISBN: 978-0-7618-4825-7 (paperback : alk. paper)
eISBN: 978-0-7618-4826-4

∞™ The paper used in this publication meets the minimum requirements of American National Standard for Information Sciences—Permanence of Paper for Printed Library Materials, ANSI Z39.48-1992

To Etta Mudeater
with best wishes
Phil Davis

To all my friends and relatives,
including especially my two daughters,
who gave me needed encouragement
and useful computer advice, and to all the
other computer geniuses, who by their expertise
and knowledge made this book possible.

Contents

Preface vii

Part I THE AUTOBIOGRAPHICAL AND HISTORICAL CONTEXT

1 Rosebud 3

2 Pine Ridge 21

3 Paha Sapa (Black Hills) 34

4 Fort Laramie Treaty of 1868 42

5 Little Big Horn and Wounded Knee 53

6 Indian Boarding Schools 64

Part II PHILOSOPHICAL REFLECTIONS AND GENERALIZATIONS

7 Scalping of the Great Sioux Nation 79

8 The Underlying Rationale for Dispossession 87

9 Custer's Extraordinary Influence 98

10 Federal Indian Law and Self-Governance 114

11 Tribal Sovereignty and Casino Gaming 131

12 Justice 145

Table of Cases 163

References 165

Index 169

About the Author 175

Preface

Before I began telling my children and grandchildren stories about my early life on two Sioux Indian Reservations, it had not occurred to me that my upbringing was in any way unusual or extraordinary. Yet when I mentioned that I attended first through fourth grade and fifth through seventh grade in a two room county schoolhouse, and that while working on my fifth grade lesson I would also listen to the teacher's instruction of the sixth grade, they were amazed. Amazed also, and somewhat shocked, to learn that all the boys (but not the girls) in the school carried pocket knives, with which, among other things, they played mumblety-peg during recess. For those who have not had the pleasure, "mumblety-peg" or "mumblethepeg," is a game played with knives in which the participants, almost exclusively boys, flip their knives, the sharper the better, from various positions on the body, such as the hip, the knee, the elbow, the shoulder, the head, or most dangerously, the nose. The object is to have the knife blade stick into the ground. The game, played by a group of cowboys, has recently been portrayed in the television mini-series, "Lonesome Dove.". The loser, the one with the most unsuccessful flips, is according to tradition supposed to pull up with his teeth a peg driven into the ground. To my knowledge my playmates and I never required anyone to pay this penalty. No one used a knife in a fight, of which there were quite a few, and if any blood flowed it was only because of a nose bleed or because he had cut himself, not someone else. Learning that many of my schoolmates were Indians has led many persons (although not my own children) to suppose that I too, like Will Rogers and Cher Bono, have Indian blood, a distinction I must admit, regrettably, I do not share with them, but even my wife has been told, "He really doesn't look Indian."

At the urging of some close friends and colleagues, as well as some inquisitive relatives, I have decided to set out the historical and autobiographical context of those early years, but having been trained as a philosopher I find that I cannot settle for the bare facts alone, interesting though they may seem to some persons looking at them from a more recent and perhaps more "advanced" perspective. I want from time to time throughout my narrative to try to understand the presuppositions of the times, white-Indian relations as they existed then and now, the implications of the entire reservation system, then, now, and for the future, and to contrast Indian and white values and practices such as the former practice of scalping engaged in by both Indians and whites.

What is needed for this kind of investigation besides the focal point of my own life, a small portion of which occurred on the Rosebud and Pine Ridge Reservations during the early 1900's (1927–1939, to be exact), is a lens, so to speak, which encompasses a much larger time—a period which is post-Civil War, after the Great Indian Wars and Massacres (both red and white), and after the wholesale slaughter of the plains buffalo, and after the vigorous reintroduction of the Reservation System during President Grant's administration; in other words, with the *aftermath* of these events—the Civil War, the buffalo slaughter, the Indian Wars, the establishment of Reservations—all of which have had profound effects on our nation as it now exists. These effects are what I wish to recount and philosophize about.

But is there some historical figure whose life (and death) unifies all these diverse historical events and trends, which might make it easier to talk about all of them as a kind of whole? I think there is and it is Custer's life and death, regardless of how one might ultimately think of him. It has been claimed by Milo M. Quaife who has edited General Custer's book, *My Life on the Plains* (first published as a series of articles from 1872 to 1874) that Custer engaged in every important battle in the Civil War (at least as far as the Army of the Potomac was involved) from Bull Run to Appomattox. General Sheridan gave Custer the flag of surrender tendered by Lee's Army of Northern Virginia, and to Mrs. Custer he gave the table on which the articles of surrender were signed. General Sheridan did so because he "knew of no one who had been more instrumental than her 'gallant husband' in bringing the surrender to pass." (Quaife xx).

It can easily be doubted that the entire war between the northern and southern states or even the surrender at Appomattox could be wholly explained in such a simplistic manner. The incident relating to Appomattox does provide some insight, however, regarding the admitted antipathy of President Grant for Custer and his military judgment. Grant, after all, had refused to accept Lee's sword at the surrender, a magnanimous act which Lee never forgot, and he allowed Lee's men to keep their horses and mules "for the spring plowing." Grant made it publicly known that he thought Custer's "last stand" was reckless and totally "unnecessary." Still there may be some truth in the observation that Custer's life *after* the Civil War neatly mirrors, in many respects, the cruelties inflicted on the Indians, the loss of *Paha Sapa*, their holy ground which had been pledged to them by the Fort Laramie Treaty of 1868, the decimation of the buffalo (ironically today the logo of the Department of the Interior), the corralling of Indian onto reservations, their bureaucratic maltreatment and neglect by the Federal Government thereafter and to this day. Frequent references will therefore be made to Custer, and extended comment in Chapter IX will be made regarding his extraordinary influence. His death left a legacy not only to those who followed his Indian-hating and Indian–killing ways, but also, and indelibly, to the Reservation System and the Bureau of Indian Affairs, which employed both of my parents until their retirements. I suspect that Custer's legacy also had its effect on me too, or at the very least on the environment in which I grew to the age of twelve or thirteen, nearly the same age as the Mark Twain characters, Tom Sawyer and Huck Finn. Stories of their adventures also affected me, in the sense that in my youth I did many of the things Tom and Huck might have done, such killing snakes, walking for miles over the prairies, swimming naked in the "crick," as we called it, and occasionally playing hooky, but I think that their influence was much less than Custer's influence on reservation life, and so consequently on mine.

Part I

THE AUTOBIOGRAPHICAL AND HISTORICAL CONTEXT

Chapter One

Rosebud

In the early 1900's, after trekking with horse and wagon and other livestock from Unionville, Missouri, to Dupree, South Dakota, my grandfather, Alonzo Grant Davis, always known as A.G. Davis, and his five young children settled down on government homesteaded land and commenced, under severe conditions, to create a farm out of previously untilled landscape. My grandmother, Laura Bradshaw Davis, had died soon after giving birth to her last child. My father was her third, and was eleven years old at the time of her death. My aunt Hazel was the eldest and consequently inherited the role of *mater familias*. Even my father confessed that "she raised us all."

The A.G. Davis family brought with them to South Dakota many Southern characteristics. Although Unionville is only a few miles from Iowa, and Missouri has always been a "border state," their southern orientation is not particularly surprising since they were descendants of one John Davis who emigrated from Wales, finally settling in western Virginia, or what is now Kentucky, early enough to have joined the Continental Army in Albemarle County, and to have chased Cornwallis' troops, so he claimed, "up and down the Atlantic coast." He and a brother, James, were also present at the surrender ceremony at Yorktown, before returning to his farm in Kentucky. Applying for his wartime pension, he was required to prove his service, and since there were no official discharge papers issued at that time, he obtained the written testimony of several neighbors who swore that he was indeed "a soldier of the revolution."

My grandfather himself came from a rather large family, he being the youngest—too young apparently to have served during the Civil War, though several of his older brothers did. Since his middle name was *Grant*, I have always supposed that he was named after General Ulysses S. Grant. Apparently a schism developed in the family. I am not at all sure but I suspect that some in the family supported the Confederate cause and others the Union. In any case, I remember my mother's telling of a nostalgic trip which my parents and my grandfather took back to the old homestead in Missouri. Driving out to the farm or to the farm house of one of his daughters, my grandfather recognized the driver of another vehicle and identified him as one of his brothers, but declined to stop, even to say hello. My mother could never understand his attitude or behavior on that occasion. She guessed that it was just a "Davis" thing. Possibly it was just his expression of a residual resentment relating to Civil War loyalties.

Although a very hardworking man, extremely devoted to the well-being of all his children, his "blood-kin" as he put it, as honest as anyone in Ziebach county, and much respected, he was nevertheless a racist in the sense that he believed blacks to be inferior in all respects to whites. Not that he disliked blacks or wished to deny them their rights, but he couldn't escape that pre-Civil War southern master-slave mentality. He once told me while visiting our family in Minneapolis, Minnesota, that whenever he was in strange or unfamiliar place he had no hesitancy in asking directions or other information from a black person, or "negro," which was the term he used. I don't recall that he ever used the derogatory "n" word. The reason he gave was that blacks were always polite and properly subservient, something he could not always count on in a white man.

After service in the United States Navy (1917–18), my father returned to South Dakota, and for a time acquired and worked a homestead of his own. All that was required for this relatively free land was a structure one could live in and an agreement to work the land for a minimum length of time. After a while, however, he was lured to the Rosebud Reservation to serve as Farm Agent. Perhaps a word of explanation regarding this job of teaching Indians how to be farmers needs to be given.

As far back as Thomas Jefferson it was Administration policy to convert Indians from hunters and gatherers to farmers. Jefferson foresaw even then that the depletion of wildlife and the destruction of forests for agricultural purposes by white settlers had, or soon would, make it impossible for the Indians to live as they previously had. Of course this was prior to the doubling of the size of the country by the Louisiana Purchase and the discovery by Lewis and Clark of literally millions of buffalo on the western plains. In time, of course, professional buffalo hunters such as William F. Cody, alias "Buffalo Bill," would decimate such herds, partly for their meat and hides, but often and licentiously "for the hell of it." The U. S. Cavalry which was later sent, after the Civil War, to protect settlers from Indian raids, were also responsible for much killing of the buffaloes. Even "friendly" Indians would kill buffalo for their hides to sell to the Army, leaving the carcasses to rot on the open plains. Custer enjoyed the sport and once expressed the view that hunting buffalo was as exciting as hunting Indians. (Ambrose, 327)

After the Great Indian Wars, one of Custer's primary duties was corralling Indians and forcing them by deceit or calculated violence to live on reservations. The Brulé Sioux, otherwise known as Sicangu Sioux, were herded onto the Rosebud Reservation, established in 1889, located in south central South Dakota bordering the State of Nebraska. It later became my father's task to teach them how to farm dry prairie land. Average rainfall in South Dakota in the Rosebud area averages about 13 to 14 inches a year. The U. S. Government through the Bureau of Indian Affairs (BIA) was supposed to supply the implements, plows, hoes, etc., and the initial seed. My father who had grown up as a farmer was fully qualified to perform this task. However, the plan never succeeded. The Plains Indians disliked the occupation and were reluctant to give it a try. Some persons have supposed that being inherently nomadic the idea of turning Indians into farmers was bound to fail. In fact, however, eastern tribes often grew crops. The tribes of Massachusetts taught the Pilgrims how to grow maize or corn, and in fact saved their lives by teaching them how to survive on what was to them unfamiliar land.

Jefferson's policy was entirely reasonable and indeed prescient with respect to American Indians nationwide. The problem lay with its implementation. As Arapaho Councilman Crawford White, a farmer in the Southwest succinctly expressed it,

> The white man placed us here and told us to survive, to change our traditional lives as hunters and become farmers. But then he took away much of our water, so white settlers could feed their crops. Now there are not enough jobs for everyone. So are we to give up our land and leave the reservations? For people who have lived here all their lives, that is not an easy thing to do. (see Mark Wexler, "Sacred Rights," *National Wildlife Magazine,* June/July, 1992, 21).

As a result of this kind of inattention and niggardliness on the part of the federal government, the Rosebud Reservation now has an extreme high unemployment rate, a poverty rate second only to that of the Pine Ridge Reservation which has the highest in the nation, a third of its residents are classed as homeless, and sixty percent live in substandard housing. Since Indians are no longer confined to the Reservation, and are free now like other American citizens to go elsewhere, the basic underlying philosophical question has to do with the extent that one sovereign state is obligated to assist another (theoretically) sovereign state within its borders, particularly one whose members still claim to be self-governing and yet full fledged citizens of the larger whole. We shall postpone this question to a later chapter.

For whatever reason, and I am not sure exactly why, my father ceased being a Farm Agent on the Rosebud Reservation and became instead a Special Agent in charge of federal law enforcement among Indians. Just when this change took place I also do not know. For a time, he was employed by a man by the name of T.C. Clark who owned the only General Store in the Agency town. The Pine Ridge Agency, to which our family subsequently moved had *three* such General Stores. Clark's store, as you might expect, sold just about everything, that is, everything which might be needed to live. In Urbana, Illinois, where I once lived and worked as a visiting professor of philosophy, it was a common saying that if the stores in Urbana didn't have what you wanted, you didn't need it. The same could have been said of shopping at Clark's store. They sold blankets (a favorite of the Indian customers), meat, groceries, hardware, dry goods, clothing (overalls, mainly), straw hats, tools, guns, ammunition, and candy consisting of licorice ropes, both red and black, horehound rock hard candy, jelly beans, and perhaps a few chocolate bars such as *The Three Musketeers*, divided separately into vanilla, strawberry, and chocolate flavors—three pieces for the price of one—sold for pennies. I once made a collection of "Indian Head" pennies—a whole jar full—which I lavishly and exhaustively spent on such items.

As a Special Agent in charge of enforcing law on the Rosebud Reservation, my father dealt with a whole gamut of crimes from outright murder to petty theft and vandalism. Often he had to jail many a drunken Indian or a belligerent white man who had sold the Indian alcoholic beverages. At Pow-Wows and other congregations of members of the tribe, he had to confront and deal with obstreperous persons, some of whom carried hunting knives and handguns. My father as a consequence had to carry a government issued revolver, usually in a shoulder holster concealed under his suit coat. Surprisingly, considering the lawlessness of some Indians as well as some conniving white salesmen, traveling circus performers, or carnival operators who would occasionally appear on the Reservation to attempt to dupe the inhabitants, my father never once had to use his weapon.

He was, even before becoming a policeman, quite accustomed to guns. As a young man growing up in Dupree, South Dakota, to the north, he, like others his age, always carried some sort of gun. Most often such guns were only used to shoot rattlesnakes which were, and I believe still are, numerous in that part of the state. In the Navy, although he never served overseas, he was instructed in the use of all kinds of firearms, so carrying one was in no sense a novelty for him.

Another reason for my father's ability to handle obstreperous Indians, individually and collectively, was a certain charisma he possessed. He was five feet, eleven and one half inches tall, just barely short of six feet, but he had a full head of naturally wavy hair which made him look taller than he actually was. He hated his wavy hair (which many a woman would kill for), and often after washing it he would try to control its springiness by wearing a section of silk stocking. Like Saul in the Old Testament (1 Samuel 10: 23), "he was a head taller than anyone else" and so was anointed King. My father wasn't anointed King in any sense, but he was as self-effacing as Saul, and so the Indians came to respect him, even when he was required by his office to send some of them off to prison. The Rosebud Sioux tribe made him an honorary member and gave him an Indian name, which I now don't recall. My mother was similarly honored and her Indian name was *Mashishaninni*, which I believe when translated means "little red rattler," so-called because of the noise she made when using her typewriter.

The biggest problem (or headache) my father faced was enforcing the federal law prohibiting the sale of liquor to Indians. This was also the biggest problem he faced after he transferred to the Pine Ridge Reservation, and later in Minnesota and Wisconsin on the Red Lake, Menomenie, and other Reservations where he was also required to enforce the Indian Prohibition Law which was eventually repealed by Congress in 1953. But more on that subject, the effects of rescinding the law, and the philosophical presuppositions of that legislation in later chapters.

Herbert P. Davis.

Nellie M. Post.

My mother, Nellie Mae Post, met my father, Herbert P. Davis, or H. P. Davis, as he was usually called, on the Rosebud Reservation. The "P" in my father's name, incidentally, stood for "Perley," "Perly," or "Pearly," not Philip. When required, which was not often, he would spell it indifferently one way or the other. No one, not even banks, seemed to find this habit objectionable. Standardization of spelling was apparently of little interest back then, although my mother often commented on his practice.

She was employed by the BIA in the capacity of an "account clerk" and "typist." She may also have been called a "typewriter, "but I think that by that time the distinction had been made between the person doing the typing and the machine. She had taught herself how to type at her previous place of employment, the Lame Deer Cheyenne Indian Reservation in Montana, under the guidance and counsel of her boss, the Agency Superintendent. The Agency had acquired a typewriter but no one knew how to use it other than to "hunt and peck" the keys. Her boss supplied her with the manual and told her to "take her time" learning how to use the instrument properly. In fact,

Lame Deer Agency Office, 1919.

he taught her, or rather allowed her to learn, many other office accounting skills as well as short-hand as a way of writing down dictation. No one, however, had to teach her how to improve her handwriting which was superb. It consisted of very small but carefully formulated letters, learned by means of a method—the name escapes me—which preceded the Palmer Method of penmanship by which I was taught to write in long hand. My mother was

Lame Deer, Montana.

Lame Deer Indians.

forever grateful to her benefactor and employer for his kind and sympathetic treatment and his regard for her as his protégé.

She secured her job at Lame Deer in a rather curious way. She had traveled from her home in Center, Nebraska, to her parents' newly acquired farm near the Reservation. They were getting on in years so she dropped everything and went to Montana to assist her parents. What they needed most was a well. She and her elder brother, Ellsworth, dug the well with the assistance of a horse. He would do the digging, placing the soil in a bucket, and my mother would hoist it using the strength of the horse to pull it up and then she would empty it out. When the well was nearly finished, she received a visit from a man named Buntin, Superintendent of the Tongue River Agency at Lame Deer, Montana. My mother must have looked awful, covered in mud from head to toe, but when he saw what she had done, he wanted to hire her immediately.

She lacked secretarial skills, although she had picked up some skills working at age 16 in an Abstract and Title Office in Center, Nebraska, and later for a County Judge for about eight years. She had only completed the eight grade (which was commonplace then), but the Superintendent was so impressed with her labor and perseverance that anything she needed to know about office work he thought she could learn "on the job" with his help.

Thereafter my mother taught herself all kinds of things. Presumably she had learned to sew, knit, and crochet from her mother, but later she bought a new Ford Model T automobile and taught herself to drive. She was probably one of the first women in the state of South Dakota, and perhaps the United States, to own and operate her own car. My father and mother drove it all the way to Denver, Colorado, and Estes Park, and back again to Rosebud on their honeymoon. She also taught herself how to swim, and on one notable occasion saved my father, who was not as adept at swimming, from drowning in a whirlpool situation. She enjoyed sports and taught herself to play tennis. She also taught herself to play the piano and the organ, well enough to lend her talent to the local Episcopal church she attended. At evening services I used to sit at her feet behind the organ and fall asleep. She also gave the ukulele and the guitar a try, although I don't believe she mastered either of

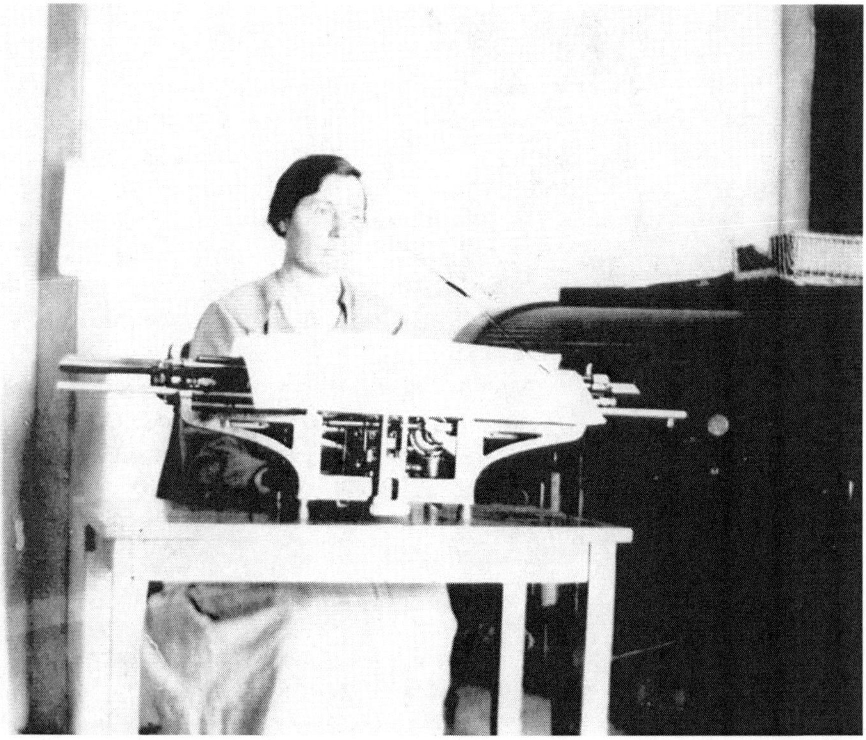

Nellie at Typewriter.

Indian Papooses at Turkey Shoot.

those instruments. Later in her long life (she lived to be 96), she undertook to learn Spanish, from records and a book. She loved to cook and although she was no Julia Child, still she was very experimental for her time. Once, she served my grandfather Davis a BLT, or bacon, lettuce, and tomato sandwich, and he became convinced that she was trying to poison him with such a strange combination of foods. Whenever persons such as Betty Friedan or Gloria Steinem tout the virtues of feminism in strident tones, I have only to think of my mother and how she anticipated their ideas with her actual accomplishments by several decades and how she did it all without fanfare while simultaneously raising a family.

Many of the persons my parents worked with were full-blooded Indians and others fractionally so. Some Indian agency employees were members of tribes other than Sioux, such as the Osage, Arapaho, Cherokee, Chickasaw, Choctaw, and other displaced tribes of Oklahoma. It wasn't at that time the policy of the BIA to hire as many Indians as possible to operate the Agency, as I believe it is now. The Superintendent, the Chief Clerk, and the Special Agents, such as my father, and the heads of other departments were all white men. As I recall, no women, whether white, red, or black, held high official positions in any branch of the BIA. Now of course they do. Also many of the federal government employees, as well as those of the county, including especially the teachers, were from the South. I don't know exactly why, but I suspect that jobs in that depression and pre-depression era were scarce, and

Our Rosebud Home.

government service even on remote and isolated Indian Reservations was better then no job at all. As one might expect, some of these Southerners, like my grandfather from Missouri, brought with them certain racial biases. One got the impression, even as a child, that they didn't particularly like Indians. I remember one such family who practically disowned their son for getting a beautiful young Indian girl pregnant. That he married her did not assuage their hatred, and when the child died soon after birth, they were elated.

Our home on the Rosebud Reservation was a two story red brick structure with a wrap-around front porch. It was located on a large square on the perimeter of which were other practically identical houses, except for the home of the Superintendent whose house was larger and far more elaborate and located at one corner near the Agency Offices, which were also constructed of red brick. In the center of the square was a tall white flag pole. Quite evidently at one time, but before my parents moved in, the quadrangle had been a military drill field, the houses quarters for military officers, and the Superintendent's house the house of the Commandant. Since the town, that is, the part of the Agency which was leased to or owned by non-military and non-governmental residents, lacked a hotel or other commercial living quarters, each of the houses on the quadrangle contained a guest room reserved for any visiting VIP from Washington, D. C. or elsewhere who might happen by. In our home we never used that room except for that purpose. We used to sit on the porch or go back and forth on a swing attached to the tongue and groove wooden ceiling on hot sultry evenings. The only hazard involved was

Superintendent's Quarters–Rosebud, Winter of 1920.

dodging the bats which nested during the day near the ceiling but became very alive and active during the night and evening. But like the weather, since nothing could be done about it, we learned to ignore it, and so also the bats.

At the end of the Quad was a building which was used for recreational purposes. I believe it also served as a kind of fire station. Parties and celebrations were held there, but most memorable perhaps were the *shivarees* or "charivari," a word derived from the Latin meaning "headache." I doubt that anybody on the Reservation knew, or even cared to know, the etymology of the word. But for those who are unacquainted with this custom, let me say that it was a noisy mock serenade to newly-wed couples, usually soon after they returned from their honeymoon. It occurred late at night after the newly-weds presumably had gone to bed. It involved the whole community who brought pots and pans and large spoons with which to awaken the couple and force them out of their quarters, sometimes in their pajamas or night clothes. They were then feted at a party attended by everyone, including the little kids.

My brother, Herbert Chandler Davis, was born in our Rosebud home, whether with the assistance and attendance of a physician or a mid-wife I do not know. I myself was born in a hospital in Valentine, Nebraska, just over the border. I don't believe the Reservation at that time even had a hospital, but they must have had some sort of clinic and at least a few resident physicians to treat the Indians who were very susceptible to tuberculosis. My mother was very aware of this health problem. When taking communion at the Episcopal Church, she, along with the clergyman's daughter, were always the first in line at the altar railing to receive the cup and the bread, and always before the tubercular Indians took their turn at the Eucharistic service. The Reverend Joyner, I believe his name was, always was the last to sip the cup, and it was suspected that he took the ambiguous injunction, "Drink ye all of it," in the sense, "Drink ye . . . "all of it," rather than as "Drink ye all . . . of it," and that he deliberately poured rather large quantities of the wine, and as a result would take a noticeably long time consuming "all of it." Surprisingly, he never contracted tuberculosis despite his many years of missionary service to the Indians. My mother, however, remained a bit paranoid and from time to time attended services at the nearby Presbyterian church where instead of drinking from the same chalice each parishioner was given his or her own individual cup (of grape juice).

Besides teaching the Indians to be farmers, another aim of the reservation system as a whole, and as envisaged by President U. S. Grant, was to "civilize" the Indians. To accomplish this task it was thought that the various denominations of the Christian Church were most appropriately suited for this task. We shall examine the presuppositions of the Indian Boarding Schools in a later chapter, but let it be noted here that the missionary arms of both the Catholic and Protestant sects were in effect given *carte blanche* to convert the Indians from pagans (or so the government bureaucrats regarded them) to God-fearing Christians. A tacit agreement (I don't think there was anything formal of official about it) among the various religious groups, particularly among the Protestant churches was that they would not duplicate each other's efforts. So if there was a Presbyterian church in one Indian

Rosebud Agency Staff.

The Davis Family.

community, no Congregational or Methodist missionary would attempt to convert souls there. There were Catholic churches everywhere, however, and the Episcopal or Anglican denomination was quite prevalent. All of them condemned native American religious ceremonies and rituals such as the use of peyote (which has a narcotic effect), the Ghost dance, and the Sun dance in which Indian braves dance about a pole with rawhide thongs attached to their pierced skin.

Vine DeLoria, Jr. has written scathingly about Christian missionaries sent to civilize the Indians in his best-selling book, *Custer Died For Your Sins* (1969). The title, as he himself explains, was originally a bumper sticker meant to refer to the Fort Laramie Treaty of 1868 in which the United States pledged to give free and undisturbed use of lands including the Black Hills to the Indians in exchange for peace. In the *Old Testament* the commission of a sin required a blood sacrifice for its atonement. The implication of the bumper sticker was that Custer represented the blood sacrifice the United States was obligated to give for its breach of the 1868 Treaty.

Vine DeLoria, Jr., of Standing Rock Sioux tribal origin, knows whereof he speaks. Not only was he the son of an Episcopalian priest (and I believe also the grandson of one), he himself spent four years in the Lutheran School of Theology at Rock Island, Illinois, where he received his theology degree in 1963, after graduating from Iowa State University in 1958. He was born in Martin, South Dakota, on the Pine Ridge Reservation, and was initially educated at Reservation schools. Our paths never crossed while we were both at about same time living on that Reservation, but my parents may have known his father, since my parents were also Episcopalians and frequently traveled through the town of Martin. Given the relatively sparse population of South Dakota, it is at least a plausible conjecture on my part.

After receiving his theological degree, he decided that the religious life, particularly as a missionary to Indians, was not for him, and he pursued and received a law degree from the University of Colorado at Boulder (1970). It must have been something of a disappointment to his father, Vine DeLoria, Sr., who had long served in the Episcopal Church and was highly influential himself.

I came across an article recently in *The Witness* on the Internet regarding a Dr. Mark Butterbrodt, who also grew up near, if not actually on, a reservation—the Sisseton-Wahpeton Reservation—in the northeastern corner of South Dakota. He claims that "it was through the wisdom and character of one man, Vine DeLoria, Sr., that I traversed that chasm [between the native and non-native populations of border towns] as an adolescent." Although of Norwegian heritage, Butterbrodt came from an Episcopalian family. His great-grandfather had left the Lutheran Church to become an Episcopalian, and all the others followed. Butterbrodt's father was a pharmacist who spoke "excellent Dakota" and taught his son the language at an early age. After graduating from high school, he went to Harvard College, then returned to finish his medical degree at the University of Minnesota. Again, like the younger DeLoria, our paths may have crossed at Harvard, or at Pine Ridge, but that is pure speculation on my part, although I sincerely wish that they had.

Butterbrodt has long been associated with the Indian Health Service (IHS) on the Yankton, Pine Ridge, and other reservations, attempting to understand why so many Sioux suffer from diabetes and are more susceptible to obesity. He has made many Indian friends on the Pine Ridge Reservation and was even "adopted" by one Sioux family. He has said that "Beyond my genuine respect for the inner character and spirituality of Indian people, my lifelong connection with them has been bolstered by the Episcopal Church, the Lakota/Dakota (Sioux) language, and the wonderful old Lakota Hymnal."

Vine DeLoria, Jr., though having in some respects the same religious background as Mark Butterbrodt, seems not to have been so impressed with Christianity—Episcopalian or otherwise—and in fact has become entirely disillusioned by it. Speaking in 1969 in his book, *Custer Died For Your Sins*, DeLoria says his faith was "shaken to the core" by a Presbyterian missionary's statement that although his denomination had preached Christianity to the Shinnecock Indians on Long Island for over 350 years, they would continue to conduct missionary activities among them "until the job is done." Although the Indians had become nominally Christian for several centuries, the white missionary establishment still had no confidence that they had done their job—which was in fact a complete confession of impotence and irrelevancy.

DeLoria speculates that the reason for such impotence and irrelevancy among other tribes as well was caused by a variety of confusions and misunderstandings of the Indian mentality. For example, he cites the case of a Roman Catholic priest who attempted to console a mother after the death of a child who had fallen from a second story window. He admonished her for crying because the child had been properly baptized and was therefore automatically now with Jesus. She should be happy. Grief was unnatural to man since Jesus had died upon the cross. Despite the priest's frantic attempt to reinforce what he had been taught in the seminary, and the disbelief which he may have discovered in himself, DeLoria contends that he misunderstood that Indians do not think of death as a judgment of an arbitrary God, but as a perfectly natural event which requires no elaborate theological justification. Indians also believe that grief is better expressed rather than suppressed. The Christian teaching seems to contradict this feature of Native American religion.

A personal comment may be in order here. I was once asked by a youthful Baptist minister what I would suggest telling a mother who had lost her child. The child had run out from between two parked vehicles and been run over by a passing car. Of course, philosophers, and especially students of philosophy, which I was at that time, have no special expertise in counseling of this sort. They are trained to analyze and criticize as objectively as possible whatever general proposition is put to them. But that doesn't necessarily make them wiser than anybody else. All I could suggest was that rationalistic proofs for the existence and nature of God would be clearly out of place, even if the mother had the patience to hear them. The pastor was clearly distressed that his own religion seemed incapable of providing the kind of comfort the mother needed.

Besides impotence and irrelevance DeLoria finds fault with the white man's religious attitude toward the land. Indians have a reverence for the land and all its animal inhabitants. The Christian sees nothing wrong with killing off whole species of wildlife, damming up rivers such as the Columbia which then destroy salmon runs, or defacing Mount Rushmore with likenesses of four United States Presidents, one of whom, Theodore Roosevelt, was by no means a friend of the Indians (but more on that topic later).

Early missionaries may well have thought that the Indians by their Sun dance ritual worshipped the Sun, and by other acts made Nature the Mother (or Goddess) of all things. Curiously, when the Sioux in particular speak of the Great Spirit (*Wakantanka*) it is a kind of monotheism they are expressing Though they might appear to worship nature, it is nature's God who is their deity, and that is how in their prayers they often describe the Creator or Holy Spirit who govern all things. It is amazing that the early Christian missionaries didn't pick up on this facet of their native religion.

In place of a "living religion" which includes fasting, sacrifice, and prayer, according to DeLoria the missionaries substituted a kind of magic involving the "regurgitation" of catechisms and creeds. He illustrates this with an account of a female missionary who asked him for advice regarding how to get her little Choctau pupils in Sunday School to understand "the technical side of being saved." According to her, there were seven steps to salvation, and if one could recite them in proper order, he or she was saved. "Apparently," DeLoria says, "the Lord would ask all people to recite the seven steps on Judgment Day." He was unable to give her the needed help, but asked her why, if it was so difficult to get them to understand, she didn't move to a different field. She replied that the Baptists had previously confused the children, and she was not about to let some other church come in after her and once again confuse them!

He also notes that both Catholic and Protestant missionaries have misconstrued the Indian concept of sharing. As an illustration he tells of an Indian woman on the Wind River Reservation who had a telephone, and how she let all her neighbors use it. The monthly bill was often rather high and sometimes she was behind in her payments. To the local priest, who could see no difference between sharing one's goods with the community and squandering them, real Christian "stewardship" meant saving money and giving a portion of it each Sunday in the collection plate.

DeLoria has many other criticisms of Christianity and of missionaries (he also has no love for anthropologists and other "friends" of the Indian), but we shall not survey them here. For himself, as he himself puts it, "Christianity has been a sham to cover the white man's shortcomings." Yet, in the end one gets the impression that he thinks that an Indian version of Christianity could do much for American society—a kind of rapprochement between traditional Christianity in which he was brought up and some of the ancient Indian concepts and practices. In a somewhat disconsolate mood, however, he says, "there is little chance for such a melding of the cards."

Of course, that was his attitude and viewpoint back in 1969, and between that time and his death in November, 2005, he may have changed his mind. I will let others decide that matter. But many changes have occurred which perhaps provide a more sanguine view. For example, when I was living on the Rosebud Reservation with my parents, the St. Francis Mission was just a few miles distant from the Agency town and was fully engaged in implementing the Federal policy of civilizing the Rosebud Sioux. As far back as 1877 Sinte Gleska (Spotted Tail) had met with President Rutherford B. Hayes and requested that the "Black Robes" or Jesuits come to South Dakota to teach the Sicangu (Rosebud Sioux). In 1886 St. Francis was officially founded, even before the Rosebud Reservation was established in 1889. By 1930 St. Francis had become the largest Catholic boarding school in the United States with an enrollment of some 479 students. During the Hayes Administration government policy changed as far as allowing Christian denominations to monopolize the "civilization" project. Not only had it been thought that the Grant policy was a failure, but questions regarding the separation of church and state had emerged. As a result of this change of policy, churches lost not only official sanction but also subsidies, and the influence of the Churches—Catholic as well as non-Catholic—tended to diminish. In 1972 the official name of St. Francis Mission changed to St. Francis Indian School. A parents advisory board was instituted, and the Jesuits finalized the complete transfer of the School to Sicangu Oyate Ho, Inc., in 1980. In 1990 a member of the Rosebud tribe became the first Sicangu to be Superintendent there. So-called "Anglo studies" are no longer completely dominant, and each day begins with a singing by students and faculty alike of the Lakota Flag Song, and a pounding of drums. The Website of St. Francis Indian School announces that the school is "Home of the Warriors and Lady Warriors," and that this month (visited in July) is *Can wape to wi* [May or Moon of the Green Leaves]. Progress? Some would say so, others perhaps not, but there has at least been change and a marked difference from the past.

Chapter Two

Pine Ridge

Living on an Indian Reservation Agency is not at all like living in a typical Hometown, U.S.A.—such as the towns of Rushville, Gordon, Chadron, or Valentine, Nebraska, to which we often resorted for special goods and services. There we could receive dental and medical examinations, arrange for family photographs, obtain groceries and spices not generally available on the Reservation, and attend movies, usually involving either Shirley Temple or Westerns in which the Indians were always the bad guys and the Cavalrymen or the White settlers were always the good guys. An Agency town such as Pine Ridge compares better with a place like West Point, where the federal government, and not the state or local government, controls what goes on. At both places a certain hierarchy of authority exists with the Commandant at West Point and the Superintendent at Pine Ridge at the top, both officers being governmentally appointed. Indeed, I believe the chief military officer at West Point and at the other military academies is also called Superintendent. They have their superiors in Washington, D. C. In the case of the military commander, the superior was the Secretary of War, as he was then called, and in the case of the reservation superintendent, the immediate superior is the Commissioner of Indian Affairs and ultimately the Secretary of the Interior.

At Pine Ridge there is no Mayor elected by the inhabitants, although there is an Indian Tribal Council whose head is, I think, democratically elected by the tribal members. That may not be the case on all reservations but I believe it was and is presently at Pine Ridge. In any case their jurisdiction was restricted to the Indian population. Perhaps that has changed now. As I understand it, the Council and Indian police now occupy the offices my parents had when they were employees at the Reservation, and the local BIA personnel are now located in a newer building. The Indian police may now have complete jurisdiction over the entire population of the Agency town, although they may share that jurisdiction with state police.

My parents, of course, like all American citizens were able to vote in State and National elections. I have a photograph of them in Spearfish, South Dakota, in the Black Hills listening to a speech by Calvin Coolidge all decked out in an Indian headdress. As a matter of party affiliation my parents were Republicans, but they were not permitted to be too vocal about it. Civil servants were (and perhaps still are) forbidden to take public stands in favor of or in opposition to any politician. Their views of course could not be kept entirely secret, and what now seems like a rather strange attitude developed among reservation employees with strongly held political opinions. I once spoke to an old gentleman who had long served on the reservations with my parents. He confessed that at that time he regarded anyone who was a member of some other party, say the Democratic party, as not only mistaken but indeed grossly immoral. Only in his later years had he realized how silly this attitude was, but I gather that he was not alone. Many other persons in the 1920's and 1930's felt that way.

It was not until June 2, 1924 that Congress passed the Indian Citizenship Act, which permitted *all* American Indians born in this country to have and to exercise all of the constitutional rights of citizens, including the right to vote. Before then some Indians, namely those who had agreed to the Government

At Home in Pine Ridge.

Phil with Dog.

Allotment policy could vote, but not the others. It seems outrageous that they had to wait so long, but then so had the women of this country. Amendment 19 giving them the right to vote was not passed until August 26, 1920, although many state legislatures, Wyoming being the first, had already given them the vote. It would be pure speculation on my part to suggest how many Indians actually took advantage of their new right, but it is likely that this franchise took time to get used to. Perhaps the same could be said regarding women voters. Suffice it to say that during the 20's the vote was predominantly that of the white male.

Benjamin Reifel or Ben Reifel, as he was generally known is one of the distinguished Indians to "graduate" from a South Dakota reservation. He was born in 1906 on his parent's farm near Parmelee on the Rosebud Reservation. His father was a German-American named William Reifel and his mother a full-blooded Lakota Sioux named Lucy Burning Breast. As an enrolled member of the Rosebud or Sicangu Sioux Tribe, Ben's Indian name was Lone Feather. I am not sure what that is in Lakota.

His grade school education was obtained at both kinds of schools which then existed on the reservations, a Boarding School and a County School. After graduating from eighth grade (presumably at the County School), he enrolled in the School of Agriculture in Brookings, South Dakota. He later graduated from South Dakota State College in 1932, received his master's degree from Harvard in 1950 (the same year I received my bachelor's degree from the same institution), and thereafter completed his doctorate in Public Administration.

Between degrees he began in 1933 a career with the BIA. He was appointed Farm Agent at Oglala on the Pine Ridge Reservation. Like my father who had held the same job on the Rosebud Reservation some years before, he stayed in the position only a short time, in fact, only one year. Obviously, those who held that job were not entirely satisfied with it, and perhaps for good reason. Ben was later made a Field Agent with offices in Pierre, South Dakota. It must have been around this time that my parents made his acquaintance, or he theirs. In any case, they always spoke well of him and even after they transferred to Minneapolis, kept track of his career.

During WWII he was commissioned a Second Lieutenant and in 1942 served in France and Germany leaving the Army as a Lt. Colonel. After the war he was appointed Tribal Relations Officer and later served as Superintendent at the Fort Berthold Reservation in North Dakota. In 1960 he resigned from the BIA and ran for Congress to become the first person of Sioux ancestry to become a U. S. Representative. He served as a Republican in that post for five terms, deciding not to seek re-election in 1970, but to devote himself to other political projects and speaking engagements.

He traveled widely throughout the world during his various careers—from Europe to Ethiopia to Asia and to Israel. His extensive travels remind me of a comment a daughter of Mrs. Helen Evans, the owner of Evans General Store in Pine Ridge, once made. After her mother had sold the store and moved to Rapid City to become the Curator of the Indian Museum there, Beverly, a childhood friend of mine, married a graduate of the South Dakota School of Mines in Rapid City. As a mining engineer his services were in demand all over the world, and his wife and children accompanied him to all those foreign destinations. "Not bad," Beverly once wrote, "for a kid raised on the Reservation!"

The Shannon County School Ben attended was probably very much like the one I attended. It may even have been the same one. I do not know for sure. In any case, such county schools were run (or perhaps I should say regulated) in very much the same way. At Pine Ridge there were multiple classes in each of two classrooms, grades one through four in one room (no kindergarten), and grades five through eight in the other. At about the time I left the Shannon County School System, after finishing seventh grade, a high school of sorts (grades nine through twelve) was instituted in the basement of the building. I believe there were three or four students enrolled. Two teachers, possibly later a third teacher to teach the high school students, constituted the faculty. I remember well Miss Fay Cantrell from some southern state, possibly Georgia. She was a tough taskmaster and I barely got out of fourth grade because of her. Note that in the enclosed copy of my report card for that year I was promoted to fifth grade "provided [I] could pass the first test in arithmetic" in the next year. Next year came and thank God I was in the adjoining room with a different teacher. I must have passed that damned test because it appears from my report card record that I wasn't demoted.

Discipline was also a very big thing with her. Any first to fourth grader who behaved badly in her classroom, according to her rather strict set of rules, would find him or herself banished to the dunce corner, or in the case of particularly rambunctious boys would have their outstretched palms whacked with a ruler. Corporal punishment was fairly common then and I don't recall that any of the parents objected. The punished students, if their parents learned of the incident, probably received even harsher treatment at home. It was not an auspicious event to receive a bad report regarding "deportment" on your report card which the parent had to sign and return.

School Classes.

TO THE PARENTS

At the end of each six weeks, this card will be sent home in the hands of the pupil. It shows the status of the pupil in the regular school work. If the grades are below 75 per cent, the matter should have attention. You should visit the teacher, determine what the trouble is, and then work with the teacher to remove the causes leading to poor work. Please sign the card in the proper place below and see that it is returned to the teacher immediately.

Superintendent of Schools.

1st period *Mrs Nellie M Davis*

2nd period *Mrs Nellie M. Davis*

3rd period *Mrs Nellie M. Davis*

4th period *Mrs Nellie M. Davis*

5th period *H P Davis.*

6th period ....

PROMOTION CERTIFICATE

This is to certify that the holder of this card has satisfactorily completed the work *except Arithmetic* of Grade *4* and is hereby promoted to Grade *5* *Provided he can pass the first test in Arithmetic next year* *F. Cantrell* Teacher.

Be Willing to Stand Alone for Frequently the Crowd Is Wrong

STATE OF SOUTH DAKOTA · GREAT SEAL · MDCCCLXXXIX

PUPIL'S REPORT

SHANNON COUNTY

NAME *Philip Davis*

INDEPENDENT SCHOOL DISTRICT No. 1

Pine Ridge School

MILLARD GYTE

Superintendent of Schools

REPORT OF YEAR

Beginning *Aug. 31*, 193*6*

Ending *May 21*, 193*7*

		STANDINGS BY SIX WEEKS						
		1st	2nd	3rd	4th	5th	6th	Yr. Av
Arithmetic		57	73	69	58	81	76	69
English Arts	Reading	82	74	81	72	70	72	75
	Writing	80	80	80	81	82	84	81
	Language & Gram.	81	92	88	79	81	80	83
	Spelling	77	77	88	83	69	89	80
Social Studies	History	89	79	80	96	92	90	88
	Geography	77	92	80	86	81	90	84
	Civics							
	Hygiene	84	81	90	87	90	81	86
Art		77	79	75	64	81	81	76
Music								
Average		78 7/9	80 3/9	81 2/9	78 4/9	80 2/9	82 5/8	80 7/9
Deportment		95	94	92	92	94	94	
Days Present		30	25	19	21½	27	29	
Days Absent		0	3	0	5½	3	1	
Times Tardy		0	2	0	0	0	0	

Attitude Toward School and Recitation	1st 6 Weeks	2nd 6 Weeks	3rd 6 Weeks	4th 6 Weeks	5th 6 Weeks	6th 6 Weeks
Excellent						
Average						
Poor						
Lessons Poorly Prepared						
Little Effort						
Inattentive						
Work Falling Off						
Promotion in Danger						
Improving					—	
Wastes Time		✓				

Recommended Grading System
A—Excellent (94 to 100 per ct.)
B—Above Av. (87 to 93 per ct.)
C—Average (81 to 86 per ct.)
D—Below Av. (75 to 80 per ct.)
F—Failure.

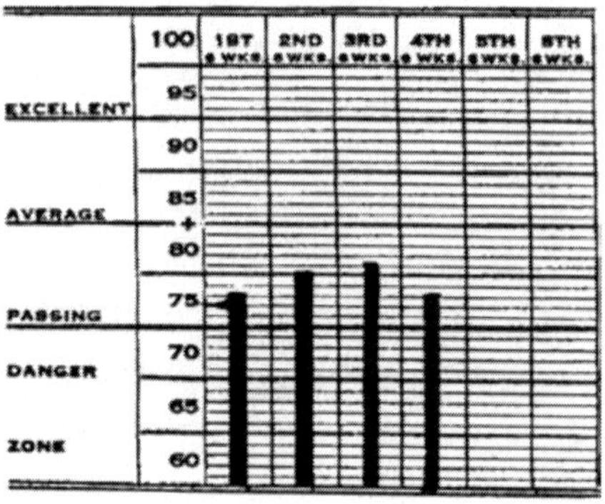

TO PARENTS

We invite your co-operation. This card is sent you regularly that you may know the teacher's estimate of your child's work.

Please sign and return at once.

Your signature is not an approval of the report but a proof that you have received it.

You are cordially invited to visit the schools.

Irregular attendance endangers promotion.

Friendly conferences help to mutual understanding

SIGNATURE OF PARENT OR GUARDIAN

1. Nellie M. Davis
2. Nellie M. Davis
3. Nellie M. Davis
4. Nellie M. Davis
5. ______
6. ______

CERTIFICATE OF PROMOTION

This Certifies That ______

has completed the work of the ______ grade and is hereby recommended for promotion to the ______ grade of the Public Schools of this county.

______ Teacher.

______ 19____

Teacher's Report of Pupil's Progress to Parents

SHANNON COUNTY

Name Philip Davis

Grade Seventh School Dist. No. 1

School Year Beginning Sept. 4 19 39

And Ending May 24 19 40

Mary R Lemen

Teacher

MRS. ELSIE HADDOCK

COUNTY SUPERINTENDENT OF SCHOOLS

ST. LOUIS PARK HIGH SCHOOL

Report of Davis, Philip 19 43 to 19 44 Grade 11

SUBJECTS	SIX-WEEKS' PERIOD 1	2	3	4	5	6	Ex.	Av.	Cr.
English 11	B	[illegible]	A	A	A	A	A	A	1
American History	A	A	B	A	B	B	A	A	1
Advanced Algebra	B	B	B	B	B	B	B	B	1
Chemistry	A	B	A	B	A	B	B	B	1
Band	A	A	A	A	A	A		A	½
Physical Education	B	B	B	B	B	B		B	
Glee Club	B	B	B	A	A	A		A	½
Times Tardy	0	0	0	0	0	0			
Days Absent	0	0	0	1	0	0			

SYSTEM OF GRADING

A—Superior 94-100
B—Above Average 87-93
C—Average 80-86
D—Unsatisfactory 75-79
F—Fail—Below 75
I—Incomplete

(Over)

Besides deportment which was graded pretty much on the same basis as regular subjects such as arithmetic, reading, and writing—note that the order was not the usual 3–R's ("reading, writing, and arithmetic"). Arithmetic came first! Not a subject in which I excelled, obviously, but by High School, fortunately I had improved. Perhaps I can thank Miss Cantrell for that! In addition to deportment there was another category of evaluation called "Attitude Toward School and Recitation." My biggest fault there was "wasting time." I have no idea now of what my teacher had in mind, but it counted as a demerit which of course didn't please my parents at all. Later in seventh grade, I notice in going over my report cards that the category was renamed "Citizenship," which included such topics as "Self-Control," "Respect for Authority," and "Cleanliness." I can't imagine teachers today seriously grading students on such matters, and indeed even then some did not. It is obvious that Mary R. Lemen, my seventh grade teacher, took this task very seriously and responded with a letter grade for each and every sub-category.

It is also obvious from the way in which the report cards were designed that moral as well as academic education was thought to be a primary responsibility of the teacher. Mottos such as "Be Willing to Stand Alone for Frequently the Crowd is Wrong," or "Friendly Conferences Help to Mutual Understanding," or on the Great Seal of the State of South Dakota, "Under God the People Rule," can be found stamped on the report cards. I also find it interesting that on my 1939–40 report card a photograph of the Mt. Rushmore National Memorial is minus the face of President Theodore Roosevelt. It was begun by Gutzon Borglum in 1927 and finished by his son, Lincoln Borglum in 1941. Because of Roosevelt's rather backward attitude towards Indians, perhaps it would have been more instructive, morally speaking, had his countenance remained as it was on my report card.

In many respects my report cards for Jr. High School (8th grade) and High School in Minnesota were quite different from those I received in South Dakota. In the first place, they contain no teacher's signature. Presumably that was because I had so many more teachers, one for each subject in each grade. The only signature on the document, aside from those of my parents, was that of the Principal. The grading system is pretty much the same. Attendance is noted, but deportment is not evaluated. The only attempt at moral education would appear to be Mr. Martinson's advice regarding "too many social engagements" and "the loafing habit."

So how did my County School education measure up with St. Louis Park's? Actually, when I first attended school in suburban Minneapolis, I was somewhat ahead of my fellow students, and I attributed that slight superiority to the *Shannon County Course of Study,* from which I learned not only arithmetic, reading, and writing, but also how to diagram any English sentence

TO THE PARENT OR GUARDIAN

The school seeks your advice and cooperation in its effort to educate your child. Some of the greatest hindrances to good school work are irregular attendance, late hours, too many social engagements, and the loafing habit. We hope you will feel free at all times to visit your school and confer with the teachers.

A. L. Martinson
Principal

Modern, American History, Introduction to Social Science, three years of English, one other elective solid and five other electives are required for Senior High School graduation. Four credits should be earned each year.

At the beginning of this year your child has earned 4½ credits.

PARENT OR GUARDIAN'S SIGNATURE

Mrs. Nellie M. Davis	H P Davis
1st Six Week's Period	4th Six Week's Period
H P Davis.	H P Davis
2nd Six Week's Period	5th Six Week's Period
H P Davis	
3rd Six Week's Period	6th Six Week's Period

REPORT OF YEAR

Beginning September 4, 1939

Ending May 24, 1940

		STANDINGS BY SIX WEEKS						
		1st	2nd	3rd	4th	5th	6th	Year Avg.
Arithmetic		B	a	a	a	a	a	a
English Arts	Reading	C	B	a	a	B	B	B
	Writing	C	B	B	B	B	B	B
	Language and Gram.	B	C	a	a	a	a	a
	Spelling	B	B	a	a	B	a	a
Social Studies	History	B	C	a	B	a	a	a
	Geography	B	B	a	a	B	B	B
	Civics							
	Hygiene	B	a	B	a	a	a	a
Art		C	C	B	B+	B	B	B
Music		C	C	C	B	a	a	a
Promotion in Danger								
Average		B	B+	a	a	a	a	a
Deportment		B	B	B	B−	C	C	C
Days Present		26	27	28	29	28	29	169
Days Absent		2						2
Times Tardy								171

Recommended Grading System
A—Excellent (93 to 100 per ct.)
B—Above Av. (87 to 93 per ct.)
C—Average (81 to 86 per ct.)
D—Danger (75 to 80 per ct.)
F—Failure.

CITIZENSHIP

Please Grade By Letter

	1	2	3	4	5	6
Co-operation	B	B	B	B	B	C
Self-Control	B	B	B	B	B	B
Industry	B	B	B	B	B	
Self-Reliance	B	B	B	B	B	B
Respect for Authority	B	B	B	B	B	B
Health	a	a	a	a	a	a
Cleanliness	a	a	a	a	a	a
Punctuality	a	a	a	a	a	a
Courtesy	B	B	a	a	B	
Sportsmanship	B	B	B	a	B	B
Initiative	B	B	B	B	B	B

The following graph can be used to show the progress of the pupil throughout the year.

Draw line on the graph to show the pupil's average standing each period. Draw the graph in red.

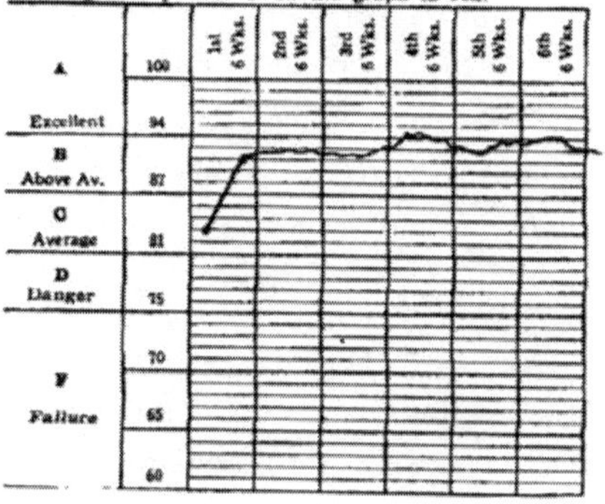

presented to me, no matter how complex, to spell like an expert, as well as everything else which that *Course of Study* prescribed for me.

Each teacher had her own copy of the *Course of Study*, and usually placed it on the corner of her or his desk. It was a mammoth volume—I would say at least twelve inches thick and must have weighed as much as a large sack of potatoes. I was really impressed. It was the biggest book I had ever seen, even larger than my parents' Family Bible, which couldn't have been over four inches thick. The State or County Board of Education had included in that book lessons in all subjects for all grades, first through eighth. All the teacher had to do was to look up the lessons for each class for which she or he was responsible, and she or he would know exactly what those pupils were to be taught on any given day, say, in November.

Of course the book also found other uses. On particularly warm days when the teacher wanted to attract a breeze from the open windows through the room to the door to the hallway leading to the "cloakrooms," she would put the *Course of Study* on the floor against the open door. Thus the mega-book was kept either on the teacher's desk or on the floor near the door. I doubt that the teachers ever carried it home with them. It would have been a cumbersome and difficult task.

I mentioned that I learned to spell from the *Course of Study*, but that is not altogether true. The *Course of Study* may have allowed for (or dictated) spelling bees, and I participated in many of those. But I think my father was mainly responsible for my progress in this feature of my education. During my early school years I was not a particularly good speller—in fact pretty awful—so my father would sit me down at a card table in the evenings and question me regarding the spelling of certain words, until I would practically fall asleep. I improved, but remained at the core a pretty mediocre speller. But because of the spelling bees and the exercises my father put me through, I did learn to recognize when I had spelled a word incorrectly, and how to use a dictionary. I have since collected quite a few dictionaries, from the usual Webster's and foreign language dictionaries, and a dictionary of philosophy, to a dictionary of architecture, a vocation I once toyed with but didn't take up, a Hawaiian dictionary, and just lately a Lakota dictionary.

I never achieved a conversational grasp of the Lakota language, spoken by both the Rosebud and the Pine Ridge Sioux, to the extent that Mark Butterbrodt, Vine DeLoria, Jr., and Ben Reifel did, but my father who was in close contact with Indian police and other tribal members, taught me a little of what he knew. For years now my wife, Laura, who is of Czech / German ancestry and spoke Czech as a child, understands when I ask for "pajuta sapa" (literally, black medicine) or "wakalyapi," both meaning "coffee," or when I offer her "mazaska" (or as I learned to say it, "mazaskow") or "money." I used to be able to count in the Sioux language and was quite pleased with myself when I discovered that a town not far from Minneapolis was called "Shakopee," which I recognized as a corruption of the Sioux word, "sakpe" meaning "six." However, I have lately learned that the town (now city) was named for a Chief Shakopee of the Mdewakanton Dakota tribe, whose ancient village on the banks of the Minnesota River was known as Teenatahotanwa, or "Village of the Praire." (http://enwikipedia.org./ wki/Shakopee, Minn.; also, Paula Giese, http://www.kstrom.net/isk/games/gaming.html). The Chief's name in Dakota means "Little Six" (and probably the same in the Lakota dialect), so I was not too far wrong in associating it with the number six. Indeed, even today near the fabulously profitable Mystic Lake Casino built on Shakopee Reservation land is another building called the "Little Six Casino." Incidentally, the only other city that I know which is named after an American Indian Chief is Winnemucca, Nevada. Chief Winnemucca was Chief of all the Northern Paiute Indians.

On August 29, 1935, an automobile accident occurred on Highway 18, about 20 miles northwest of Pine Ridge, South Dakota, in which my mother, a friend of hers, my brother and I were involved. Today such accidents are so common that they are hardly worth mentioning, much less describing. But this one in South Dakota in the thirties had several features which were, at least from today's perspective, rather unusual, if not absolutely unique. Most prominent was the fact that Sicangu Chief Short Bull was riding in the other car and was killed. I have been able to ascertain that he was probably not the same Short Bull who was a medicine man and prominent leader of the so-called Ghost religion who died in 1915 at about the age of 70 (see Sprague, *Pine Ridge,* 68). The Chief Short Bull who was killed in the accident, however, may have been old enough to have fought in the Little Big Horn Battle, or been involved with Chief Big Foot's band of Indians at Wounded Knee. Also in the car with him were Charles Short Bull, who was declared unconscious at the scene of the accident and later died of his injuries; his wife, Susie Short Bull; Kermit Short Bull; Andrew Blue Horse, Kate Blue Horse—a total of six persons in a Model A Ford Sedan.

Andrew Blue horse, age 19, was the driver. Whether he had a license is not specified in the official report by Special Officer R.S. Pinkerton, who had been summoned from the Pine Ridge Agency to the scene. He gives the license plate numbers of both cars, but no information regarding the drivers' licenses. That probably is not surprising in itself since in those days driving tests and licenses were not strictly required. I know that in Minnesota in the 1940's all that was required to get a driver's license was the payment of a fee, being at least 16 years of age, and an affirmative answer to the question, "Do you know how to drive?" I received my license at that age and could answer truthfully because my father had previously taught me to drive. My wife never learned to drive until after we were married because she could not truthfully say that she knew how to drive and so she never even applied, as some of her less truthful friends did. As a result she did not obtain her license until she was considerably older than 16.

My mother was the driver of our car, a Willys Eight Sedan, manufactured by the Willys-Knight Company. As I recall, it was a large, rather square, heavy, eight cylinder, "Hummer" type of vehicle, certainly as compared with the Ford Model A. God knows what the average gas mileage was for the Willys, but in those times, gasoline was relatively cheap, a few cent, maybe 16 or 18 cents a gallon. Seat belts were unheard of, and as a consequence I received a rather painful bruise across the cheek of my face, as a result of being thrown from the rear seat against the back of the front "bench" seat, and perhaps also against the steel railing attached to it, the purpose of which now escapes me. Perhaps it was meant to help you get up and out of the back seat, or more likely it was only there to hold blankets or other "robes" in case the heater didn't work or one's feet and legs felt cold. In fact, I believe it was not until much later that automotive heaters were made to heat the back seat passengers as well as those in the front seat.

At the time of the accident at about 12:30 Noon, my mother was driving south on Highway 18 enroute from Hot Springs, South Dakota, to our home at Rosebud. I forget the exact circumstances, but we must have been returning from a visit to Evans' Plunge in Hot Springs. The car containing the Indians was traveling north. The main culprit involved in the accident was a large red truck which passed us going up a small rise in the dirt road, raising a lot of dust, the weather being very dry. The dust made visibility nearly impossible and my mother slowed down and applied her brakes. The occupants of the Model A also testified to the passing truck traveling in their direction and causing a dust storm. Of course no one recorded the license number of the truck or otherwise identified it. It sped past both cars and was never seen again.

What happened next was a collision of the two cars, both drivers blinded by dust. Probably the left front wheel and fender of the Willys and the left front of the Ford entangled and twirled them about blocking the road. Conflicting claims were made by both parties regarding who was driving near or at the center of the road, a conflict never resolved and probably in the circumstances irresolvable.

Fortunately there were two Indian bystanders, Norman Pipe On Head and Alex Scabby Face, who were only a short distance from the road when the accident occurred, but because of the dust they didn't actually see the event;

they heard the crash and rushed over to help the survivors and direct traffic around them.

Today Highway 18 still runs through the Pine Ridge and Rosebud reservations and in fact across the state and into Iowa. It runs south of and parallel with Interstate 90, which of course didn't exist then. In 1935 Highway 18 was a dirt road, not even a gravel road, and probably not as wide as the paved version is today.

The first car to arrive at the scene was driven by a man named Frank Olds, who notified Officer Pinkerton of the accident and transported the Davis car occupants, including myself, to the hospital. Pinkerton then drove a doctor and a nurse to the scene. A few miles south of the scene they met a Field Nurse who was transporting the occupants of the other car to the hospital.

The report of the accident doesn't mention the matter, but I recall that there were even then apprehensions regarding the reactions of the Oglala Sioux community, not only because of the deaths of two members of their tribe, one of whom may have fought against Custer at the Battle of the Little Bighorn, but also because there was a hint of favoritism as far as the white survivors were concerned. They were the ones first taken to the hospital even though their injuries were far less serious.

As it turned out, there were no after effects—no Indian uprising, revolt, public protest, or lawsuit. Both parties apparently were willing to accept the judgment of the investigating officer that "this was an unavoidable accident caused by the extremely dusty condition of the road and the passing of the truck which raised the dust and obscured the vision as they were about to pass." In retrospect, however, the incident does strongly suggest that some 59 years after the Little Bighorn Battle, and 40 years after the Wounded Knee Massacre, which occurred less than 18 miles northeast of Pine Ridge, Indian resentments were still very much alive.

Chapter Three

Paha Sapa (Black Hills)

The Lakota name of the Black Hills is Paha Sapa, which, in at least one of several meanings, is literally translated as "Black Hair of the Head," or "Black Scalp," which is a fairly apt description of both the spruce and pine forests which cover it and its location in the center of what the Treaty of 1868 calls the Great Sioux Reservation and surrounding Hunting Grounds (or Unceded Indian Territory).

Perhaps there is an authoritative scientific explanation of why the Hills appear to be black, but I have yet to encounter it. However, I have heard several other explanations. One is that the soil gives the spruce a dark or blackish color to both their needles and their bark, so that at a distance the otherwise green trees appear black. Another is that the spruce trees emit an effluvium, gas, or vapor which discolors the atmosphere. The same sort of phenomenon is present in the Blue Ridge Mountains of Virginia. At a distance they definitely appear, not black, but blue.

Regarding the location of the Black Hills and its status as a kind of scalp of the region, we shall defer discussion to Chapter VII, except to say that it is a rather big scalp (approximately 7.7 million acres or 6000 square miles), most of which is located in what is now the state of South Dakota, and the rest in what is now Wyoming.

Before those states were admitted to the Union in 1889 and 1890 respectively, the Sioux and Cheyenne tribes who lived there knew it as Sacred Land, not to be defiled by anyone, Indian or white man. It contains many streams containing trout, and mountains as high as 7,242 feet (Harney Peak). Yet it also contains deep canyons and geological rock formations and spires. It also sports a lake (Sylvan Lake), which is unusual for South Dakota which is otherwise landlocked. There are many species of wildlife—deer, antelope, etc., and on the northern side, and in Custer Park, herds of buffalo. Minerals are to be found in abundance—silver, copper, lead, iron, and of course gold discovered in 1874. The Homestake Mining Company near Lead, South Dakota, and its mine are no longer in operation, but until its shutdown in 2002 was the richest gold mine in the Western Hemisphere.

In my youth growing up on the Rosebud and Pine Ridge Reservations, I was not fully aware of the history of the Black Hills, especially the fact that the U.S. Government with the help of Lt. Colonel Custer had stolen all this land from the Indians. However, I was personally acquainted with the natural and recreational features of the area—the beautiful forests, the gold mining, the sale of "Black Hills jewelry," of which my mother had several pieces, the outdoor camping, as if in a big park, visiting the Mt. Rushmore Memorial as it progressed, eating buffalo burgers, and of course swimming in the warm mineral springs of Evans' Plunge in the city of Hot Springs, on the edge of the Black Hills, and closer to our homes in Pine Ridge and Rosebud.

My older brother, Herb, and I learned to swim there under the tutelage of my mother. The building which houses the pool contains what seemed to us an enormous and very scary slide which stretched nearly to the ceiling, higher than any Olympic diving platform. After overcoming the fear of climbing so many steps, sitting or lying down, and nervously letting go, we came sailing down the slide and into my mother's or another experienced swimmer's arms—time and time again until we needed to turn in our rented woolen swim suits and return home. No one brought their own swimwear in those days. Everyone was issued a suit and towels upon payment of their admission fee. The only problem with the suits, aside from lacking a snug fit, was that after they got wet they seemed to weigh a ton. Women's suits were even worse since they were larger one-piece outfits. And of course the warm, almost hot, mineral water was debilitating. We enjoyed every minute of it.

My mother and father were married in Hot Springs by a Justice of the Peace. I don't know why but the decision to marry must have been a sudden one and there was no time to arrange for a proper Episcopal ceremony. Possibly there was a problem such as that in Clarence Day's play, "Life With Father," starring William Powell and Irene Dunne. I am not sure that my father was ever baptized, and if that was a prerequisite for marriage, as it may well have been, my father probably concluded that it was simply too much trouble. I am guessing, of course, but I do know that my brother received infant baptism. I, on the other hand, was nearly twelve when it occurred to my mother that I had been neglected. We were about to visit my Grandfather ("Granddad") Davis and other relatives in Dupree, South Dakota, so she arranged to have me baptized in the Dupree Episcopal Church by their itinerant priest. By George, I was not going to Hell just because of a little oversight on her part!

What even a casual reader of the literature, or should I say propaganda, regarding the Mount Rushmore Memorial observes is that it is decidedly one-sided. It usually starts out with the announcement that that the mountain was named after Charles E. Rushmore, a non-indigenous Easterner from New York (how much eastern can you get?) who was also a lawyer who had been in South Dakota to investigate, what else but certain mining claims. The latter distinction is not always mentioned. Next it is pointed out that the initial aim of the project was the promotion of tourism in the Black Hills and South Dakota generally. As Borglum's plan developed and Congressional approval sought, the aim became more political, or some would say more patriotic. President Coolidge insisted that before he would support the project two republicans and one democrat be portrayed in addition to Washington. The whole scene is now rationalized as follows: Washington represents the struggle for independence; Jefferson, government by the people; Lincoln, the permanence of the Union; and Roosevelt, America's place in world affairs. It might also be noted that they were all actively involved in our national wars; Washington and Jefferson of course in the Revolutionary War; Lincoln in the Civil War; and Roosevelt in the Spanish-American War.

Not a word is said regarding the Lakota Sioux or the Cheyenne Indians who preceded the Sioux there. Or that it was regarded as a religious sanctuary. Only rarely is it even mentioned that in 1937 a bill proposing that the head of a woman—Susan B. Anthony—be added to the group. The legislation, as one might have expected, was derailed. The emphasis now is almost entirely on the recreational benefits of the Black Hills and on the giant sculptures as artistic celebrations of our nation's greatest leaders. How Borglum ever thought that his granite sculptures would, as he said, "show posterity what manner of men they were" is a bit of a mystery. However, perhaps a word or two about their presidential policies toward the treatment of Indians might not be out of place here, even though their Indian policies were never one of the considerations which led to the creation of the project in the first place.

George Washington's closest encounters with Indians occurred during the so-called French and Indian Wars (1754 to 1763) while serving as a colonial officer of the Virginia Militia with the British Army. Most Indian tribes involved in that fracas sided with the French rather than with the British, but as it happened also during the Indian Wars of the 1870's in the West, some Indians could be found on both sides of the conflict. Even Custer had his Osage guides in his attacks on the Washita and Powder River Indian villages. Washington has the distinction of being fired upon by one of his own guides and nearly killed. Instead of pursuing the treacherous would-be assassin who might alert others of their whereabouts, Washington and his companions, upon Washington's own orders, let the Indian go, and then hurried to the safety of their fort. Despite this rather harrowing experience, Washington as President worked out a six-point program regarding relations with Indians in which he tried as best he could to befriend the Indian while also meeting out justice to bad Indians who sought to murder and massacre early settlers.

It is worth noting that the Continental Congress in 1787, even before the Constitution was adopted passed an ordinance under the *Articles of Confederation* "for the government of the territory of the United States, north west of the river Ohio." It declared that

> The utmost good faith shall always be observed toward the Indians; their lands and property shall never be taken from them without their consent; and in their property, rights, and liberty, they shall never invaded or disturbed, unless in just and lawful wars authorized by Congress; but laws founded in justice and humanity, shall, from time to time, be made for preventing wrongs being done to them, and for preserving peace and friendship with them.

Washington personally subscribed to this policy during his administration as did Thomas Jefferson and indeed all the Presidents through John Q. Adams until Andrew Jackson, an experienced Indian fighter, took a hard line and refused to give credence to any treaties with Indians.

In accordance with his policy to treat Indians fairly but to punish Indian wrongdoers, Washington once sent General Josiah Hamar's army to bring the leaders to Justice. In this action he failed and the Shawnee warrior Little Turtle ignominiously defeated the General's troops. Regarding this affair, Jefferson who was Secretary of State at that time privately expressed the view that the government had yet to discover "what experience has long ago taught us in Virginia, that rank and file fighting will not do against Indians." Since Washington was also a Virginian, he should have said, "what all Virginians in his part of the country, i.e. Albemarle County, knew." Jefferson preferred a less militant approach and in his instructions to Lewis and Clark he made a point of encouraging good relations with all the tribes they encountered. They were to provide medical help (smallpox vaccinations, e.g.) and given needed items, e.g. pots, knives, axes, etc. to the extent that the voyagers were able. Jefferson himself made a study of several Indian languages—their vocabularies—which unfortunately were lost in transit from Washington to Monticello. He also encouraged Indians to become educated and ultimately citizens of the country. Unfortunately he felt differently about the capabilities of Blacks to become citizens or otherwise integral members of American society. But he was very proud of the fact, if it was a fact, that on his mother's side, he may have been related to the Powaton princess, Pocahantas.

Lincoln's position vis-à-vis the Indian is harder to determine. It is known that he interrupted his first political campaign for Illinois State Senator in

1832 to fight the Sauk and Fox Indians who had resisted the encroachment of white settlers first in Wisconsin and then had been forced to move southward to Illinois and then by the government forced to move to Iowa. An attempt by the Indians to regain their lands in Illinois led to the so-called Black Hawk War, named after the Sauk leader, Black Hawk. Lincoln was only 23 years old at the time, his service lasted only three months, and he was not involved in any actual fighting.

During the Civil War, although his mind was preoccupied with other matters, he still found time to deal with some of the repercussions of the Santee Sioux uprising in Minnesota during 1862. Their reservation land along the Minnesota River near New Ulm had been invaded illegally by white settlers, and the annuities due the Indians for 1862 had been delayed. Food and other supplies were in the Agency warehouses, but the Agency Superintendent refused to distribute them. Traders cut off credit to the Indians. The Indians were desperate and one thing led to another, such as the taking by the Indians of a few eggs from a settler's chicken, which eventually resulted in the killing of three white men and two women, and later still others. Troops were sent out and many Indians were either killed or captured. The captives were taken in chains to Fort Snelling near St. Paul where a gallows was erected. An Episcopal Bishop, the Right Reverend Henry Whipple, appealed to President Lincoln proving to him that the Indians had good reasons for their hostility. Lincoln's response was that none should die merely for fighting in a battle, but should be treated as prisoners of war. Hundreds of Indian lives were thus saved, although some 38 were hanged for either murder or rape.

Lincoln seems not to have had any specific Indian policy and his record with respect to them is rather spotty, but it would appear that his view that there be "Charity to all, and Malice toward none" was intended to apply as much to Indians as it was to Blacks and to slaveholders.

Theodore Roosevelt did much to promote the conservation of forests and other natural resources of this country, and he was definitely fond of the western part of this country. He even bought two cattle ranches in North Dakota (then Dakota Territory next to the current Montana border) in 1884, near the Little Missouri River, during a lull in his political life. He lived there himself for a time and even spent some 14 hours in the saddle on occasion. But his policies regarding the Indians were totally unenlightened, to say the least. In his book, *The Winning of the West* (I, 90) he clearly states that "The settler and pioneer have at bottom had justice on their side; this great continent could not have been kept as nothing but a game preserve for squalid savages." In a speech made in New York, January, 1886, he also said, "I don't go so far as to think that the only good Indians are the dead Indians, but I believe nine out of ten are, and I shouldn't like to inquire too closely into the case of the tenth. The most vicious cowboy has more moral principle than the average Indian." He even arranged to have the captured Apache chieftain, Geronimo, ride in his inauguration parade, as a kind of "trophy," because, as he said, "I wanted to give the people a good show." Although Geronimo pleaded with Roosevelt to let him die "in my own country," he died at Fort Sill, Oklahoma Territory, as a prisoner in 1909. (Debo, 282).

In many respects Theodore Roosevelt compares very nicely with George Armstrong Custer, whom he must have admired. Both were expert horsemen, and both enjoyed warfare. Roosevelt viewed his achievements in war at least as great as his achievements in peace. Initially he opposed the League of Nations in favor of a war pact with Britain and France. Ironically, this man of war was the first American recipient of the Nobel Peace Prize! His eager service during the Spanish-American War, an ill-conceived project, and his audacious ride up San Juan Hill, reminds one of Custer's audacious, but less successful, foray up the Little Bighorn Ridge. Custer had the impression that in proceeding against the Indians he was only punishing rebels for their traitorous acts against the people. Roosevelt was under the impression that in prosecuting the war against the Spaniards he was only punishing them for their maltreatment of the Cubans people, and their sabotage of the battleship, *The Maine*, which, as naval historians and other investigators have discovered was not the work of the Spanish at all.

It is probably not at all surprising that someone would come up with the idea of a sculpture in the Rushmore region of the Black Hills of a leader of the Sioux Indians. It is not at all clear whose idea it was, but a group was formed and some ten Lakota chiefs sponsored the project. Although it may never be completed as it is now envisaged (so far only the face and part of the outstretched arm are completed), there is something troubling about the attempt to out-do the Rushmore Memorial. When completed it is expected to be several times larger than the heads on Mt. Rushmore, but that means that even more of the surface of this holy mountain will be scared. Is that really what the Indians want?

Also, why did someone choose Crazy Horse? Crazy Horse was of course a fierce warrior and led the Indian tribes against Custer's regiment at the Little Bighorn. He survived and Custer didn't. But what else is he known to have done to benefit his people? There is no authenticated picture, photograph, or other likeness of him in existence. Apparently not even Korczak Ziolkowski claimed that the sculpture was a true likeness of Crazy Horse, but only a "metaphoric tribute to the spirit of Crazy Horse and Native Americans." (http://enwikipedia.org/wiki/Crazy Horse Memorial). But did Crazy Horse speak up for his tribe when they were starving on the reservation? Did he guide them to temporary safety in Canada, as Sitting Bull did, and as Chief

Joseph of the Nez Percé at least tried to do? Did he engage in any diplomatic efforts, such as Red Cloud and Spotted Tail attempted?

Edgar I. Stewart describes Crazy Horse as "fanatical" and calls him the "Stonewall Jackson of the Sioux" (Stewart, 436) a clever Civil War analogy which could easily be extended by calling Sitting Bull the "Robert E. Lee of the Sioux." The relationship between the two is well illustrated by a story Stanley Vestal tells (127–131) about a battle with a military escort of the Northern Pacific Railroad Company in which both Crazy Horse and Sitting Bull were involved. Too many braves were being killed and Sitting Bull wanted to end the conflict. Crazy Horse did not and kept racing his horse back and forth in front of the soldiers. Sitting Bull decided he had to remind his Indians who was in charge of this frantic but ill-chosen battle. He did something that was truly remarkable although fraught with danger. Like Socrates of ancient Athens who, tiring of a war, simply got up, walked through the enemy lines, and so astounded his enemies that they failed to attack him, Sitting Bull simply gathered up his pipe and his long beaded bag of kinnikinick, tobacco, or whatever he smoked, strolled out in front of his tribesmen within sight of the soldiers across the way, sat down, took out his pipe, filled it and began smoking as if he were sitting outside his own tepee. He then invited the other Indians to join him. Two young and foolhardy Cheyennes accepted his invitation and with bullets from the soldiers' rifles flying all around them proceeded to smoke the pipe. When finished, Sitting Bull carefully cleaned the bowl of the pipe and slowly returned to the Indian line. So astounded were his compatriots with his sheer bravery (and good luck) that when he said, "That's enough," they stopped their fighting and returned home.

Crazy Horse at first ignored Sittiing Bull's command, had his horse shot from under him, and barely made it back to the others without getting killed. Vestal sums up the episode by saying, "Crazy Horse was brave as a lion, but he lacked the intelligence, imagination, and originality displayed by his Chief." (Vestal, 130).

The Crazy Horse Memorial thus immortalizes a man whose countenance is totally unknown to any living person; whose burial place is undiscoverable; whose exploits were wholly those of a warrior whose exalted title of "Shirt Wearer" was once stripped from him (Ambrose, 341); a man who cared for his people and sympathized with their poverty and their hardships but did practically nothing to help them; who was not a man of great intelligence, of little imagination, and yet fanatical in all his relationships with his friends and relatives as well as with his foes. He was never a man of peace, as Sitting Bull tried to be, and his credentials for being a benefactor of his race are negligible. His countenance no more deserves commemoration on Paha Sapa than do the other four on Mount Rushmore.

If the Rushmore Memorial had been conceived differently, as it should have been, as a commemoration, indeed, as a celebration, not so much of the manliness and militancy of our national leaders, but of America the beautiful, and of the Black Hills in particular as a sanctuary of rest, repose, and peace, then all persons of whatever race could identify with it. Because of its unique location, special tribute ought to have been made to the Indians, and because of its national significance, perhaps not merely to the Sioux or Cheyenne Indians who inhabited the region before the coming of the white population, but also to other tribes who share this continent. Deference to the Indians at the very least is what they are due.

It seems to me that the figures for this memorial should not have been selected simply or primarily because they were warriors. If that were the proper criterion, then the countenance of Custer as well as Crazy Horse should also have been included, but I doubt that many who know the details of Custer's life, and certainly no Indians, would consent to that selection. Persons known for their contributions to the general welfare of Indians should have been chosen. If it could all be done over, which it cannot be of course, and assuming that the whole sculpture was inevitable, I think the following arrangement would have been preferable. Since Paha Sapa was literally stolen from the Indians, at least two of the carved faces should be of Indians. My personal candidates would include Sitting Bull of the Hunkpapa Sioux (1843?-1890); Chief Joseph of the Nez Percé (1840?–1904); Benjamin Hawkins (1760?-1816), one of the first and best Indian Agents to the southern tribes of the Cherokee and the Creeks; and President Ulysses S. Grant (1822–1885; President 1869–1877), who *as President* did his best to prevent total Indian genocide by Generals William T. Sherman, Philip H. Sheridan, who held the view that the only good Indian was a dead Indian, and George A. Custer, who appears to have shared the same view. A woman's face should also have been included My choice would be that of Sacagawea, a Shoshone captive of the Hidatsa Sioux who became the indispensable guide of Lewis and Clark on their expedition to the Pacific and back (May 14, 1804 to Sept. 22, 1806).

Chapter Four

Fort Laramie Treaty of 1868

Having been raised in the shadow of the Black Hills and a Monument dedicated more to the war-related experiences of our national leaders than to their love of peace, I should have had curiosity enough to inquire why, and have delved more deeply into the history of the region. But I didn't. I do recall being taught American history, including South Dakota history, but I am sure that it was the kind of thing one could read in an ordinary encyclopedia. I have more definite recollections of the landing of the Pilgrims in Massachusetts and of Columbus' voyage to America. One project I recall (it was probably prescribed by the *Shannon County Course of Study*) involved carving out of a bar of Ivory soap a replica of either the Niña, the Pinta, or the Santa Maria—you could take your pick. My Indian schoolmates always seemed to do a better job than the rest of us. Perhaps because of their greater artistic talent. In any case, my historical studies up through high school were clearly "Anglo-dominated." Not a word was said about Indians, except for some comments regarding their encounters with the Pilgrims, or their assaults on westward bound land-grabbing white settlers.

Vine DeLoria, Jr., in his book, *Custer Died For Your Sins*, recounts several Columbus jokes as told by Indians. They are almost as numerous as jokes about Custer. One he tells is that Columbus began his journey with four ships, but when one went over the edge, he arrived in the new world with only three. That is not a story (or joke) I ever heard from any of my teachers. Nor was another DeLoria tells that goes more or less as follows. When Columbus finally landed an observant Indian said to another, "Well, there goes the neighborhood." Such spoofing would have earned me several demerits in deportment, maybe even an 'F' grade.

Had I inquired more deeply into the history of the Black Hills, examined more critically what I was taught, and broken through the wall of silence regarding the property and other civil rights of Indians which was then imposed upon all persons living in reservation country, I might have come across the Fort Laramie Treaty of 1868. When Vine DeLoria, Jr., and I were both living on the Pine Ridge Reservation, he had not yet brought all this background information to the public's attention. Nor was a reformer-protestor such as Russell Means of American Indian Movement (AIM) around to focus attention on these matters of intense interest to Indians and their white supporters. It is worth noting, however, that in 1980 a federal legal case demanding reparations for the Black Hills take-over was filed, but the settlement awarded by the Supreme Court was rejected by the Sioux plaintiffs, and so the problem still awaits a solution.

The ultimate basis for all such appeals is the Treaty of 1868. Although it was modified in 1889 by statute (25 Stat. 888), and many parts of it totally and illegally rescinded, it is still worth while to examine its provisions. But perhaps before examining the treaty in detail a word or two needs to be said regarding why such a treaty was sought after in the first place. Ulysses S. Grant became president on March 4, 1868 just a month before the treaty was actually signed. Prior to his administration there of course had been sporadic bloody encounters with Indians, such as the uprising of the Santee Sioux in Minnesota during 1862 and the Chivington or Sand Creek, Colorado, massacre of November 29, 1864, but white-Indian relations on the western plains had been relatively calm and peaceful until after the Civil War, during which the U.S. Cavalry, of which Custer was a part, and other units of the U.S. Army were fully engaged. Even General Sherman who made an inspection of the Plains region in the summer of 1866 said, "God only knows when, and I do not see how, we can make a decent excuse for an Indian War." (Debo, 215) However, when Sherman replaced Grant as commanding General of the Army, and Sheridan became commander of the army units assigned to the Plains, the relationships with the Indian tribes of the Plains and the Southwest became more bellicose.

In the spring of 1866 the peace advocates of the Indian Office in Washington, D.C. sent E. B. Taylor, commissioner of Indian Affairs, to Ft. Laramie to attempt to get the hostile Sioux, Cheyenne, Arapahoe, and other tribes to sign a peace treaty. It turned out to be a total and disastrous failure and an outrageous attempt at trickery. Red Cloud and Man-Afraid-of-His-Horses came to see what presents the great White Father had to offer, and to have the entire treaty read and explained to them. In this treaty the government was to be given the right to build forts and roads in Indian country, namely the Powder River and Dakota Territories. When hearing these provisions the main chiefs all refused to sign the treaty. Taylor then tried to explain, untruthfully, that the treaty did not contemplate the construction of any new roads, other than the Bozeman Trail which then already existed, but which the Indians wanted closed. He also dissembled regarding the plan to build a series of forts near the Bozeman Trail. They had not yet been built, but he probably knew that the army under the command of Colonel Henry B. Carrington was preparing to do just that. Once this intended deception was discovered by the Chiefs there assembled, including Red Cloud and Standing Elk (a Brulé Chief), they told the peace commissioners that they would resist this invasion of their territory, and abruptly left the meeting. Back in Washington, Taylor falsely reported that most of the hostile tribal leaders had signed the treaty, and that Red Cloud, who had not, was but a leader of small influence.

Naively, the government adopted this version of the treaty, and ordered the erection of Fort Reno, Fort Phil Kearny, and Fort C.F. Smith, which were thereafter periodically attacked by Indians, as were also the travelers of the Bozeman Trail. Then in December of 1866 the Fetterman Massacre occurred. Attacks on the wood train which supplied timber and supplies to the forts had become common and Captain William J. Fetterman was dispatched to defend the train. Fetterman was known for his boast that with one company he could whip one thousand Indians and with a regiment he could clear the plains of all the hostile tribes. Disobeying strict orders of his superior, Colonel Carrington, Fetterman chased the Indians away from the wood train, which was his assignment, but then continued to follow the Indians into an ambush from which none of his command of some 80 men survived. Carrington's report of the incident to President Grant, Carrington claimed, was later suppressed because it contained evidence of the mismanagement of Indian affairs. (Stewart, 42, 45.)

General Winfield Scott Hancock was of the opinion that the Plains Indians needed to be punished for their continued depredations of wagon trains, railroad stations, and thefts of goods and horses. He apparently felt that if one tribe, such as the Cheyenne, were to be punished (by killing as many of them as possible), then the others would be taught a lesson and stop their attacks upon the white settlers. The problem was actually finding them. He sent out Lt. Colonel Custer with the seventh cavalry to track them down without much success. Finally, Custer discovered some Cheyennes and Arapahoes camped on the upper Washita River on the western edge of Indian Territory (what is now Oklahoma). His cavalry attacked the camp, killed Chief Black Kettle, one of the few who had survived the Chivington massacre, and his wife and an uncounted number of Indians. Some 53 women and children were taken prisoner. General Sheridan, his superior officer, was delighted with his protégé's success.

After this "Battle of the Washita," two Kiowa chiefs, Satanta and Lone Wolf, came to General Sheridan to make peace. He arrested them and let their tribe know that they would be hanged unless the entire tribe came to Fort Cobb. Custer pulled the same trick with the Cheyenne. He invited the chiefs to his camp, jailed three of them, and prepared to hang them if their tribesmen didn't turn over two white women captives and do as they were told.

The debate between the War Department, which favored all out warfare, and the Interior Department, in Washington, D.C., which favored peace, had been going on for some time, but suddenly it ended by a decision, surprisingly, to make peace. Whether Grant had a hand in this decision so near his election as president, or whether it was clear to almost everyone that too many disastrous and shameful actions by the Army had been committed and it was time to try a different strategy, it is difficult to determine. The United States government actually apologized for the Chivington or Sand Creek massacre (Debo, 198), and although the ambush at Washita wasn't quite in the same category, there must have been many who deplored it, although as we shall see later in Chapter VII there were many who applauded it.

In any case, Congress created a Peace Commission, which included General Sherman even though he had come to the conclusion that "we must act with vindictive earnestness against the Sioux, even to their extermination, men, women, and children." (Debo, 234). After several failed attempts to get the chiefs of the various Sioux bands to agree to a meeting, one was finally arranged at Fort Laramie during April of 1868. All the Commissioners except one signed the treaty. Nearly all of the Chiefs who represented the Sioux bands as well as the Arapahoes also signed or "touched the pen." These included Red Cloud and Man-Afraid-of-His Horses for the Oglalas, and Spotted Tail and others for the Brulés. Most notably, however, is the fact that neither Sitting Bull, who was not a Hunkpapa Chief but an influential Medicine Man, and Crazy Horse who also was never a Chief but a prominent Oglala Warrior, did not attend the conference and did not sign the treaty. Both were opposed to making any concessions to the white man.

The Treaty of 1868, however, turned out to be the only treaty to have been ratified by the U.S. Senate which was on the whole favorable to the Indians. Article I contains a mutual pledge on the part of the Government of the United States and the Indian parties to the Treaty to cease all war between the parties "forever," and it provides a method of punishing any bad men among the whites who violate the treaty, and also any bad men among the Indians who "commit a wrong or depredation upon the person or property of any one, white, black, or Indian."

This is the only mention of black persons in the document and one wonders why the Commissioners included it. How many Blacks were there in that part of the country for the Indians to harm? Of course, one must remember that the commissioners were all acutely aware of the recent war in the South and the emancipation of slaves some of whom may have decided that their futures lay in the West. The commissioners may also have been aware that some of the slaveholders in the South had been Indians. The reference to bad men among the Indians may have been intended to cover not only "hostile" Sioux who might not accept the terms of the Treaty (such as Sitting Bull and Crazy Horse) , but also members of other tribes such as the Crows and Shoshones with which the Sioux tribes were constantly, if sporadically, at war. As a peace document it was indeed quite extensive in its coverage of possible contingencies.

Article II delimits what became known as the Great Sioux Reservation. The language, which is not without a certain vagueness, goes as follows:

> Commencing on the east bank of the Missouri river where the forty-sixth parallel of north latitude crosses the same, thence along the low-water mark down said east bank to a point opposite where the northern line of the State of Nebraska strikes the river, thence west across said river, and along the northern line of Nebraska to the one hundred and fourth degree of longitude west from Greenwich, thence north on said meridian to a point where the forty-sixth parallel of north latitude intercepts the same, thence due east along said parallel to the place of beginning; and in addition thereto, all existing reservations on the east bank of said river shall be, and the same is, set apart for the absolute and undisturbed use and occupation of the Indians herein named.

Besides allowing in Article II for the possibility that additional territory may be added to the reservation, the Treaty in Article XVI also stipulates "that the country north of the North Platte River and east of the summits of the Big Horn Mountains shall be held and considered to be unceded Indian territory."

The included map represents one attempt (there have been many by others) to indicate the extent of the treaty territory. Since the Great Sioux Reservation (GSR) was carved out of existing Dakota Territory (North and South Dakota had not yet become states), it turns out that the northern part of the GSR overlaps slightly with what became North Dakota. The Black Hills which were meant to be included also overlap with part of what became Wyoming although signers of the Treaty refer to Fort Laramie (not to be confused with the current city of Laramie) as being located in Dakota Territory. The only state with fixed borders is Nebraska which was admitted to the Union in 1867.

The unceded territory was intended as hunting grounds but the boundaries are very vague. No northern boundary is specified, and presumably the territory could extend to all of North Dakota and up to Canada. Similarly, although the southern boundary is specified as the North Platte and not the Platte River itself, it is unclear just how far along Nebraska's southern border

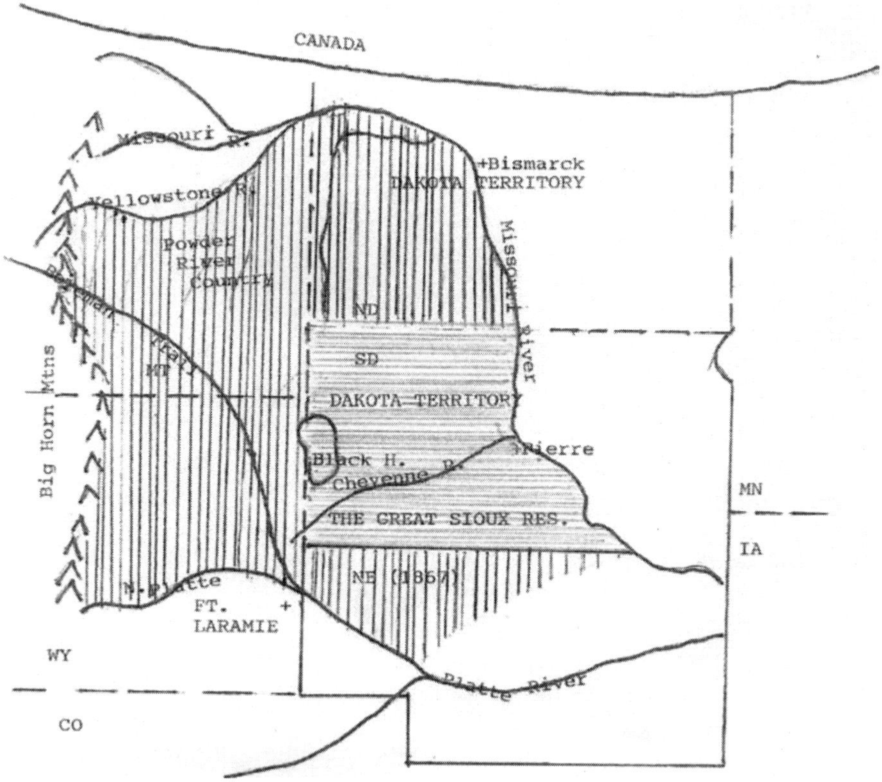

Great Sioux Reservation & Hunting Grounds. Fort Laramie Treaty of 1868.

it extends. Also unclear is the reference to "all existing reservations on the east bank" of the Missouri River. How far east? Was it meant to include the Sisseton Reservation on the Minnesota border, or the Santee Reservation which is actually in Nebraska?

Despite its vague references which the Sioux chiefs probably didn't even understand (many later claimed that the entire document had not been read to them), they were pleased with several of its provisions. One was that "no persons except those herein designated and authorized so to do, and except such officers, agents, and employees of the government as may be authorized . . . shall ever be permitted to pass over, settle upon, or reside in the territory." Another was that the U. S. government would supply a physician, carpenter, farmer, blacksmith, miller, engineer, and a teacher and school house "so soon as a sufficient number of children can be induced by the agent to attend school." The teacher was to be "competent to teach the elementary branches of an English education."

The unceded lands would be reserved for Indians only to hunt upon "so long as the buffalo may range therein in such numbers as to justify the chase." The Commissioners even at that time must have realized how greatly the buffalo herds had been diminished.

The part of the Treaty which must have most impressed Red Cloud and the other chiefs, however, was the promise on the part of the United States that "within ninety days after the conclusion of peace with all the bands of the Sioux Nation, the military posts now established in the territory . . . shall be abandoned, and that the road leading to them and by them to the settlements in the Territory of Montana shall be closed." The road mentioned was the Bozeman Trail and the other roads suggested were roads and trails in the unceded lands which led to the mines of Montana where gold had already been discovered.

Just when Red Cloud himself signed the Treaty of 1868 is a bit unclear. He withheld his signature until the three forts along the Bozeman Trail were abandoned by the U. S. Army and subsequently burned by the Indians. That may have occurred after the specified 90 day period or perhaps before depending on how anxious the military was to leave.

But peace between the parties did not occur. Sporadic attacks by Indians and the consequent responses of the soldiers continued. Then someone in Washington, D. C. got the bright idea of bringing Red Cloud and some other hostile Indians (in all, 17 men and 4 women) to visit the Great White Father (President Grant). The motive behind the invitation was to convince Red Cland his contingent that the power of the U.S. Government far exceeded any power the Indians had. Red Cloud reiterated his opposition to the white man's invasion of Indian territory, called the Treaty of 1868 a swindle because not all of it had been read to him, but nonetheless accepted the huge amount of "presents" given to him although, or perhaps because, he regarded the presents as a sign of weakness on the part of the Government. He and his entire group were taken to New York City where he again spoke at the Cooper Union causing a great sensation among the pro-Indian pacifists. Nothing was accomplished by either side. Sitting Bull, upon hearing of the trip dismissed it for what it was, a kind of charade. (Stewart, 55; Brown, 183).

Yet, for a time after the signing of the Treaty of 1868, the soldiers tried their best to enforce the terms of the Treaty. They arrested white settlers, miners, and others invading Indian territories, and there were many of them. They included settlers determined to use the Bozeman Trail to get to Oregon and other destinations in the Far West; surveyors for the Northern Pacific Railroad and their construction crews which never stopped laying rails even though their activities were in clear violation of the treaty; and miners intent upon developing the gold mines in Montana and later in the Black Hills. As one might have expected, the Army found their task not only difficult, in fact nearly impossible, since those arrested always found ways to return, but it was also not a task that Lieutenant General Philip H. Sheridan, who was commander of the Division of the Missouri, really supported or agreed to. He recommended that new forts be constructed in the midst of Indian Territory, a proposal which Congress failed to fund. Nonetheless a whole series of forts had been built in the general area, some before the Treaty of 1868 and some after: Fort Rice (1864), Fort Buford (1866), Fort Ransom (1867), Fort Totten (1867), Fort Stevenson (1867), Fort Pembina (1872), Fort Stewart (1872), Fort McKeen (1872), later renamed Fort Abraham Lincoln near present day Bismarck, North Dakota, and also Fort Sheridan (1874) and Fort Robinson (1874). Sheridan later contended that if Congress had gone along with his recommendation of two more to be constructed on the Big Horn River and the junction of the Tongue and Yellowstone Rivers (in the center of the unceded Powder River hunting grounds) the Sioux War of 1876 would not have occurred.

Most of the white violators of the Treaty—settlers, miners, railroaders, and the like—took the position that Indians have no rights, and who was the Government anyway to deprive settlers of perfectly workable and inhabitable land? Theodore Roosevelt later expressed essentially the same idea in his book, *The Winning of the West.* The Sioux, Cheyenne, and the other tribes, for their part were quire aware that wrongful trespasses were occurring, and that the government was attempting a grand and ominous encirclement of them. Naturally they fought back and Sheridan was hard pressed to prevent their depredations on settlers and attacks on the forts. So in addition to his requisition of more fortifications and troops and failing to get them, he also requested that Custer and his Seventh Cavalry be ordered from the southern Indian territories of Oklahoma and Kansas, where he had spent most of his time on the plains, to Dakota Territory.

Once there Custer and the Seventh Cavalry accompanied General D. S. Stanley on an expedition along the Yellowstone River, the purpose of which was to support the Northern Pacific's surveying parties, all of course in violation of the Treaty of 1868. Custer, in typical egotistical style, assumed command of the entire expedition, an act of insubordination which totally exasperated General Stanley, his superior, but avoided a court martial on this occasion because Stanley was a known alcoholic. More on this episode in Custer's life later in Chapter IX. The entire expedition was attacked by the Hunkpapa Sioux under the leadership of Sitting Bull. Two non-combatants who strayed from the main body of the troops were killed by Indians, but for some unexplained reason neither was scalped.

A persistent rumor existed about this time that gold could be found in the Black Hills. Gold had earlier been discovered in California (1849); in Colorado

(1858); and in Montana (1860). Had gold been discovered in the Black Hills before the Treaty of 1868, no doubt the Treaty would never have been written as it was. The rumor may have been started by members of an earlier exploration of the Black Hills by Lieutenant General G. H. Warren. His small party skirted the western edge of the area until they were met by a group of Sioux chiefs who demanded that they leave. Warren obeyed but encircled the area to Bear Butte without really entering the heart of Paha Sapa. Nonetheless they may have been there long enough to have discovered some gold. Various individual trappers, probably French, may also have helped to spread the rumor that there was gold just beneath the grass. Also, despite a dire warning by the Sioux that any Indian providing information about gold in the Black Hills to a white man would be punished by death, a story was circulated about a couple of Indians who brought some nuggets and gold dust into a nearby trading post, and admitted that it came from the Black Hills. The story was instantly relayed to every prospector in the West. Since the Sioux's own penalty for such a disclosure was so severe, there is reason to doubt the truth of the story, but it became part of the general rumor. In any case, General Sheridan decided that the question should be resolved and ordered Custer who was then headquartered at Fort Abraham Lincoln near present day Bismarck to make reconnaissance of the Black Hills which he did starting on July 22, 1874.

After a march of more than 227 miles, he arrived at the northern edge of the Black Hills with a complement of over 1200 Cavalry and Infantry, some sixty scouts (mostly Santee) and four Gatling guns. Fred Grant, the President's son, of the Second Cavalry, was on Custer's staff and accompanied him. One can easily speculate upon Custer's motive for arranging to have the President's son on his staff. The troops were followed by a huge train of provisions. It is reported that the whole procession was led by Custer's own brass band playing what has become the unofficial "fight song" of the Seventh's Cavalry, *The Garry Owen.* More on this topic in Chapter IX.

Of course the whole expeditionary invasion was a clear violation of the Treaty of 1868. Custer's official orders from General Sheridan were to make a reconnaissance of the area to obtain information regarding the trails of hostile Indians from the Yellowstone River through the Hills to the Missouri River. That was the ostensible reason for the invasion, although gold was the real reason. Neither was justification, however, for the clear violation.

Surprisingly, Custer's illegal but one might say "musical" entry into the Black Hills met with no resistance on the part of the Sioux Indians who were then living there. Yet, the Indians were well aware of Custer's presence—perhaps a little awed by the fanfare—but they let other Indians know of it by means of smoke signals. At first his Indian scouts refused to enter the Sacred Land, but Custer dismissed their fears and apparently at least some of them accompanied him into the interior. They discovered five Indian lodges in a valley and notified Custer who then sent his chief scout, Bloody Knife, to inform them of his friendly and peaceful intentions. To forestall any treachery on their part he surrounded their camp, gave presents of sugar, coffee, flour, and bacon to them and more or less coerced their chief, One Stab, to serve as his guide for the next three days. Custer stayed in the Hills from July to September.

Custer discovered, besides the gold which his geologists ascertained as being there, also what he named The Floral Valley. Like many later visitors, he compared it to a vast part, indeed even to New York's Central Park with which he was personally acquainted. The valley was so profuse with flowers that one could pluck them without dismounting. The cavalrymen adorned their horses with many different varieties of beautiful flowers. (Stewart, 64; Monaghan, 355; Ambrose, 377–8.)

In his own report of the expedition Custer noted the discovery of gold, as did the newspaper reporter he purposely brought along with him. Besides informing his commander in chief, President Grant, he saw to it that the whole world knew about the gold, fully aware of what the consequences would be. Keeping out fortune hunters became totally impossible and finally Grant had to order the Army not to try to enforce the provisions of the Treaty of 1868 which prohibited white settlers and prospectors from entering Paha Sapa without the express permission of the Indians.

Grant's next step was to send another Commission to negotiate with the Lakota (Sioux) Nation for the outright sale of the Black Hills. The commissioners finally offered to buy it for six million dollars ($6,000,000). Some Indians such as Red Cloud and Old Spotted Bear were willing to accept the offer (if raised to $7,000,000). The translator of Old Spotted Bear's remarks mistook the figure of $7,000,000 for $70,000,000, which the astounded commissioners immediately rejected. The Indians for their part learned that the $6,000,000 offer was also attached to another offer to purchase the unceded hunting grounds in the Powder River country of Montana and Wyoming as described in the Treaty of 1868 for an additional $50,000. This additional offer only infuriated the Indians who rejected it, packed up their belongings and left the meeting without signing anything. The Commission which had managed to assemble some 7000 Indians from all of the affected tribes in hopes that they could get the necessary ¾ vote as required by the Treaty to sell any part of the Great Sioux Reservation (GSR) found that they could get none to agree to sell anything. Exasperated, and under great pressure from the white population, the U. S. Congress in 1877 passed the Black Hills Act which, again contrary to the terms of the 1868 Treaty, unilaterally and without a vote of the Indian tribes transferred the Black Hills to the United States.

If today one consults the Internet regarding "Paha Sapa," one will find a catalog of the history of attempts by the U.S. Government and the Courts to make the sale of the Black Hills a reality. Since Custer's time, of course, uranium has been discovered there so its value has increased. The latest Court approved "settlement offer" is $107,000,000, but the Sioux tribes of South Dakota, individually and collectively, have refused the settlement, so the political if not the legal issue remains undecided. On the Internet the Sioux position is bluntly stated: "Paha Sapa Kin Wiyopeya Unkiyapi kte sni yelo!" or in English, "We will not sell the Black Hills!"

Chapter Five

Little Big Horn and Wounded Knee

Custer returned to his headquarters at Fort Abraham Lincoln where he spent the entire winter with his wife, except for their usual fall/winter sojourn in New York City. Surrounded in his quarters in Dakota Territory by mounted heads of buffalo, antelope, wolf, bear, and panther, all of which he had killed, and in some cases, mounted himself without the aid of a taxidermist, he was content, fully knowing perhaps that his recent venture into the Black Hills had set the stage for all-out war with the Sioux Nation.

Custer's involvement did not occur right away. During 1875 he spent his time attempting to prove that the Hunkpapa Indian, Rain-in-the-Face, was the one who murdered the two noncombatants mentioned earlier in connection with the Stanley expedition who had strayed from the main column of the Seventh Cavalry. Dr. Honzinger had been the veterinarian for the Cavalry and Mr. Baliran the sutler, or supplier of goods to the regiment. Custer managed to extract, or recalling his prior treatment of captive Indians, perhaps it could be said that he "extorted" a confession from Rain-in-the-Face by means of a lengthy four hour long interrogation of him while locked alone with him in his cell. His tribesmen assumed that Custer would hang him as a criminal, with or without a trial, and requested that they be allowed to visit him. Custer granted their request; afterwards Chief Iron Horn thanked Custer for his care of Rain-in-the-Face, and gave him the ornamented buckskin shirt he was wearing. It is pure speculation but one can't help but wonder whether it was this shirt which Custer wore during his last battle. Custer, as all the world knows because of various paintings of his "last stand," often dressed "out of uniform," much as many modern day generals, such as General George C. Patton have done.

While awaiting marching orders during 1875 and the spring of 1876, Custer was also involved in discovering why so much grain and corn had been stolen from the warehouses of Fort Lincoln. He suspected that the civilians running the trading post as well as even the Mayor of nearby Bismarck were implicated in the thefts. By numerous apparently warrant-less searches he managed to identify the thieves who were subsequently tried in Fargo, which was then either in Dakota Territory or Minnesota.

In February, 1876, the *New York Herald*, published by James Gordon Bennett, called for a full investigation of fraudulent practices in the War Department relating to traderships in Indian country, and at military bases such as Fort Lincoln. The main culprit, the newspaper alleged, was W. W. Belknap, then Secretary of War, who was solely responsible for the distribution of trader positions at military posts and who allegedly received kick-backs from the persons he appointed. These persons, including allegedly the President's brother, Orvil Grant, in turn received kick-backs from those actually assigned to handle the trading posts and to receive goods from the government intended for the Indians but often never distributed to them. It was widely understood that Custer attempted to protect both his own troops and the Indians from the rapacious acts of the traders, but was often unable to do anything about the fraud which was then affecting practically the entire western theatre of action.

Representative Heister Clymer, a Democrat (Grant was a Republican), chaired the Committee investigating the War Department and found enough in the records of the War Department to call for an impeachment of Belknap, who resigned his post. Since Orvil Grant was extensively involved, his testimony was demanded and given, much to the chagrin of the President. Clymer also decided to demand by subpoena the testimony of Lt. Colonel George Armstrong Custer for further details of the post traders' illegal behavior and his personal knowledge of Belknap.

By this time General Sheridan had already formulated his campaign against the "hostile" Indians. Upon the advice of his Secretary of War and Secretary of the Interior, President Grant had decided to notify all the Indians in the unceded lands that they must retire to the existing Indian Agencies and Reservations or be treated as "hostile" and be herded in. This decision, of course, allowed Sheridan and company to proceed with their all-out assault which they regarded as essentially punitive, not protective. It was three-pronged. General George Crook would come up from the North Platte in the south; General John Gibbon would proceed east up the Yellowstone River country from Fort Ellis; and Custer, with his Seventh Cavalry, under the overall command of General Terry would come west toward the Powder River country from Fort Lincoln. General Crook started his assault on March 1; Gibbon and Terry were to commence their marches somewhat later.

Custer didn't know exactly when his Cavalry would join the attack but he knew it was immanent (not later, he surmised, than April 15), and wanted desperately to be a part of it. He appealed to Representative Clymer to allow him to submit answers to their questions in writing and by deposition. Clymer, who may have had political motives, such as embarrassing the Administration, rejected his appeal, and although Custer claimed that all he could give by way of testimony was hearsay, he was forced to go to Washington for an indefinite period beginning with his testimony on March 29. He was recalled April 4 for more testimony. On the 17th of April, when the impeachment trial of Secretary Belknap began, he was still in Washington. He telegraphed General Terry to see whether he could speed the process but without success. He was also unsuccessful in obtaining an interview with President Grant who nonetheless kept him waiting in his outer office for several hours, on each of three occasions. After he had been released by the Investigating Committee bringing charges against Belknap, Custer left Washington for Chicago without getting the permission of the War Department. Upon learning that, Grant had him arrested and ordered that he not be allowed to join Terry's expedition against the hostile Indians. After intercessions by both General Terry and General Sheridan, Grant agreed to allow Custer to accompany the expedition but only in command of his own regiment. There is some evidence that Custer, upon being permitted to return to Fort Lincoln and the campaign, had already devised ways to avoid the supervening command of General Terry just as he had done previously with respect to General Stanley.

It wasn't until May 7, 1876 that Terry and Custer received their orders to begin their long trek from Fort Abraham Lincoln to Montana Territory. Meanwhile General Crook's force of some 1300 men had come up from the North Platte and on June 17 encountered a large war party of Sioux and Cheyenne Indians along the Rosebud Creek where a fierce battle was fought by the two opponents which ended in a draw. Although the exact number of Indians Crook met is unknown, Crook had the impression that he was fighting the entire Sioux Nation. He retreated with minimal losses to his base camp on Goose Creek, thereby avoiding Custer's fate. His defeat was heralded in the press as a victory, but his part in the campaign against the hostiles had been stopped for the rest of the summer. He also became the recipient of much criticism for his actions from General Sheridan.

General Gibbon with a force of about 450 infantrymen met with General Terry's troops, including Custer's Seventh Cavalry at or in the vicinity of the junction of the Yellowstone River and mouths of the Rosebud and Bighorn Rivers. Terry's scouts convinced him that the bulk of the hostile Indians were located on or near the Little Bighorn. The plan was for Gibbon, with his 450 men, and Terry with his approximately 900 men would move up the Bighorn toward the Indian encampment. Custer with his 31 officers and approximately 585 enlisted men, plus a few Arikara and Crow scouts, would circle around and strike the assembled Indians from above.

Custer got exactly what he had wanted—his own regiment entirely free from the control and guidance of his superior, General Terry. Custer's rapid march up the Rosebud and to the valley of the Little Big Horn, a distance of approximately 90 miles in two days and one night, was quite obviously made in order to beat the forces of Terry and Gibbon to the Sioux villages. Although totally ignorant of the number of Indians he was pursuing, Custer was convinced that his regiment could defeat any number of Indians he encountered, and so achieve for himself alone the glory of a decisive military victory. Nobody seems to know exactly how many Indians took part in the battle which occurred on June 25, 1876. Estimates vary from 1500 to 5000. Major Marcus Reno guessed that his troops were outnumbered five to one. But so confident was Custer that he turned down Terry's offer of a battalion of the Second Cavalry and a platoon of Gatling guns.

In what follows I shall not attempt to give a detailed account of the battle which followed. There have been many accounts from persons such as Major Reno and Captain Fred Benteen, both members of Custer's regiment, from Mrs. Elizabeth Custer herself, and from scores of military experts since then. Many of the accounts are inconsistent with each other in many respects. Since none of the Custer party survived, there were no living witnesses other than the participating Indian combatants who survived, and even their accounts do not always agree. I leave the ultimate analysis of the battle to the military scholars at West Point, where, incidentally, Custer's bones are now buried.

The following commentary is concerned only with the generally agreed upon facts relating to the incident in the hopes of clarifying President Grant's own judgment that the Battle of the Little Big Horn was totally "unnecessary." It is also hoped that such a discussion may, to use Gutzon Borglum's expression, help tell us "what manner of man" Custer was and how his death helped to shape the lives of the Indians who were thereafter so ignominiously assigned to reservations.

It is fairly clear that if Custer had not insisted on a forced march of approximately 90 miles in two days and one night, his regiment would have met the infantry and the Second Cavalry of General Gibbon and General Terry, and together they may have convinced Sitting Bull and his many thousands of warriors either to give up or at least retreat. How, after all, would they have been able to stand up to all those Gatling guns? Custer's motive and behavior on this occasion marks him not only as a self-serving egotist but also as a reckless commander.

Once given complete control of his regiment, Custer proceeded to split it into three parts, Captain Benteen in charge of one part, Major Reno in charge of another, with Custer himself leading the main part. It was actually four parts if one counts the "pack" or ammunition train with its 130 men which followed behind. This three-pronged approach to the battle was the same one the campaign started with before General Crook was sidelined. It was also apparently the tactic Custer himself had used successfully during the Civil War. In this case, however, it failed to work because Reno who was to support Custer if he ran into trouble also ran into massive numbers of Indians intent on killing him. He simply could not, he argued at his court-martial, have blindly forged ahead through the Indians surrounding him without great loss of life. Benteen also, instead of going to Custer's aid found it necessary to rescue Reno. Custer and the remainder of the regiment had to battle the Indians who greatly outnumbered them by themselves alone. The Indians included Crazy Horse, but not Sitting Bull who had masterminded the entire engagement.

The ultimate aim of the plan embarked upon was to surround the Indians and prevent them from escaping. It was naively assumed that the Indians would attempt to flee once they discovered the extent and might of the U.S. forces. But the Indians were well aware of the presence of the soldiers in the unceded lands of the Powder River region, and they did not flee. Custer managed to put himself in a position where neither he nor the Indians could do anything but fight to the death.

In his hurry to kill Indians, and so enhance his military reputation, and perhaps secure a chance at the White House, Custer failed to ascertain just how many Indians were aligned against him. It seems incredible that he would risk life and limb (his own as well as that of his men) until this intelligence regarding the enemy was known. Yet Custer was willing to chance it. His regiment could defeat any number of Indians, he thought. Of course this action meant going contrary to (that is, actually disobeying) the orders of his superiors.

The fact is that Custer had no more regard for Indian lives than he did for the lives of the animals he had hunted down and mounted in his living room. After the Battle of Washita during which many Indian lives were destroyed by him and his Cavalry, he also slaughtered 900 Indian ponies, rather than allow them into the hands of other Indians. He did not share President Grant's hope (which was also Jefferson's) of incorporating Indians into American society. Toward the end of the Civil War he belatedly decided to oppose slavery as an institution, but objected to giving negroes the right to vote. As he said, "I should as soon think of elevating an Indian chief to the Popedom of Rome"—which rather concisely expresses his bigotry towards Indians as well as his bigotry toward Blacks. He sympathized far more with the genocidal aims of Generals Sherman and Sheridan.

It is difficult to say what would have happened if Custer had not made the mistakes attributed to him, or if his ultimate purpose in fighting the Indians was different from what it actually was. But in the light of what subsequently happened following the Battle of the Little Bighorn, it is quite clear that President Grant was quite correct when he judged the whole conflict "unnecessary." It is equally clear that Custer proved by his actions what an essentially self-promoting and amoral person he has often been described as being.

Another reason that the Battle of the Little Bighorn was unnecessary, besides the fact that it would have ended in victory rather than defeat if only Custer had obeyed orders, is that the Indians by this time had really no place to go. The buffalo herds, which had supplied the Plains Indians with food, shelter, and clothing, were severely diminished. Constantly pursued by the Army, the Little Big Horn Mountains offered little refuge and kept them moving from camp to camp. With winter approaching, they really had little choice but either to head for Canada or settle on one of the reservations.

Colonel (later General) Nelson A. Miles, after whom Miles City, Montana, is named, became head of the Army of the Western Territories after Custer's death. He, with General Crook and others, chased Sitting Bull and his Hunkpapa Sioux all over the Powder River country, engaging in battles with them, destroying their winter villages, and preventing them from hunting and settling down. Sitting Bull, with about 400 lodges (approximately 3000 persons) crossed over into Canada in September, 1876, and stayed there until 1881 when, because of the extremely cold climate and a paucity of buffalo and other game, and a lack of material support from the Canadian government, except for protection, he and a remnant of his tribe returned and agreed to live on the Standing Rock Reservation in Dakota Territory (which is now in South Dakota and part of North Dakota). Although offered a pardon, his return was treated as a surrender and he was imprisoned at Fort Randall in South Dakota near the Nebraska border for two years. In 1883 he rejoined his people at the reservation, but because of the neglect of the Government, he found that they were being starved to death. Buffalo Bill Cody rescued Sitting Bull for a time during the summer of 1890 making him the star attraction in his *Wild West Show*. In December, 1890, while back at the reservation, Sitting Bull continued to protest his living conditions. The Army ordered his arrest. Indian police found it necessary to shoot him in the back. (see Chapter X for more details.) Many white persons as well as Indians regarded it as murder.

Colonel Miles, whom the Sioux called "Bear Coat" because of the bear fur he trimmed his overcoat and uniforms with, was responsible, directly or indirectly, for hunting down the Apache Chief Geronimo and exiling him to a Florida jail. He was also responsible for Chief Joseph's attempt to lead his Nez Percé tribe, who were starving, into Canada. When he and his tribe were within 30 miles of the border, Miles captured them, corralled them into reservations in the Northwest, from which they were exiled to miserable living conditions in Indian Territory (Oklahoma).

But by far Bear Coat Miles' greatest sin against the Plains Indians was his hand in the Massacre at Wounded Knee in 1890. He did not personally participate in the event but gave orders which were transmitted, apparently from his headquarters in Chicago, to Major Samuel Whitside of the Seventh U.S. Cavalry to arrest, disarm, and dismount Chief Big Foot's band of Minneconjou (Sioux) Indians. Later the remainder of the Seventh Cavalry joined in the operation with Colonel James W. Forsyth in command. It is mainly because of him that the massacre took place.

To his credit Miles may have had severe regrets about the massacre. In a letter to the Commissioner of Indian Affairs on March 13, 1917, twenty-seven years after the event, General Miles wrote

> "In my opinion, the least the Government can do is to make suitable recompense to the survivors for the great injustice which was done to them and the serious loss of their relatives and property. "The action of the commanding officer, in my judgment at the time, and I so reported was most reprehensible. The disposition of the troops was such that in firing upon the warriors they fired directly toward their own lines and also into the camp of the women and children, and I have regarded the whole affair as most unjustifiable and worthy of the severest condemnation."

This quotation is supplied by James H. McGregor in his book, *The Wounded Knee Massacre—From the Viewpoint of the Sioux* (92–3). McGregor was a superintendent first at Rosebud and later at Pine Ridge. My parents served under him at both reservations. McGregor may have actually known Miles because he speaks favorably of him in several places in his book, calling him a "great, good and wise leader." (98), and says that in their retirements certain Army officers such as General Miles and General Scott "realized the importance of Indian civilization and became true friends of the Indian people and often visited them." (8). Nonetheless, his criticism of Colonel James W. Forsyth, who was court-martialed and for a time deprived of his command, does not entirely relieve him of his responsibility for giving the order which initiated the entirely unwarranted, unnecessary, and inhumane slaughter of innocent defenseless men, women, and children.

Two other factors played a significant part in the tragic event of December 29, 1890. One was the news of Sitting Bull's assassination. Chief Big Foot's band, who were camped on the Cheyenne River Reservation near Cherry Creek, were joined by about a hundred Hunkpapa Sioux from the Standing Rock Reservation to the north trying to escape the fate of Sitting Bull, their former leader. They had been invited, as had Big Foot himself and his band, to the Pine Ridge Reservation by Chief Red Cloud not only for their protection but also for a Council of Sioux Chiefs to discuss the mutual problems of the Indians, particularly their internment on reservations and imprisonment there and in Florida and Oklahoma (Indian Territory) far from the homelands they knew best. Big Foot's band had already been decimated. Only 120 men were left, along with 230 women and children. In order to avoid being stopped and possibly killed by the soldiers, Big Foot decided that they had to leave their camp at Cherry Creek on the Cheyenne Reservation immediately and stealthily. They left at night and despite a lack of food, adequate clothing, and near blizzard conditions, they made it in approximately three days to within 14 miles of their destination of about 150 miles away before they were apprehended by Major Whitside, approaching from the south. Although exact figures are hard to come by, their forced march appears similar in many respects to the one Custer made up the Little Big Horn, and even more remarkable since it was made in the dead of winter.

The other cause of their hasty and fearful march was the apprehension on the part of the white population and the U.S. Army that the entire Sioux Nation was about to rise up again to attack them. Indians on the various Dakota reservations seemed agitated, no doubt in part because of the death of Sitting Bull, and because of memories of the manner in which Crazy Horse only 13 years before had been stabbed to death. White settlers were abandoning their farms and coming to the Agencies for what they thought was needed protection. The main reason for their unrest, however, was the attempt to crack down on a newly introduced religion which had attracted widespread acceptance by the Indians.

A Paiute Indian named Wovoka from Nevada had initiated a new religious movement which became known as the Messiah or Ghost Dance religion. It is interesting to note that Chief Short Bull, a friend of Crazy Horse, but not as I once supposed the same Chief Short Bull who was killed in the 1935 automobile accident in which my family and I were involved, became very attracted to the movement, so much so that he became part of a delegation of Indians chosen by a Council called by Red Cloud to go to Nevada to investigate the claims of Wovoka. The delegation included Good Thunder, Flat Iron, Yellow Breast, and Broken Arm from Pine Ridge; Short Bull and another Indian from Rosebud; and Kicking Bear from the Cheyenne River Agency. They were warmly received, learned the Ghost Dance, and returned to their respective reservations. Short Bull came back claiming to be a representative of, and later the actual Messiah of the Sioux people. The religion and its salient feature of the Ghost Dance caught on rapidly with many on the Rosebud, Pine Ridge, and Cheyenne River reservations. In order to insure that the participants might be out of sight of white people, the Ghost Dance, which went on for hours, was often staged in the Bad Lands.

The religion itself, apart from the Ghost Dance, was very compatible in many of its tenets with those of Christianity. It was monotheistic, pacifistic, moralistic, and prophetic. It predicted a time when the real Messiah would return from Heaven, reunite all Indians with their dead relatives and friends, and make the world a more pleasant place devoid of death, sickness, and old age. The buffalo herds would return, the white people would disappear from the Plains, and things would be much as they used to be. It is little wonder that many of the weary, hungry, aging, and more credulous Indians would rally to such a religion.

Dancing had always been a part of the native Indian religion, so that feature did not seem odd to the Indians, nor to Sitting Bull when he heard about the movement. He remained somewhat skeptical of the claim about the resurrection of the dead (Vestal,271), but on the whole he found little to object to. The white people, however, had associated the Sun Dance of the Sioux with uprisings and wars against them, and so looked upon the Ghost Dance as another indicator that the Indians were about to assemble for another all-out attack.

I mentioned that Big Foot was surprised when Major Whitside and a portion of the Seventh Cavalry came toward their column from the south. They had been expecting troops to pursue them from the north, from the Cheyenne River and Standing Rock Agencies. Probably Whitside received his orders to arrest Big Foot as a "Fomentor of Disturbance" while stationed at either Rosebud or Pine Ridge. That circumstance, if it occurred, would account for the direction from which they came. Whitside intercepted Big Foot's Minneconjous on December 28, near a place called Porcupine Creek. Big Foot, suffering from terminal pneumonia, ordered his men to hoist white flags to indicate their peaceful intentions. Whitside told Big Foot his orders were to accompany him to a cavalry camp near Wounded Knee. He had intended to disarm him and his men then and there, but his half-breed scout, John Shangreau, warned that to attempt to take their guns and horses might cause a fight. Whitside wisely countermanded his order and allowed the Indians to travel under escort to Wounded Knee, with the intent of disarming them on the next day.

The Indians were assigned an area to the south of the military camp. Whitside supplied them with rations and several tents. He also sent the regimental surgeon to attend to Big Foot. To make sure no Indians escaped during the night, he stationed two troops of Cavalry around their camp and set up two Hotchkiss guns on a rise above the camp. These Hotchkiss guns or "cannons," as they were also called, could fire two pound explosive shells at a speed of fifty per minute, sending shrapnel over a wide area.

During the night the rest of the Seventh Cavalry, under the command of Colonel Forsyth, came into camp from the east (possibly from the Rosebud

Agency). He had orders to take the Big Foot band to the Union Pacific Railroad and ship them to a military prison in Omaha, Nebraska. He assumed control of the entire operation and placed two more Hotchkiss guns near the other two, then settled down with a jug of whiskey to celebrate with Whitside and the other officers their victory over and capture of the ailing Big Foot.

In the morning of December 29, 1890, the Indians were all required to assemble in one place near Big Foot's wagon and told to disarm. Not satisfied with the number of weapons collected, Forsyth ordered that the tents all be searched, and all weapons, including knives, axes, awls, and any sharp cooking utensils be removed and placed with the rifles and guns. The men then had to open their blankets and be searched. The soldiers found only two rifles, one belonging to a young Minneconjou named Black Coyote who raised his Winchester above his head and shouted that he had paid much money for it and that it belonged to him. This particular scene has lately been reenacted in the movie, "Hidalgo." Dewey Beard (Wasu Maza) who survived both the Little Big Horn Battle and the Wounded Knee Massacre, later claimed that the young man was deaf. In the struggle with the soldier for the rifle, apparently the gun accidentally went off, and indiscriminate killing of the assembled Indians began. Many Indians who were not killed immediately ran off with soldiers following after them. Most were women and children. Dewey Beard's wife and baby were killed. The soldiers made no distinctions and killed as many as they could. Some 25 soldiers were also killed, and 35 wounded, so some persons at the time and even today talk of a "battle." It is patently obvious that the soldiers were killed or wounded by their own men in a cross-fire. How could it have been otherwise? The Indians by that time had no weapons, and were completely surrounded by soldiers. Obviously some of the bullets and explosive shells from the Hotchkiss guns intended for the Indians made their way to the soldiers on the opposite side with deadly results. In no way was Wounded Knee a "battle." It was simply and unquestionably a bloody "massacre."

But why the ferocity of the engagement? Why did the soldiers chase down the relatively few survivors and penetrate the bodies of babies and children with lead? Revenge for the humiliating defeat of Lt. Colonel George Armstrong Custer—that could be the only explanation. Custer's famous Seventh Cavalry had been outfoxed by Sitting Bull and out-fought by Crazy Horse. It was not enough that both Sitting Bull and Crazy Horse were now dead. The Seventh Cavalry had not in its opinion completely settled the score.

Mary Zeiss Stange, who raises bison on a ranch near Ekalaka, Montana, concludes her article entitled, "Living with the Ghosts of the Indian Wars" (see References) with the following statement:

> This is our history, and it is one of savagery. It's surely time to exorcise the ghosts of the 19th century Indian Wars, banishing them from the 21st century landscape. And the first ones to go should be those of the army of the West's conquering "heroes."

And by "conquering heroes" she means to include Custer, Miles, Crook, Terry, Sheridan, and Forsyth, all of whom, despite all their misdeeds, have had towns named after them.

Chapter Six

Indian Boarding Schools

The provision in the Fort Laramie Treaty of 1868 which required the U.S. Government to supply teachers and school houses for the education of Indian youth was included with the consent and hearty approval of the Indian delegates to the meeting, especially by their spokesman, Chief Red Cloud (Oglala). In 1870 he, along with other Indian leaders, were invited to visit President Grant in Washington, D.C. where he reiterated his opposition to the white man's invasion of Indian lands, and criticized the 1868 treaty because not all of the provisions had been read to him, but there is no evidence that he objected to the education clause. He repeated his performance at Cooper Union in New York to the delight of the pro-Indian pacifists. It is reported that Red Cloud along with Chiefs Red Dog, American Horse, Little Wound, Lone Bear, Slow Bulls, and Young Man Afraid of His Horses, were present on February 8, 1879 at the laying of the cornerstone of the school house at Pine Ridge Agency, originally called the Oglala Indian Trading School. It burned down in 1893, was replaced in 1897, and again in 1995 when a new High School and other educational buildings were constructed. In 1883 enroute to Washington for a second time, Red Cloud stopped at the Carlisle Indian School at Carlisle, Pennsylvania, to visit Lakota and other Indian students and to inspect the institution which, it seems, he generally approved.

Another influential Indian leader, Chief Spotted Tail (Sicangu) who had accompanied Red Cloud to Washington in 1870 to visit the "Great White Father," was also very pro-education. He himself had learned to read and write in English while incarcerated at Fort Leavenworth. He sent four of his own sons and two granddaughters (Spotted Tail had five wives and some 34 children) to Carlisle Indian School, but later while visiting Carlisle discovered that his sons wore military uniforms and were made to drill like white soldiers. Like Thomas Jefferson who abruptly removed his daughters from a convent school in Paris, once he learned that the nuns were having an unexpected religious influence on them, Chief Spotted Tail immediately removed his children and returned with them to Rosebud.

As mentioned in Chapter II, Spotted tail. or Sinte Gleska, to use his Indian name, met with President Rutherford B. Hayes in 1877 to request that the "Black Robes" (or Jesuits) be permitted to come to Dakota territory to teach the white man's ways and the English language. Why he requested the "Black Robes" (the Catholics) rather than the "White Robes" (the Episcopalians) or the "Short Coats" (the Presbyterians)—distinctions mentioned by a former Reservation Superintendent, James H. McGregor, (see bibliography) under whom my parents once worked, is unclear, but the fact remains that St. Francis Mission Indian Boarding School was founded in 1886 even before the Rosebud Reservation itself was established in 1889.

One might wonder why these charismatic leaders, who were themselves so little exposed to any formal education, would be so committed to what amounted to a very dramatic change in Indian life-style and culture. When one reflects upon their ardent commitment to education, it is nothing short of astounding. But even before and certainly after the Battle of the Little Bighorn and the Massacre at Wounded Knee they must have become aware that the invasion of white settlers could not be stopped and that there might be some advantages in cooperating with the white population. Of course not all Indians felt that way. Sitting Bull did his best to keep the whites from taking all of the Indian lands while at the same time maintaining the autonomy and unity of the bands of Hunkpapa, Oglala, Sicangu, Arapahoe, and Osage Indians who followed him to Canada, or as it was then known, the North American "British Possession." Chief Joseph attempted to do the same thing, but was apprehended by General ("Bear Coat") Miles before he and his Nez Percé tribe reached the border. Crazy Horse, like Sitting Bull, adamantly refused to meet with white commissioners, travel to Washington, or sign treaties. Of course both met with violent deaths, and undoubtedly their deaths only added to the general realization that complete independence from the white society was not to be had.

Richard H. Pratt, the founder and superintendent of Carlisle Indian Industrial School, made the following argument to Spotted Tail who apparently was convinced by it. Pratt told him:

> Spotted Tail you are a very great man. You are the chief of all these people. You have no education. If you had been educated like the white man you would have known that there was gold in the Black Hills, and might lead all these people to dig it out. If you were all as smart as the white man, you could take care of yourselves, just as the white man does, and would not need an agent. The white man gets ahead of you all the time, because he is educated and you are not. You

> have to leave your affairs in the hands of some white man, and there are so many changes of your agents you come to grief all the time. The way to avoid that is to become the equal of the white man. You may not greatly change yourself, because you are too old, but your children can easily equal the white man by being educated. You can remember when you did not see a white man out here. You had all this country to yourselves, and you were not disturbed; but the white man is coming on and on, and you cannot help it. He will walk right over you, unless you get up and stand in front of him as his equal. The way to do this is to get his education. (David Wallace Adams, 258; reprinted from *Native American,* 29 Nov., 1913, 503)

Of course the federal government for their part had their own reasons for wanting to educate Indians. The policies of the War Department, under the control of Generals Sherman and Sheridan ("the only good Indian is a dead Indian") varied from outright extermination to the restriction of all Indians to reservations where even Lt. Colonel (brevet General) Custer said that he himself would rather not live (Monaghan, 352). Nonetheless, he cooperated, as a good soldier, with the policy of forcing the Indians to live in confinement without the freedom to move about the plains, much less to hunt for buffalo which no longer existed in abundance as they once had, Quite obviously this more militant approach did little or nothing to amalgamate Indians into white society. On the other hand, the Department of the Interior, the Indian Office (later *Bureau)* and the "Peace Party" of the Grant and subsequent administrations attached themselves to the idea that the way to make co-habiting with Indians possible was to "civilize" them, and what better mechanism was there for doing that than the schools?

At first the government established day schools on the reservations, run primarily by religious groups, particularly the Catholic, Episcopal, Presbyterian, and Quaker denominations which were also encouraged to set up private parochial or "mission" schools, subsidized to some extent by the federal government. The Grant administration concluded that the persons most capable of civilizing Indians were the churches, particularly since he and they understood "civilization" first and foremost to be synonymous with Christianity. Additionally, their notion of civilization included teaching Indian youngsters how to speak, read, and write English; how to count, calculate acreage, participate in the free market economy, and own property. Negatively, the process of civilizing Indians, at least initially, meant cleaning them up (i.e., delousing and bathing them); discouraging the speaking of Indian languages and dialects; exchanging Indian names for more pronounceable English names (e.g., Ruth Miller for Chesehesbega; or Thomas Goodwood for Hehakaavita) [Adams, 109–110]; cutting Indian boys' long hair and braids; eliminating all distinctively Indian clothing, e.g., moccasins, blankets, leather dresses, loincloths, leggings, etc.; changing attitudes toward work, punctuality, ownership of property, saving and accumulating but not sharing money. The Sun Dance was outlawed and students were prevented from participating in Pow-Wows and other Indian festivals.

As more and more Indian children enrolled (recall that the Treaty of 1868 provided schools "as soon as a sufficient number of children can be induced by the agent to attend school") it seemed necessary to add reservation boarding schools such as the one established and "blessed" by Chief Red Cloud at Pine Ridge. It appears initially at least that the Indian Agent (a position later abolished) had little difficulty recruiting students.

Some of the Indian students (perhaps the "overflow") ended up in the public or county schools which I attended through seventh grade. I never really inquired about their presence. I assumed that some of them were the children of Agency employees, or sons or daughters of professionally trained Indians such as Vine DeLoria, Sr., a prominent and influential Indian Episcopal priest on the Pine Ridge Reservation. All the Indian children I played and studied with spoke English, although they undoubtedly also spoke Lakota at home. But some of them may have been children for whom there was simply no room in the Indian Boarding School on the hill across from White Clay Creek.

It was my distinct impression that the teachers at my school hailed from either the Eastern or Southern regions of the United States, and I suspected that what was true of the county public schools was also true of the teachers who were hired to teach in the Indian School Service. According to David Wallace Adams, however, the vast majority of applicants for the latter positions were from regions of the Midwest, the Plains, and the Far West. (Adams, 830) He claims that in 1892 the Indian Office employed some 418 superintendents and teachers from the following regions: Northeast, 40; South, 11; Midwest, 76; Plains, 181; and Far West, 110. His 1892 statistics contradict my general impression several decades later, but still his statistics apply only to teachers hired to teach in schools specifically set up for Indians, and my school, which nonetheless included a goodly share (perhaps a quarter to a third) of Indian students, was governed by state and county authorities. It is pure speculation but there may have been different hiring practices in the two school systems, or they had radically changed their policies from the 1890's to the 1930's, which, of course, is perfectly possible.

Another feature which this comparison of county public schools and federally sponsored schools illuminates is the rather curious emphasis, at least from today's perspective, on deportment and "citizenship." The whole aim of Indian education, from the standpoint of the government, was to make citizens out of them, people who might eventually live next to you as neighbors. But who would want to associate with "filthy" or "squalid savages" (an epithet commonly used in the literature of this period, and by none other than Theodore Roosevelt), or send their children to a school populated by lice infested, unhealthy, and "lazy Indian" children? To assure the attainment of the goal of citizenship it was imperative that all children, white as well as Indian, be clean, healthy, and industrious. It also helped to be cooperative, self-controlled, self-reliant, and respectful of authority (especially that of the teachers). Punctuality had never been regarded as a tribal custom or virtue; most Indians, regardless of tribal affiliation, were generally revolted by the idea of living by the clock, but these virtues were expected of them, as was the custom of courteous behavior (especially toward women); and good sportsmanship e.g., the ability to admit defeat when unavoidable. Individual initiative, rather than collective tribal prejudices, it was thought, should characterize the truly "white (i.e. civilized) Indian."

It is patently clear that the list of civic virtues which defined deportment on my 7th grade report card, even though I attended a public school, was but a reflection of current thinking about how to redirect Indian children from their wild ways toward the manners of a U.S. citizen. I managed to do pretty well in *cleanliness*, *health,* and *punctuality*, less well in the other categories. But I wonder how my Indian colleagues were graded in these respects. I would not be surprised today to learn that they did less well owing to differences in our upbringing, my greater access to medical facilities, and the difficulties white teachers may have had in shedding stereotypical prejudices. Mary Lemen may have been supremely enlightened and objective and totally unaffected by the color of her students' skin or native background; but of course I shall never know for sure.

Another oddity in the curriculum of the county schools I attended was the priority given to arithmetic. We are all familiar with the ditty, almost a limerick, which goes,

> "Reading and writing and arithmetic,
> Taught to the tune of a hickory stick.
> You were my gal in calico;
> I was your bashful, barefoot beau.
> You wrote on my slate, 'I love you so,'
> When we were a couple of kids."

Captain Richard Henry Pratt of the Carlisle Industrial Indian School, as well as the U.S. Office of Indian Affairs, consciously tried to invert the customary order of study, giving arithmetic a certain priority. Of course, a knowledge of the English language remained the presupposition of any course of study aimed at providing what the Treaty of 1868 Commissioners called "an English education." But beyond learning the language the other studies, including reading, writing, geography, history, and science came in secondarily. David Wallace Adams, in his book *Education for Extinction*, succinctly summarizes the position regarding arithmetic in the course of study adopted by Thomas J. Morgan, Commissioner of Indian Affairs in 1890 as follows:

> In arithmetic the first couple of years were [to be] spent on numbers and simple measurements. After eight years students were expected to be able to add, subtract, multiply, and divide whole numbers, fractions, and decimals. During this time some attention was also given to the solution of practical or word problems. As citizen-farmers, Indians must be able to count bushels of wheat, calculate their worth, avoid being cheated by the local trader, manage financial obligations, and construct a house or barn with mathematical precision. For the discerning student, there was a larger lesson as well: the culture that was engulfing him placed a high priority on measuring things; space, time, goods, and money were divided and subdivided to the nearest fraction. The white man's culture was a culture of calculations. This indeed was an important lesson, one that if not taken to heart might bring disaster later on. (see Adams, 143; Annual Report of the Commissioner of Indian Affairs, 1890, clvi-clix.)

Just as the list of civic virtues for Indians was judged equally applicable to white county school children, so it seems was the priority of arithmetic in the school curriculum. Without the realization that the white man's culture was a "culture of calculations," disaster loomed. For myself personally, my near failure to take arithmetic to heart in the 4th grade nearly resulted in my not advancing to the 5th grade. Apparently, what my teachers worried about the most, however, were the long term effects of growing up in a society which prized mathematical abilities, much as today they might be concerned with students who lack basic computer skills and can hardly function in a modern library, laboratory, or business.

One of the difficulties faced by the Indian day schools and the reservation boarding schools, aside from the question of their interrelationship, was the problem of whether and how to make attendance compulsory. South Dakota in 1883, while then a part of Dakota Territory, passed a compulsory school attendance law even before South Dakota became the 40th state in 1889. Congress didn't get around to passing a similar law affecting federally sponsored schools until 1891. Two years later it authorized the Indian Office "to withhold rations, clothing, and other annuities from Indian parents or guardians who refuse or neglect to send and keep their children of proper school age in some school a reasonable portion of each year." (see Adams, 63–4; Stat. at Large, v. 26, 1014; v. 27, 635)

Obviously even though chiefs such as Red Cloud and Spotted Tail had publicly given their imprimatur, some of the Indian youth, fearing perhaps that they would have their hair cut, be forced to speak only in English, or suffer other indignities, declined the invitation to go to the schools. It was understood early on by even the Commissioners of Indian Affairs that parental consent was to be obtained; yet often they withheld it. As the number of schools multiplied, the superintendents of these schools had to compete with each other for students. Exactly how many of the approved sanctions were actually employed is difficult to determine. In some instances the Indian Agent, the main recruiter of students, and the Indian police were required forcibly to remove eligible students from their homes and transport them to the reservation schools.

The biggest flaw in the day/reservation school system, however, was not the problem of recruitment, but their failure to achieve their primary mission which was to "civilize," "Americanize," and "Christianize" the students. It soon became apparent that by allowing day school students to return to Indian villages or camps on a daily basis, or giving reservation students the option of returning home on weekends and holidays (including, especially, Indian festivals, scheduled dances, and pow-wows), whatever the students had learned about white culture and language was wiped from their minds, and the indoctrination had to begin all over again.

Thus, to use a couple of homely metaphors, like a light bulb's being turned on, or a streak of lightning's striking a nearby tree, the idea for federally funded off-reservation schools occurred to several educators, the most enthusiastic of which was Richard Henry Pratt. The basic notion was that if you wanted to civilize Indians you had to remove them totally from their native environments and provide them with nothing but "Anglo" culture. Or as Pratt is famous for phrasing it: "Kill the Indian in him and save the man."

About the same time or perhaps somewhat before the idea of off-reservation schools occurred to Pratt, the Canadian government in 1857 passed a bill entitled the Gradual Civilization Act which aimed at the assimilation of "First Nation" peoples. A system of "residential" schools operated by religious denominations (about 60% Catholic; 30% Protestant) was set up. The purpose of the schools was "to take the Indian out of the Queen's Red Children" (see http://en.wikipedia.org/wiki/Canadian Residential School System). Pretty much the same problems which plagued U. S. boarding schools also arose with respect to Canada's residential schools. Attendance became compulsory in Canada at the "First Nations" schools, e.g. at "St. Paul's Indian Industrial School," as it became in the United States at "Carlisle Indian Industrial School." Forcible removal of children aged 7–15 (6–16 in the U.S.) became necessary. Parents were threatened with prison terms for failing to send their children to school. Students were subject to corporal punishment if they spoke aboriginal languages (other than English or French), or participated in non-

Christian religious ceremonies or rites. The parallels between Pratt's Carlisle educational experiment and that attempted by the Canadians are numerous, too many to be described here in detail. Perhaps the idea of non-reservation or non-reserve boarding schools was simply "in the air," as novel ideas, inventions, and policies often are, and both the U.S. and Canada authorities simply implemented them quite independently of each other. It is tempting to regard the Canadian experiment merely as a reflection of Pratt's and that of others in the U.S., but because of the Canadians' earlier involvement with the problem, that may not have been the case.

Richard Henry Pratt's personal history is a story well worth retelling. Shortly after the attack on Fort Sumter, Pratt volunteered for service in an Indiana cavalry regiment to fight for the Union cause. After the war he returned to Indiana, married, and tried to succeed in the hardware business. Unhappy in that occupation, in 1867 he joined the regular army as a second lieutenant and was assigned to the 10th U.S. Cavalry—a primarily black regiment, except for the officers. It was one of the army units, like Custer's 7th Cavalry also, which were ordered to the western plains to fight Indians and protect white settlers. Pratt spent some eight years in the West before he was ordered to escort some 72 Indian captives of the so-called Red River War of 1874 from Fort Sill in Indian Territory (later Oklahoma) to Fort Marion (formerly the Castillo de San Marcos built by the Spanish in the late 17th century) in St. Augustine, Florida.

The captive Indians, most of whom were young men, had been charged with crimes ranging from theft to rape and murder, but the Army had a problem of knowing what to do with them, a situation somewhat reminiscent of the problem the George W. Bush Administration has had with regard to the Muslim prisoners being held at Guantanamo in Cuba. Initially the army authorities thought they would try the Indians in military courts, but the attorney general ruled that a military trial would be illegal because a state of war could not exist between "a nation and its wards." A civilian trial was prohibited because, given the western white prejudices against the Indians, a fair trial would be simply impossible. The resolution of the problem, like President Bush's resolution regarding the Muslim captives, was simply to treat them as "enemy combatants," and incarcerate them indefinitely. (In Bush's case the captives have been denied POW status, the protections of the Geneva Convention, U.S. Laws, and even the Code of Military Justice). Pratt's orders were indefinite. After securing them in the prison at Fort Marion, he was to "oversee" their incarceration.

Pratt, who had become acquainted with certain Cherokee Indian scouts in his western assignment and discovered that they had already acquired a modicum of English education, decided that the solution of the problem of assimilation was to be found in education. Without specific orders or higher supervision, he decided to turn his prison into a school. At first he had to make life in this Florida fortress tolerable and healthy. He made the cells less damp by putting boards on the dirt floor and installing beds. He removed their heavy leg irons to give them greater freedom of movement, cut their long hair, and gave them uniforms and shoes to which they became accustomed but only begrudgingly. After a time the Indians began to look like and behave like ordinary soldiers. He met with them every evening and in a fatherly role tried to convince them as he did Spotted Tail later on in his career that in order to survive in the white dominated society, and become their equals, they had to give up their savage ways and adopt the ways of the white man.

Pratt took special care to augment their freedom. Instead of white soldiers as their guards, he substituted Indian guards. He took them on visits outside the prison, allowed them to fish and swim in the gulf waters and compete in races along the beach. The local citizenry became interested in the Indians and Pratt arranged for them to visit the prisoners. In time selected prisoners were allowed to leave the prison in pairs. This interaction between the ordinary citizens and the Indians was a deliberate part of Pratt's philosophy of education, which he later called his "outing program." He felt that assimilation of white culture as well as a divestiture of "Indianness" required a direct acquaintance with white ways and practices.

In an effort to involve the Indian prisoners in the economic life of St. Augustine, Pratt found various ways they could be productive and make money. He discovered that the local curio dealers were willing to pay ten cents for polishing each sea bean they found on the beaches. They polished 16,000 beans and earned $1,600. They also made and sold canes, bows and arrows, and painted scenes of Indian life which were also sold at a profit. Later the prisoners were hired out as laborers to the local farmers and fruit growers.

With the aid of some equally dedicated teachers, he proceeded with teaching the Indians the English language, arithmetic, and of course lessons in Christianity. One of the early visitors to his educational prison was none other than Harriet Beecher Stowe who became one of his strongest supporters. She was then herself a resident of St. Augustine. Another was Episcopal Bishop Henry Benjamin Whipple who was much impressed by Pratt's educational experiment when he visited the prison while wintering in St. Augustine in 1876. He later wrote the following:

> I was never more touched than when I entered this school. Here were men who had committed murder upon helpless women and children sitting like docile children at the feet of women learning to read. Their faces have changed. They have all lost that look of savage hate, and the light of a new life is dawning on their hearts. (Adams, 42)

He paid regular visits to the prison and preached to them about Christianity. As a result of his preaching, some of the Indians appeared "to have discarded their native beliefs for the so-called 'Jesus book,'" according to some accounts.

This was the same Bishop Whipple who in 1862 had pleaded with President Lincoln to save the lives of several hundred Santee Sioux Indians who were about to be hanged at Fort Snelling for their participation in the uprising near New Ulm, Minnesota. Lincoln agreed that they shouldn't be executed merely because they participated in a war, but should be treated as prisoners of war. Except for some thirty Indians who were hanged for offenses such as rape and murder, several hundreds of Indians were jailed and after a few years released.

Although many private citizens acknowledged Pratt's success in civilizing Indians, he himself worried about what was to become of them. He recommended to the Indian Office and to the Army with which he was still connected, having risen to the rank of Captain, that the older and more notorious prisoners be sent to penitentiaries to learn a trade, and that the younger ones who were more amenable to education be sent to agricultural and other vocational schools. Both requests were denied. In 1878, however, the Departments of War and Interior had a change of mind and informed him that the prisoners could be released. Some 22 of the younger Indians requested further education, and five of them were taken in by private citizens. The remaining 17 were at last accepted by the Hampton Virginia Normal and Industrial School run by a Union veteran of the Civil War by the name of Samuel Chapman Armstrong, an abolitionist whose father had been a missionary in the Sandwich Islands.

Hampton was itself an interesting educational experiment. Initially all of its students were black. Like Pratt's prison school at St. Augustine it aimed not only to upgrade the culture of its students in terms of the 3–R's, but also to provide moral and Christian instruction along with a large dose of industrial training. Pratt stayed on as Armstrong's assistant to oversee the integration of the Indians with the Black students who were initially afraid that they might be scalped. One of the supervisors at Hampton at this time was the black educator, Booker T. Washington.

Pratt, however, was not used to having a superior over him and had some reservations about how the public would respond to the attempt to educate Blacks and Indians together, so he applied for Congressional funds which had been appropriated for the purpose of educating Indian children in special schools. (Adams, 47) After obtaining appropriate funding and the use of some unused military barracks at Carlisle, Pennsylvania, he set out to recruit some 125 students, both boys and girls, from the Sioux tribes at the Rosebud and Pine Ridge Agencies. On November 1, 1879, the Carlisle Indian Industrial School opened its doors with Captain Pratt as headmaster and superintendent.

Although Pratt was early known for his view that schools should "kill the Indian but save the man," he never subscribed to total genocide—extinction of the entire race—as Generals Sherman and Sheridan had. He believed that "civilization was not in the genes," and that given the proper environment and training the Indian could be made to give up his Indian traits and adopt those of the white man. If B.F. Skinner had been around in his day, Pratt would have become his most earnest disciple. He was a thoroughgoing behaviorist. To prove this fundamental belief of his, he liked to tell about the turkey egg which when hatched along with those of chickens produced a creature who acted like all the other chickens, and also about the cases of white infants raised in savage surroundings and Indian infants raised in exclusively white circumstances. The Indian, he claimed, will learn the English language and civilized social habits and the white infant will learn the Indian tongue and "uncivilized" habits. Pratt claimed to have known some of the latter cases. (Adams, 52)

Among other presuppositions of his theory of education was his view that only off-reservation schools could succeed in "killing the Indian" in his students, although reservation schools (both day and boarding) could serve as stepping stones. In fact, however, Pratt disliked the very idea of reservations which he thought only prevented the total abolition of Indian ways. After Carlisle and Hampton were well established, other off-reservation schools were started in Oregon, Oklahoma, Nebraska, New Mexico, Kansas, Colorado, Arizona, Nevada, South Dakota, Montana, Minnesota, Michigan, Wisconsin, and California.

Pratt's ultimate goal was to so train the Indian youth so that they could integrate with other students in the public schools throughout the nation. I am sure he would have heartily approved the kind of schooling I myself received in fully integrated county schools.

But Pratt had plenty of critics not only in the Indian Office but also from the Army. When he once requested another officer from his regiment to help him at Carlisle, he was rebuffed by General William T. Sherman who told him that officers better served their country in their regiments. In response Pratt wrote an ill-tempered letter, not to Sherman, but to his commander-in-chief, President Rutherford B. Hayes:

> I am at this time, 'fighting' a greater number of 'enemies of civilization,' than the whole of my regiment put together, and I know further that I am fighting them with a thousand times more hopes of success. Here a Lieutenant struggles to evolve order out of the chaos of fourteen different languages! Civilization

> out of savagery! Industry and thrift out of laziness! Education out of ignorance! Cleanliness out of filth! And is forced to educate the courage of his own instructors to the work, and see that all the interests of his Govt. and the Indian as well are properly protected and served. (Adams, 55)

There is little doubt that some of the methods Pratt employed to achieve his educational goals were ingenious. In order to prevent the Indians from using their own languages, he deliberately grouped students together who spoke different Indian tongues and so to communicate with each other had to rely on English. He assigned students to different industrial tasks, e.g., farming, laundry, etc., not only to help reduce the school's expenses, but to teach them what these jobs involved. In theory at least, they were to be kept at their assigned jobs only until they "got the hang of it," and were transferred to other work. Whether this actually happened is a matter of debate. He also, in theory at least, forbid corporal punishment, but in those days a whack on the bottom, or a slap on the opened palm with a ruler, was tolerated (as it was also at my school).

The addition of sports to the Carlisle curriculum is another example of Pratt's stern but innovative policies. Initially the Carlisle football squad played against the nearby team of Dickinson College. One of his players broke his leg. Pratt declared the game too dangerous to play (he didn't want his Indians physically killed), and so for three years there was no more competitive football at Carlisle. Then a large group of students begged him to allow the game, and he consented, provided the team brought no dishonor on the school as a result of bad sportsmanship, and that it beat all its competitors. In 1894 they won only a single game, but in 1895 they won all they played. The teams they played included the University of Pennsylvania, Navy, Bucknell, and Yale. It seems a little strange that a mere Indian Industrial School, with a graduation rate of only about 8%, could play in such a collegiate league, but in fact they did. In 1903 they played and beat Harvard, but their proudest victory was against Army, and perhaps in their minds, against Custer! The moral Pratt derived from these athletic activities was that if given the opportunity the Indians were quite capable of competing against whites as their equals.

In 1904, Pratt, because of his domineering personality and his zealous attempts to assimilate Indians into white society, was forced to resign as superintendent of the Carlisle School. This was the same year that Jim Thorpe became a student there and became their star football player. Dwight Eisenhower, while playing for the West Point team against Carlisle, injured his knee, but nonetheless commented about Thorpe: "He could do anything better than any other football player I ever saw." (Wikipedia. org/wiki/Jim Thorpe). Thorpe later went on to win gold medals in the 1906 and 1912 Olympics and to achieve further fame in professional baseball, football, and basketball. It is small wonder that today the football team and stadium at the Pine Ridge High School are named after him. The students there call themselves the "Thorpes." Associated with the High School is one of the few government sponsored Indian boarding schools which still exist.

Carlisle continued as an off-reservation boarding school until 1918 when it closed and the Army reclaimed the property. It is now occupied by a U.S. Army War College. Its demise was hastened partly perhaps by WWI but also by changes of policies toward the education of Indians. Many persons in Washington, D.C. and elsewhere had second thoughts about the government's attempt to "Christianize" the Indians (separation of church and state doctrine), and the advisability of attempting to totally eradicate Indian cultures. Certainly Pratt's view was extreme. Even Jefferson who favored turning Indians into American citizens never advocated a total assault on their languages (he himself made a special study of them) or their culture. He enjoyed their company and often invited Indian Chiefs to the White House (or President's House as it was then called) where he spent more time with them than with ambassadors from Europe. He even favored intermarriage between whites and Indians and was proud of the fact (if it was a fact) that his daughters may have been descendants of Pocahontas, the Powhaton princess, on his wife's side of the family.

Part II

PHILOSOPHICAL REFLECTIONS AND GENERALIZATIONS

Chapter Seven

Scalping of the Great Sioux Nation

By an act of 1871 Congress terminated the negotiating of treaties with Indian tribes, thereby enacting a policy contrary to the one adopted by the first five presidential administrations but similar to the view expressed by Andrew Jackson as early as 1817 in a letter to President Monroe in which he said that he had "long viewed treaties with Indians an absurdity not to be reconciled to the principles of our government." (Spicer, 228.) The rejection of making treaties with the Indians did not mean that the United States couldn't enter into agreements with them. The difference was that only a majority vote was required for ratification as opposed to the two thirds vote of the Senate required for treaties. As a consequence, most of the reservations established after 1871 were established by statute or executive order.

In 1875 it became apparent that many Indians were not living on the Great Sioux Reservation as set forth in the Treaty of 1868, but in the unceded lands of the Dakota and Montana Territories. These included not only "hostile Indians" such as Sitting Bull and Crazy Horse who had never signed the treaty, but also many others who had gathered in the Powder River Country in response to Sitting Bull's call for them to join him there. By the time of the Little Big Horn battle, the Indian village along the Little Big Horn River ran to over three miles long. On the advice of his Secretary of War, William W. Belknap, who was shortly thereafter to be threatened with impeachment, and his Secretary of the Interior, Zachariah Chandler, President Grant issued an order directing that unless the Indians "remove within the boundaries of their reservation before the 31st of January next [1876], they shall be deemed hostile and treated accordingly by the military force." (Welch, 53).

The winter of 1875–76 in Montana Territory was extremely severe, with frequent blizzards, which are not that uncommon in that area, with deep snow drifts, and sub-zero temperatures. It is doubtful that the Indians could have met the deadline to return to the reservations even if they had tried. But a winter campaign against the Indians was exactly what General Sheridan had really wanted. Custer had proved how successful such a campaign had been at Washita. Grant's order gave Sheridan exactly the justification he needed for his vendetta against the Indians ending with the Battle of the Little Big Horn.

Frustrated by the Sioux's refusal to sell the Black Hills, Congress passed in 1877 the Black Hills Act which unilaterally and without a vote of the Indian tribes transferred the entire area of 6000 square miles (7.7 million acres) to the United States Government. It was clearly in violation of the 1868 Treaty and can only be regarded by persons who appreciate the morality of promise-keeping as nothing but grand theft.

Having taken away the Sioux Holy Land (Paha Sapa) which was held in common, it was only a short step to taking away other Indian lands, either by way of allotments or by splintering the Great Sioux Reservation of 1868 into several individual and much smaller reservations. The first method had been recommended as early as 1877 and later by various Secretaries of the Interior and by Commissioners of Indian Affairs; and also by President Cleveland in 1886. (Debo, 300.) On February 8, 1887, it was finally signed into law and was known as the General Allotment Act, or Dawes Act, after Senator Dawes of Massachusetts who sponsored it. The general idea was that the President was empowered to allot tribal land to all individual Indians who applied for an allotment. The average share envisioned by the legislation was 160 acres or a quarter section to each head of family and lesser amounts to unmarried men and orphaned children. A bonus feature was that all such allotees were to become citizens of the United States, those who did not seek allotments did not become citizens (until the Indian Citizenship Act of 1924). The land—some 11 million acres—not allotted theoretically became available for homestead to white settlers. In fact, although it was argued that the only way of incorporating Indians into American society was to make them fee simple holders of property (i.e., real estate), the chief motive for allotments was to satisfy the white population's demand for Indian lands. The allotments were to be held in trust for 25 years after which the Indians would be free to sell them. But white traders and farmers soon found ways to by-pass this restriction by signing leases for the land owned by Indians. Subsequently many Indians were wheedled out of their land by fast talking white men who paid them a mere fraction of its actual worth. According to Vine DeLoria, Jr. many churches supported the Dawes Allotment Act as a way of Christianizing Indians, believing somehow that religion and private property were intimately related. (DeLoria, 1969, 53.)

In 1889, after several earlier relatively unsuccessful attempts to get a majority of Indians to accept the Dawes Allotment or Severalty plan, Congress passed the Great Sioux Agreement (25 Stat. 888). Note that unlike the *Treaty* of 1868, this statutory legislation is called an *Agreement*. Under one of its provisions (Section 8) the President

> is hereby authorized and required, whenever in his opinion any reservation of such Indians, or any part thereof, is advantageous for agricultural or grazing purposes, and the progress in civilization of the Indians receiving rations on either or any of said reservations shall be such as to encourage the belief that an allotment in severalty to such Indians, or any of them, would be for the best interest of said Indians, to cause said reservation, or so much thereof as is necessary, to be surveyed, or re-surveyed, and to allot the lands in said reservation in severalty to the Indians located thereon as aforesaid, in quantities as follows: To each head of a family, three hundred and twenty acres [320]; to each single person over eighteen years of age, one-fourth of a section [160 acres]; to each orphan child under eighteen years of age, one-fourth of a section [160 acres]; and to each other person under eighteen now living . . . one eighth of a section [80 acres]. (DeLoria, 1971, 83).

Obviously in this document the pot had been sweetened—from 160 acres to 320 acres. Also General George Crook, who this time was part of the Commission along with a clever Indian Agent named James McLaughlin, were able to segregate the various tribal chiefs and cajole them into signing the agreement in the manner required by the document itself in Section 28, namely:

> That this act shall take effect, only, upon the acceptance thereof and consent thereto by the different bands of the Sioux Nation of Indians, in manner and form prescribed by the twelfth article of the treaty between the United States and said Sioux Indians concluded April twenty-ninth eighteen hundred and sixty eight. (DeLoria, 1971, 96.)

Article 12 of the Fort Laramie Treaty of 1868 reads:

> No treaty for the cession of any portion or part of the reservation herein described [the GSR] which may be held in common shall be of any validity or force against the said Indians, unless executed and signed by at least three-fourth of all the adult male Indians . . .

General Crook and Agent McLaughlin without doubt threatened the Chiefs with losses, not only of their lands, if they didn't sign, as happened in the case of the Black Hills, but also losses of their food rations (they were not above starving Indians to death), but also possibly with their very lives (as happened at Sand Creek, Washita, and later at Wounded Knee). Despite efforts by Sitting Bull, who was not invited to the conference and who everyone knew was

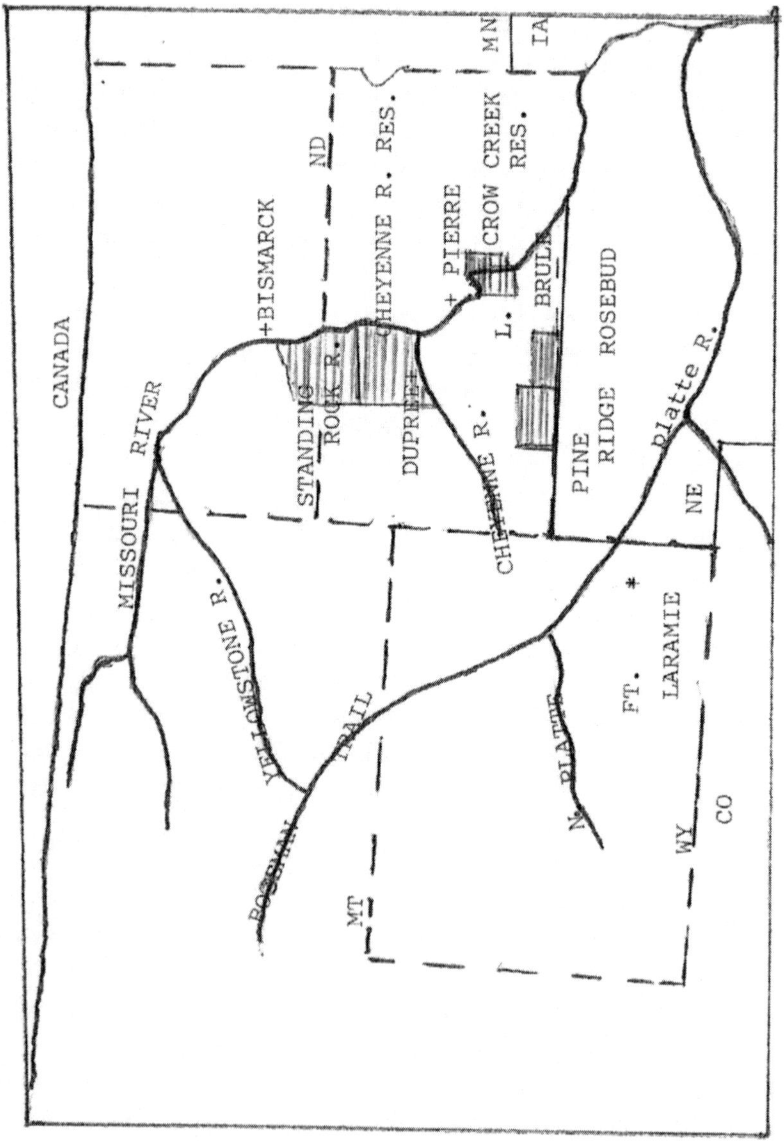

Result of the Sioux Agreement of 1889.

opposed to selling any Indian lands, the Commission managed to get the 75% vote required. Sitting Bull, incidentally, was around at this time because he had refused an offer by Buffalo Bill Cody to join him on his European tour of his Wild West Show, in which he had appeared the previous summer. The reason for his refusal was "I am needed here; there is more talk of taking our lands." He wanted to be around to prevent that from happening. (Vestal, 255.) Congress promptly approved the "Agreement" and on February 10, 1890, President Benjamin Harrison, himself a grandson of an old Indian fighter, proclaimed that the Great Sioux Reservation was no more.

The 1889 Agreement also splintered the GSR in another way. Six smaller permanent reservations and agencies were established, namely, those of Pine Ridge, Rosebud, Standing Rock, Cheyenne River, Lower Brule, and Crow Creek. Donations of Indian land were made to the cities of Pierre, S.D., and an island in the Niobrara River, then part of the GSR, to the city of Niobrara, Nebraska. Lands for highways, four rods or 66 ft. wide, were reserved around every section of land, as was acreage for at least 30 school houses. Land was granted to any religious society engaged in educating and civilizing the Indians. Rights of way were given to the Chicago, Milwaukee & Saint Paul Railroad Company and the Dakota Central Railroad Company.

All the other parts of the GSR became available for white settlement under various previously enacted Homestead laws. For 50 cents or at the maximum of $1.25 an acre a farmer could acquire as much land as he wanted or could afford. My own grandfather, in the early years of the 1900's took advantage of this situation and purchased land near Dupree, S.D. in Ziebach County in the very center almost of the Cheyenne River Indian Reservation, not more than one hundred miles from Sitting Bull's home and birthplace on the Standing Rock Reservation to the north.

What I have described so far, namely, the Congressional and Presidential actions regarding national policy toward Indians from 1871 to 1889 is what I should like to call the collective scalping of the Great Sioux Nation. It started with the 1871 termination of treaty negotiations, and continued with the 1875 executive order to treat all non-reservation Indians as "hostiles;" the failed attempts to buy the Black Hills in 1877 and the passage of the egregiously immoral Black Hills Act which transferred ownership to the Federal Government; the passage of the Dawes Allotment Act of 1877; and the final termination of the Great Sioux Reservation by the passage of the Great Sioux Agreement of 1889.

Some may think that the metaphor of scalping has been too widely or inappropriately construed. Recalling that the literal meaning of Paha Sapa is "Black Scalp" or "Black Hair of the Head," perhaps the metaphor should be restricted only to that part of the Great Sioux Reservation. I think, however, that if one seriously reflects on the nature of scalping and its history, one can easily see how a wider construal is not only possible but justified.

The usual dictionary definition of scalping is the act of cutting off the skin of the top and back of the head from an enemy as a trophy in war. The *Oxford American Dictionary* goes somewhat further and gives two definitions of "scalp" as follows: "1. the skin of the head excluding the face. 2. this with the hair, formerly cut from an enemy's head as a trophy by American Indians." The reference to American Indians is totally superfluous and in fact historically inaccurate. Not all American Indian tribes engaged in the practice. The Navajos, who regarded it as a barbaric practice introduced by the Spaniards, did not engage in scalping even though soldiers under the command of General James Carleton and Kit Carson, a former friend of the Indians who became an Indian fighter, paid bounties for Navajo scalps. (Brown, 25.) Vine DeLoria, Jr., in his book, *Custer Died For Your Sins*, claims that scalping was introduced prior to the French and Indian Wars by the English, and quotes a proclamation dated 1755 which offers a bounty of forty pounds for every scalp of an adult male Penobscot Indian, and twenty pounds for every female or male under twelve years of age. (DeLoria, 1969, 14.) During the 1960's a theory was prevalent among anthropologists that the Europeans who had long practiced scalping introduced the practice to the American Indian. That theory has met with considerable opposition and is not now generally regarded as a true description of how this practice ever caught on in America. One thing is clear, however; the American Indian was not the first to invent the practice.

The Sioux Indians were indeed practitioners of the art, and were totally indiscriminate regarding the scalping of anyone who was an enemy, even other Indians including other bands of Sioux with which they were at war. They scalped white persons, and it didn't matter whether they were men, women, or children. They had no compunctions regarding such killings. The only requirement was that you were their enemy. Crazy Horse was apparently an exception to the Sioux custom. According to Stephen Ambrose's account, on one occasion Crazy Horse killed an enemy Omaha Indian and rushed over to take the victim's scalp, but discovered that it was a woman who looked surprisingly like his own sister, so he left the scalp to his companions who thereafter teased him about his hesitation, much as Theodore Roosevelt was once teased about refusing to shoot a bear cub, and thereafter was called "Teddy." (Ambrose, 70). In Crazy Horse's case there was a sequel. He apparently revealed to a white army officer later in his life that he morally disapproved of the Sioux custom of scalping enemy women. But perhaps in this case we can only say that "the exception proved the rule."

Furthermore, scalping was not always limited to the taking of scalps. Just as some unscrupulous white men and soldiers often took the nose and ears of a victim, they were also known to have taken the skin and pubic hair of Indian women as scalps. Some white men such as Governor Alexander Ramsey of Minnesota, after the Santee uprising in 1862, took the position that "The Sioux Indians must be exterminated or driven forever beyond the borders of the state," (Brown, 52) and encouraged payment by the State of Minnesota of twenty-five dollars per Indian scalp. (Brown, 62.) Other persons in authority, such as Colonel Henry H. Sibley who was largely responsible for rounding up the Santee Sioux Indians after the massacre at New Ulm, took a different view. After discovering that many of his soldiers had scalped and mutilated the bodies of Santee warriors, he issued an order that "The bodies of the dead, even of a savage enemy shall not be subjected to indignities by civilized and Christian men." (Brown, 56.) The names of Ramsey and Sibley, incidentally, are as well known in Minnesota as are the names of Custer and Miles in Montana.

The main point of this digression regarding scalping is to illustrate that the line between scalping and mutilation, particularly the dissection of the body, is not very great, so that if we speak of the Black Hills as a kind of scalplock, and its taking a kind of scalping, that is not so very different from the cutting up of the entire Great Sioux Reservation into six smaller reservations. Since the scalplock as well as the other parts of the GSR belonged collectively to the Great Sioux Nation it makes good sense to speak of the acts of Congress and the various Presidents who were responsible for these destructive acts as the scalping (in the broader sense) of the Great Sioux Nation.

A feature which scalping in the literal and in the broader sense share which strengthens the metaphor is that scalping in the ordinary sense does not always bring about the death of the victim. People are known to have survived being scalped, although that is not usually the case nor the intention of the attacker. Indeed, the reservation system may originally and by President Grant been intended as a way to prevent the wholesale genocide of the Indian population, but attempts to eliminate Indians and their reservations altogether have persisted. The Dawes Act of 1887 aimed to make individual property owners out of the Indians, thus assimilating them into the greater white society of private property owners and making them less dependent on the communal property of the tribes of the reservation. It succeeded, however, only in greatly diminishing both land ownership by Indians and the size of the reservations. For example, the Sisseton-Wahpeton Sioux reservation in eastern South Dakota lost 660,000 acres of land because unalloted and so eligible for white settlement. Allotment among the Crows yielded a "surplus" of

1,800,000 acres. (Debo, 304.) Similar "yields" or losses to the tribes occurred on other Sioux and Cheyenne reservations.

During the administration of President Franklin D. Roosevelt and with the active support of Secretary of Interior, Harold L. Ickes, and Commissioner of Indian Affairs, John Collier, Congress had a change of heart, so to speak, and passed in 1934 the Indian Reorganization Act, otherwise known a the Wheeler-Howard Act. The Act put a stop to allotments in severalty to individual Indians, and restored tribal ownership to any remaining "surplus" lands. It also authorized the appropriation of two million dollars ($2,000,000) per year for the acquisition of land, water rights, and surface rights for Indians, and set up a ten million dollar ($10,000,000) revolving fund from which to make loans to Indian chartered corporations. If it possible to reattach a scalp, this legislation went a long way towards doing that for the Sioux Nation and Indian tribes generally.

Other important features of the Wheeler-Howard Act were that for the first time it allowed tribes on the reservations the possibility of self-government by means of elected Indian Councils, and gave Council control over tribal funds. It exempted qualified Indians from civil service requirements in obtaining positions with the Office of Indian Affairs and in fact gave them preferential status with respect to appointments to vacancies in any such positions.

But the surgical (in this case, legislative) reattachment of the scalp of the Sioux Nation did not meet with total Congressional approval. Nor have the Indians succeeded in their attempts to have the Black Hills as a whole returned to them.

Chapter Eight

The Underlying Rationale for Dispossession

The motives for depriving Indians of their lands, their forests, their mountains, their rivers; as well as their gold, their buffalo, their beaver, and other wildlife; their religion, their dances, their languages, and general way of life are numerous. Some of them have already been touched upon. They include an almost insatiable desire for their lands by some settlers, including the homesteaders who simply wanted to establish farms and ranches, and others such as the railroad companies who wanted a direct passage overland to the Pacific; and by still others who wanted access to mineral deposits—gold and silver especially. Some sought the land simply to make a living for themselves and their families, some sought to enrich themselves at the Indians' expense. Meriwether Lewis on his return from his western expedition envisaged a lucrative and perhaps mutually beneficial commerce with Indians with respect to fur trading. My grandfather Davis merely wanted a farm on which to raise his children and saw an opportunity to obtain one cheaply by means of government sponsored homesteading. Others were merely greedy and convinced that the Indian had no rights anyway. Theodore Roosevelt was largely of this opinion and acquired two large ranches in what is now North Dakota for himself. Generals Sherman, Sheridan, and Custer thought that American society would be better off without Indians and did their level best to achieve their actual extinction.

But aside from these personal motives, most of which are questionable on almost any theory of ethics, is there any legal or moral justification for all these more or less successful attempts to dispossess the Indian of everything he owned—including his life, his liberty, and his property? One has to ask, sooner or later, did the Indians own all of North America? Did they even possess it? Was it their private property? The American president, Andrew Jackson, took a decidedly negative stance with respect to such questions.

Another was President Theodore Roosevelt who wrote in his book, *The Winning of the West* (I, 90) that "The settler and pioneer have at bottom had justice on their side; this great continent could not have been kept as nothing but a game preserve for squalid savages."

The Founding Fathers of this country appear to have adopted a quite different view. The policy of the United States Federal Government from George Washington's administration (through those of Adams, Jefferson, Madison, Monroe, and John Q. Adams) until the time of President Andrew Jackson was largely one of benevolence toward Indians. Even before the adoption of the Constitution in 1789, Congress passed in 1787 an ordinance under the Articles of Confederation "for the government of the territory of the United States, north west of the river Ohio." The following passage from it has been mentioned already but because of its importance it is reproduced here again:

> The utmost good faith shall always be observed toward the Indians; their lands and property shall never to taken from them without their consent; and in their property, rights, and liberty, they shall never be invaded or disturbed, unless in just and lawful wars, authorized by Congress; but laws founded in justice and humanity, shall, from time to time, be made for preventing wrongs being done to them, and for preserving peace and friendship with them.

Washington as President maintained the view that the United States should treat Indians as friends and deal with them on terms of justice and humanity. He was adamant, however, that "the United States will not suffer the depredations of the bad Indians to go unpunished." Rather even handedly, in a six point program for dealing with Indians, he proposed an arrangement "for punishing those who infringed Indian rights, violated treaties, and thus endangered the peace of the nation." The other five points of Washington's program (as summarized by Francis Paul Prucha in *American Indian Treaties: A History of a Political Anomaly*) were: (1) An impartial dispensation of justice toward the Indians; (2) A carefully defined and regulated method of purchasing lands from the Indians, in order to avoid imposition on the Indians and controversy about the reality and extent of the purchases; (3) Promotion of commerce with the Indians, "under regulations tending to secure an equitable deportment toward them;" (4) "Rational experiments" for imparting to the Indians the "blessings of civilization;" and (5) Authority for the president to give presents to the Indians.

Perhaps a comment or two are in order here. Richard Henry Pratt's efforts to educate and civilize Indians would presumably fall under the heading of "rational experiment," I suppose; whether Washington would have approved is a wholly different matter. Throughout the negotiations with Indians during the late nineteenth century "presents" were often given to the Indians, and

Indians such as Chief Red Cloud came to expect that they would be forthcoming even when he totally disagreed with the Indian Office or the "Great White Father" in Washington, D. C. Washington's Six Point Program may have established this custom.

In *Johnson v. McIntosh* , 8 Wheaton 592, 5 L.Ed. 693 (1823), Chief Justice John Marshall reiterated the European principle of discovery (namely, that discovery followed by conquest extinguishes Indian rights of ownership), thereby giving the United States exclusive title to all Indian lands. Yet Congress continued to authorize suits based on aboriginal Indian title or "right of occupancy, " and even Marshall admitted, perhaps inconsistently, in *Johnson v. McIntosh* that "It has never been contended that the Indian title amounted to nothing. Their right of possession has never been questioned." In *Mitchell v. United States,* 9 Peters 746, 9 L. Ed. 283 (1835), it is stated that the Indian "right of occupancy is considered as sacred as the fee simple of the Whites."

Jefferson's views were very much the same as Washington's and to a lesser extent those of Marshall. As Secretary of State, and in response to inquiries by President Washington, Jefferson said:

> I consider our right of pre-emption of the Indian lands, not as amounting to any dominion, or jurisdiction, or paramountship whatever, but merely in the nature of a remainder after the extinguishment of a present right, which gave us no present right whatever, but of preventing other nations from taking possession . . . that the Indians had the full, undivided and independent sovereignty as long as they choose to keep it, and that this might be forever. (Quoted in Prucha, 227; Washburn, 56.)

In addition to honorable land cessions from the Indian tribes, conceived as sovereign nations, Jefferson, as President, foresaw the conversion of the Indians from hunters to farmers and their ultimate incorporation into white society.

> I consider the business of hunting as already become insufficient to furnish clothing and subsistence to the Indians. The promotion of agriculture, therefore, and household manufacture, are essential in their preservation, and I am disposed to aid and encourage it liberally. . . . While they are learning to do better on less land, our increasing numbers will be calling for more land, and thus a coincidence of interests will be produced between those who have lands to spare, and want other necessaries, and those who have such necessaries to spare, and want lands. This commerce, then, will be for the good of both, and those who are friends to both ought to encourage it. . . . In truth, the ultimate point of rest and happiness for them is to let our settlements and theirs meet and blend together, to intermix, and become one people. Incorporating themselves with us

> as citizens of the U.S. , this is what the natural progress of things will of course bring on, and it will be better to promote than to retard it. Surely it will be better for them to be identified with us, and preserved in the occupation of their lands, than be exposed to the many casualties that may endanger them while a separate people. (*Letter,* Peterson, 1115)

Jefferson, like Washington, had his troubles with Indians, both during the early days of the Revolution and while a war-time Governor of Virginia. He too felt that the terrorist behavior of some Indians with respect to white settlers had to be dealt with severely, but he took a somewhat less military approach. After the overwhelming defeat by the Shawnee warrior, Little Turtle, of General Josiah Harmar's army which had been sent by Washington to quell the northwest Indian tribes, Jefferson, then Secretary of State, was of the opinion that the government had yet to discover "what experience has long ago taught us in Virginia, that rank and file fighting will not do against Indians." (Since Washington was also a Virginian, perhaps Jefferson should have said, "what experience has taught us in my part of Virginia, Albemarle County"). In any case, his view was to avoid open warfare and promote other ways of controlling Indians, many of which Washington himself approved, such as promoting commerce with them and assimilating them to colonial civilization through education. Of course, it helped if the Indians were sufficiently fearful of the superior might of the United States government. As he wrote to William H. Harrison, this time as President, "It is essential to cultivate their love. As to their fear, we presume that our strength and their weakness is now so visible that they must see we have only to shut our hand to crush them, and that all our liberalities to them proceed from motives of pure humanity only." (Peterson, 1118) Compared to Washington, Jefferson preferred the threat of force to force itself, but he did foresee its possible use.

Assuming as he did that most Indian lands would eventually and inevitably become occupied and acquired by westward moving white settlers, the method of acquisition Jefferson favored was purchase by agreement, in other words, by treaty, the same method employed by his predecessors and successors up to Andrew Jackson. As early as 1787 when the first edition of Jefferson's *Notes on the State of Virginia* was published, Jefferson commented:

> That the lands of the country [i.e., Virginia] were taken from them by conquest, is not so general a truth as is supposed. I find in our historians and records, repeated proofs of purchase, which cover a considerable part of the lower country; and many more would doubtless be found on further search. The upper country we know has been acquired altogether by purchases made in the most un- exceptional form. (Jefferson, *Notes,* 96)

In a footnote to this passage, editor William Peden adds:

> Here, in his original manuscript, Jefferson wryly commented and later crossed out: "it is true that these purchases were sometimes made with the price in one hand and the sword in the other. (Peden, n.4, 281)

Sometimes, of course, it is said that *all* such treaties have been not only "bought by the sword," but also abrogated by acts of the federal government. For example, according to Vine Deloria, Jr., "America has yet to keep one treaty or agreement despite the fact that the United States government signed over four hundred such treaties and agreements." (*Custer Died For Your Sins*, 35) Francis Paul Prucha, who is probably the chief authority on American Indian treaties, has pointed out, however, that there are cases in which the Indian signatories "broke" the treaties. He also points out that subsequent changes and modifications in treaties, duly enacted by Congress, can not properly be regarded as abrogations. Furthermore, there are treaties on the books (such as the Ft. Laramie Treaty of 1868) which the federal courts uphold today and to which Indian tribes constantly refer.

Sometimes it is argued, even by Justices of the Supreme Court, that treaties with the Indians are invalid or at the very least suspect, because they were written in a language that was foreign to them, and in the form of a contract which the Indians were unaccustomed to and didn't understand. That at least some Indians fully understood the significance of the documents is suggested by the case of a treaty made with the Cherokees in Georgia in 1804. It became lost in the War Department files for twenty years. In 1824 a Cherokee delegation brought up the matter and the War Department found no record of the treaty. Thereupon, the Cherokees produced their own copy and asked that it be sent to the Senate to complete the process of ratification, which the Senate did, after sending it to Thomas Jefferson, by then retired as President, who examined the document, pronounced it genuine, and apologized for this "slip of executive functionaries." (Prucha, 111–12)

The fact of the matter is, however, that the use of outright force, coercion, and fraudulent payment has characterized so-called "Jeffersonian Policy" toward Indians, but the use of this expression requires some explanation. In his *Notes on the State of Virginia*, Jefferson summarizes not only his own views but also those of his contemporaries regarding White-Indian relations, much as he summarized his own and others' views in the *Declaration of Independence*. Because he did it so persuasively and so eloquently, and because he pursued those policies so tenaciously himself, some authors have used the term "Jeffersonian" to characterize the whole gamut of administrative policies regarding Indians adopted by the government both prior to Jefferson's time and afterwards. (Cf. Sheehan, *Seeds of Extinction,* 5–7)

Relocation or removal of whole tribes from the eastern states has occurred, e.g., the Cherokees from Georgia and North Carolina to Indian Territory (Oklahoma). Jefferson himself envisaged the possible need to transplant Indians beyond the Mississippi, but never undertook the project. President Monroe did. Many Indians were coerced, some with alcohol, to sell their lands, others by threat of extinction. And of course payments for lands were often miserably inadequate. William Henry Harrison, e.g., arranged a treaty with the Miami and other Indians of the Northeastern United States which amounted to the sale of "upwards of two millions and a half acres" which he said "will cost less than two cents per acre. " Spelled out, that amounts to 2.5 million for less than $50,000!

But having pointed out such injustices and egregious inconsistencies in government policy, which all persons today would probably agree are morally reprehensible, the underlying philosophical issue is whether the dispossession of the American Indians from their lands even if done in the manner Jefferson intended, is in any way justified, or as Bernard W. Sheehan has expressed it, did Jeffersonian Philanthropy sow the seeds of the ultimate extinction of the American Indian? Actually there are a plethora of issues involved, some specifically involving genocide and cultural extinction which have already been discussed to some extent in previous chapters, so let us concentrate on questions regarding possession, dispossession, and ownership—in other words with questions dealing with Indian rights.

Generally speaking, Thomas Jefferson as well as others who have perceived the difference between motivation and justification, including Theodore Roosevelt, have based their justification for "taking" Indian lands (a term perhaps less offensive than "dispossessing") on John Locke's theory of property, which perhaps we should now review to see whether indeed it makes sense or is less persuasive than other possible views, such as that of the philosopher, Immanuel Kant, who was also well aware of the problem of Indian ownership of land in America at the close of the 18th century.

In the fifth chapter of his *Second Treatise of Civil Government,* Locke, who helped draft a constitution for the new world colony of Carolina in 1667, sets forth his theory in its most distinctive form. It is interesting that in this relatively short chapter he mentions "America" no less than five times and "Indians" no fewer than three times. These references could hardly have escaped Jefferson's notice. But in any case, in all his comments regarding Locke specifically (e.g., in his letter to Thomas Mann Randolph of May 30, 1790), and in the framework of the Declaration of Independence and his comments on the U.S. Constitution, it is clearly Locke's views which pervade his thinking as well as that of the other founding fathers. As a lawyer, Jefferson was of course acquainted with the English common law of property and its concepts of possession and ownership. But regarding the origin, or as Locke would put it, the "original" of property, it was Locke's theory he appealed to as far as Indian rights regarding land were concerned. One might therefore expect that insofar as Locke's theory makes sense, so does Jefferson's.

Locke's theory is relatively simple. According to Locke, God gave the whole world to mankind in common. The derivation of private property occurs when anyone mixes his labor with an object, e.g., land. Why this converts common property to private is because, Locke reasons,

> Every man has property in his own person; this nobody has any right to but himself. The labour of his body and work of his hands we may say are properly his. Whatsoever he removes out of the state that nature hath provided and left it in, he hath mixed his labour with, and joined to it something that is his own, and thereby makes it his property. It being by him removed from the common state nature hath placed it in, it hath by this labour something annexed to it that excludes the common right of other men. (*Second Treatise of Civil Government,* Hafner, 134)

Locke's rather common sense theory has had a long and influential history and yet it has been severely criticized. One objection is that Locke's notion of a primitive state of nature on which the theory is based is a pure fiction. Of course, Locke himself never meant to identify the state of nature with any remote historical condition of mankind. It is for him a recurrent condition of mankind, and he on occasion remarks that "In the beginning, all the world was America . . ." This appeal to a beginning state of affairs is unnecessary, it is said, to account for and to justify property and private ownership.

Another complaint against Locke is that his theory, entailing initially as it does a physical relation of labor between the prospective owner and the object, cannot account for property that is unearned in the physical sense, e.g., gifts and cases of inheritance, or of owning something one doesn't know exists, e.g., valuable minerals such as gold on one's land, or cases of owning property created by another's labor.

Locke limits his theory by the restriction that one can only justifiably own what one can profitably use. To claim land, for example, which one could not himself cultivate, or to produce more crops than one's family could eat, was to create waste, which God never intended, and encroaches on the property rights of other. He saw, however, no reason to limit the acquisition of gold, silver, or diamonds, since they do not spoil. And he contended that while hoarding such items would create economic inequalities, the person who did it "invaded not the right of others." But as W.T. Jones has put it:

> It is not self-evident that massive accumulations of capital in a few hands is harmless. Indeed there may well be a contradiction between the political equality on which Locke insisted so eloquently and the economic inequality that his doctrine of property approves. (*Jones,* 273)

Jefferson's views regarding the dispossession of the lands of Indians, or to put it more positively, Jefferson's views regarding the possession of lands by Indians, do not necessarily entail an acceptance of the whole of Locke's theory (he does not accept Locke's theological premise, for example), but the cardinal point is whether Indians could be said to "own" or even to "possess" millions of acres of land which they neither cultivate nor are in a position to exclude others from. Locke's answer would undoubtedly be No. They could claim as their own only that which they could use and control. All the rest was for others to claim as their own. Jefferson certainly agreed with this thinking, but he never denied that Indians had rights of first or prior possession. And he did his utmost in the process of dispossessing them of this right to get for the Indians just compensation.

But is this a morally sufficient justification? Immanuel Kant, writing his *Rechtslehre* or philosophy of law in 1797, raises the question,

> . . . whether, when neither nature nor chance but just our own will brings us into the neighborhood of a people that holds out no prospect of a civil union with it, we should not be authorized to found colonies, by force if need be, in order to establish a civil union with them and bring these human beings (savages) into a rightful condition (as with the American Indians, the Hottentots and the inhabitants of New Holland); or (which is not much better), to found colonies by fraudulent purchase of their land, and so become owners of their land, making use of our superiority without regard for their first possession. Should we not be authorized to do this, especially since nature itself (which abhors a vacuum) seems to demand it, and great expanses of land in other parts of the world, which are now splendidly populated, would have otherwise remained uninhabited by civilized people, or, indeed, would have to remain uninhabited, so that the end of creation would have been frustrated?

His answer:

> But it is easy to see through this veil of injustice . . . which would sanction any means to good ends. Such a way of acquiring land is therefore to be repudiated. (Kant, *Rechtslehre*, 417–18.)

What is indeed easy to see is that Kant disagrees totally with Locke's view on this subject, and partially, as we shall see, with Jefferson's, but the reasons for his disagreement are by no means evident. To understand them we have to sketch Kant's own theory of property, which, unlike Locke's more commonsensical view, is not easily grasped. Part of the difficulty with Kant's theory of property is that it is written within the context of a continental legal system derived from Roman law, as our Anglo-American legal system is not, and partly because it is based on his general moral theory which he himself calls "the metaphysics of morals." No one has ever accused Kant of being an "easy" philosopher either to read or to comprehend. But we must do our best.

Kant's theory of property is based on a particular set of assumptions regarding rights and obligations. According to Kant, rights and obligations are correlatives. For every right there is an obligation and for every obligation there corresponds a right. Only rational beings can be the bearers of rights or the subjects of obligations because only such beings have free will. One cannot be said to have a right or be obligated unless that person is free to act wrongly or do what a person ought to do. Kant also attributes to all rational beings an "innate right to freedom." All other rights, including what Kant calls "acquired rights" are derived from this most basic right. From all these assumptions Kant draws the rather startling conclusion that no one can have a right to a thing—if one interprets that claim to refer to a direct relation to a corporeal being. For since rights are correlative with obligations one would have to suppose that corresponding to the right in the person is some correlative obligation in the thing. "It is therefore absurd to think of an obligation of a person to things or the reverse, even though it may be permissible, if need be, to make this rightful relation perceptible by picturing it and expressing it in this way."

A right to a thing, such as land, has to be conceived as a relation of one person to other persons. Here Kant speculates that if someone were the lone inhabitant of the earth he "could really neither have nor acquire any external thing as his own." Furthermore, the right to a thing is really a right to the private *use* of a thing possessed in common with all others. Note that Kant is not really speaking of "private property" in the usual English sense of the term. He speaks of "use" here rather than "ownership." Rarely does he ever employ the word "property" (*Eigentum*, in German), but usually the rather awkward expression, "the external mine or yours." (Mulholland, 234.)

But what can he mean by the expression "possessed in common with all others"? To understand that we have to see what role physical possession has in determining property in Kant's thinking. Contrary to Locke, he denies that physical possession creates rights. I may hold an apple in my hand, have physical possession of it, but it may not be mine. (Kant's example.) I may have stolen it, or taken it simply to inspect it. Nor, unlike Locke's view, does the development or cultivation of land give property rights. As he says, "developing land is nothing more than an external sign of taking possession." Even my "taking control" of land by excluding others is not conclusive of property rights. I can own land even if I do not physically possess or control it—this kind of possession he calls "intelligible possession."

Possession of a thing is, for Kant, however, a precondition for having a right to it, and the capacity for intelligible possession is necessary for having what he calls "peremptory right" as opposed to "provisional right." But neither of these kinds of rights are based on empirical considerations such as a physical taking and control. Nor are they dependent upon need or self-preservation as Hobbes would have it. Granted that all persons need land and its produce to survive, that practical biological fact does not, for Kant, create any right or obligation.

What then does? The innate right to freedom, according to Kant, implies an innate right to land which is essential for one's existence as well as one's right to be treated equally. Thus, given the original common possession of the whole world, not some supposed empirical condition as Locke, Hobbes, Rousseau and other social contract theorists would have it. but an a priori presupposition on which all rights in a civil society are based, one acquires peremptory rights as long as all others are willing to relinquish their equal claims to particular lands. Kant seems to be saying that what is right depends, not so much on a supposed social contract (although he does talk in this manner at times), but upon the notion of a universalizable maxim that my use of the common property be respected as long as I possess it on condition that I respect others' such possession. Such a condition for property rights rests, he claims, on no empirical considerations whatsoever, only rational ones and the notion of universalizability (or in other words, law).

Such a property-owning arrangement requires a civil society which all are morally obligated to join. What if some aborigines such as the America Indian or the Hottentots choose not to join? In that case of course they remain in a state of nature (a pre-civil state), but they nonetheless have rights of "occupation," as he calls them—provisional rights, not peremptory rights which can only exist in a civil society. In this regard, Kant's view differs from that of Hobbes, who denies that the notion of "mine and thine" has a place in a State of Nature, and from that of Locke, who suggests that in a State of Nature there are property rights, though practically unenforceable, since in a State of Nature there are no agencies to enforce them. Kant wants to claim that even in a State of Nature there are rights to property which everyone must respect, as long as there is an expectation that those who have these provisional rights will eventually join the civil society.

Why should anyone, including Indians, join a civil society? Hobbes cites a fear of death; Locke cites the inconveniences of life in a State of Nature.

Kant apparently thinks that practical reason will prevail (as a motive) and all truly rational beings will see the wisdom of doing so. (Kant, *Practical Reason,* 164)

One difficulty with Kant's theory is that since everyone has an equal right to land, there seems to be no reason why anyone would agree to respect anyone else's claim. Furthermore, since all lands are contiguous, there is seemingly no reason all persons individually couldn't claim all of it, i.e., the entire world, for themselves alone. To attempt to do so would, of course, invite conflict, and Kant is not unaware that conflict will result. But that is precisely the main reason for civil society, with its capacity to judge property rights and enforce its decisions regarding them.

Enough has perhaps been said to indicate some of similarities between Kant's views and Jefferson's, even though Jefferson for the most part follows Locke. Kant's notion of a "provisional right," or "right of occupation," bears a certain resemblance to the "right of occupancy" which Jefferson, Justice Marshall, and other jurists of his period recognized and which has become part of our American legal heritage. Some call it "aboriginal" or "primordial" right, which is "as sacred as the fee simple of the whites." Jefferson, like Kant, was hesitant to found society and its institutions, such as the institution of private property, upon the notion of an original convention, set of rules, or social contract. Both opposed the taking of land from Indians by brute force or by fraudulent manipulation. Both entertain the hope (or expectation, in the case of Kant) that the Indians would eventually join the civil society. Both were a bit fuzzy about exactly how this transition would take place, but both agreed that until accomplished, which might be never, according to Jefferson, their "provisional" or "aboriginal" rights were to be respected, and that, as the Continental Congress declared, "utmost good faith" should always be observed toward them.

Chapter Nine

Custer's Extraordinary Influence

More than a century after Custer's defeat and death at the Battle of the Little Bighorn, on June 25, 1876, his name and fame continue to reverberate throughout American history. One cannot help but compare this phenomenon with other famous cases of military defeat such as George Pickett's futile charge against Union forces at Gettysburg, Pennsylvania, and Robert Gould Shaw's unsuccessful assault against the Confederate stronghold at Fort Wagner, Charleston, South Carolina. There are significant similarities as well as differences between the three cases, but all have captured the American public's imagination; movies and videos have been made regarding each of them and their exploits; and monuments of one kind or another have been erected by their admirers to honor them. One might wonder, however, why their respective defeats have received such attention. Normally in matters of war one would suppose that only cases of outright victory would generate such admiration and enthusiasm. Among the three, of course, Custer's notoriety and influence has been the greatest, but perhaps a comparison of the three might reveal something about what William James called "the variety of military experience," and the factors which turned these military losers into quixotic national heroes.

One significant difference between Custer's battle at the Little Bighorn and Pickett's charge at Gettysburg is that Pickett personally survived and Custer did not. Over fifty percent of the men under Pickett's immediate command also did not; one hundred percent in Custer's case. Of course, Pickett survived mainly because, unlike Custer, he chose to lead his troops from behind rather than in front of them. To his dying day (some 12 years later), however, he blamed General Robert E. Lee for ordering him to lead his troops against impossible odds, resulting in the deaths of so many of the men under his command.

On the other hand, Pickett and Custer were alike in many ways. Both barely managed to graduate from West Point, Pickett in 1846 and Custer in 1861, each the "goat" of his class, last out of 59 in Pickett's case, and last out of a class of 34 cadets in Custer's case. Both were pranksters and loved to wear flamboyant uniforms, mustaches, and long hair perfumed with Araby in Pickett's case, cinnamon-scented hair oil in Custer's. Both received rapid advancement in the military. Pickett rose from Lieutenant to captain (in the U.S. Army) and after Virginia seceded, from major in the Confederate States Army of Artillery to colonel (within a month) and to brigadier general in January of 1862. In October of the same year, he was promoted to major general. Custer was made a brevet brigadier general when he was only 23 years old, and later a brevet major general. Pickett's promotions were also brevet or temporary battlefield promotions. Custer ended his career as a Lieutenant Colonel in the regular army.

Just as Custer had distinguished himself by rash and impulsive attacks during the Civil War, earning the respect and mentorship of General Philip H. Sheridan, so Pickett distinguished himself during the Mexican-American war by retrieving an American flag from his wounded fellow soldier, the future Confederate General James Longstreet, and unfurling it over the fortress during the Battle of Chapultepec in 1849, with bullets whizzing all around him; and later in the Washington Territory in 1859 on San Juan Island in a boundary dispute with British forces. He has been quoted as telling his outnumbered men, "We'll make a Bunker Hill of it."

After the disaster of Gettysburg, Pickett's fame went decidedly downhill. His troops were defeated at the Battle of Five Forks. The attack of the Union forces in that battle occurred while Pickett was two miles away enjoying a shad bake with some friends. He was later relieved of his command, although he was present at the surrender site at Appomattox Court House (the name of the town, not the building). It has been claimed that his defeat at Five Forks was a pivotal moment in the war which caused Lee to evacuate Richmond and retreat to Appomattox, which effectively ended the war.

Just as Sheridan claimed that Custer, who also was present at Appomattox, was the one whose "gallant efforts" brought about the surrender, so it would appear that Pickett is now said to be the one who single-handedly and inadvertently brought about Lee's ultimate defeat! Such claims and actions only re-enforce the notion that war is absurd as well as obscene, and that as the French statesman, Georges Clemenceau, during WWI once said, "War is too important to be left to generals." Two films have portrayed Pickett's tragic career, namely, the 1993 film, *Gettysburg*, in which Sephen Lang plays George Pickett, and the 2003 film, *Gods and Generals,* in which Billy Campbell plays the part.

Another example of a failed military effort in the Civil War, which nonetheless generated great admiration and respect, is the case of the Massachusetts 54th Volunteer Infantry composed exclusively of black Union soldiers, led by Colonel Robert Gould Shaw, a white officer, against the Confederate stronghold or battery at Fort Wagner, located on Morris Island just south of the approach to the Charleston, South Carolina, harbor. The 1989 Academy Award winning television movie, *Glory*, depicts the story of Shaw, played by actor Matthew Broderick, and his black soldiers, and includes actors Morgan Freeman and Denzel Washington. Leading his men forward, on foot, Shaw was one of the first killed as were most if not all of his men. It was a clear victory for the Confederates who suffered only 200 casualties as opposed to about 1600 casualties suffered by the combined Union forces, including Shaw's. In a prior attack, the Union forces had lost over 330 lives as opposed to only 12 Confederate losses. The Union forces continued to shell the Fort for another 60 days, after which the Confederate forces abandoned it. Militarily it was no great achievement for the Union forces, but rather, an immensely bloody one. It would appear that persistence and stupidity in war go hand in hand.

Although the battle was an anticipatable and hopeless defeat for the Union and for the Massachusetts 54th, not only was the likeness of Shaw, astride his horse, and the likenesses of many of his fellow soldiers commemorated on a bronze plaque sculptured by Augustus Saint-Gaudens, but his official eulogy was delivered to a large Boston audience by America's most noted philosopher, William James, one of whose brothers had earlier been wounded in the war. However, the commemoration did serve the purpose of proving once and for all that black soldiers could be as valiant and brave as white soldiers. This final recognition helped greatly in the North's recruitment abilities. Yet even this celebration of fallen heroes could hardly match the fuss created by the funeral and burial of Custer's bones at the West Point Cemetery with full military honors. In addition to the Saint-Gaudens plaque in Boston, however, memorials to Shaw can be also be found on Staten Island, New York; at Harvard's Memorial Hall, even though Shaw dropped out before graduating; and in Washington, D.C. where the neighborhood of Shaw is named for him. A poem, "My Hero," has been written in praise of him by African-American, Benjamin Griffith Brawley. (http://en.Wikipedia.org/wiki/Robert Gould Shaw)

An important footnote should perhaps be appended here since it indicates an underlying reason why Shaw's moral stature now seems so much greater than that of either Custer or Pickett. After the July 18, 1863, Battle of Fort Wagner, the Union dead were buried by Confederate soldiers. Shaw's shoes were removed and he was buried "with his niggers." The act was intended as an insult but it was not regarded as such by his ardent abolitionist father who was proud that his son had been buried with his black brothers. Although at first hesitant to command a black regiment, Shaw soon learned to respect them and to despise racism. To his credit Pickett, although born in Richmond, Virginia, with southern sympathies all his life, detested the institution of slavery, but did nothing to eliminate it. Custer once expressed his views of blacks as follows:

> I am in favor of elevating the negro to the extent of his capacity and intelligence, and of our doing every- thing in our power to advance the race, . . . but I am opposed to making this advance by correspondingly debasing any portion of the white race. As to trusting the negro with the most sacred and responsible privilege —the right of suffrage—I should as soon think of elevating an Indian Chief to the Popedom of Rome. (Ambrose 251–2.)

After the war he was reduced in rank from brevet Major General to Captain in the regular army. With the support of General Sheridan, he was offered the command of the 10th U.S. Cavalry (an all black regiment called the Buffalo Soldiers) with the rank of full Colonel, but turned down the offer in favor of a Lieutenant Colonelcy of the 7th U.S. Cavalry which he took charge of at Fort Riley, Kansas Territory.

Part of the Custer phenomenon may be due to the fact that even before his death he had entertained readers of *The Galaxy*, a popular magazine, with accounts of his Life on the Plains, which were later combined into a book of the same name. Easterners with little knowledge of the West were eager to hear of his exploits in what they had been led to believe, by Lewis and Clark among others, was "The Great American Desert," a place fit only for Indians and other exotic animals. To his credit Custer, in his articles and book, endeavored to disabuse them of that myth. He started them thinking about how they too might travel the western plains, enjoy the same pleasures Custer enjoyed while shooting, buffalo, Indians, and other wildlife. Indeed, on occasion Custer personally escorted Russian royalty such as the Grand Duke Alexis and others on hunting expeditions, and otherwise gave them a taste of the wild, wild, West. Dreams that many had of riding across the miles and miles of apparent emptiness on an "iron horse" (railroad car) or by coach or wagon were made to seem to be entirely feasible as well as fascinating.

The "Great American Desert," in which so many believed and which was mentioned on maps of the time included most of the territories west of the states bordering the western side of the Mississippi River, that is, all the states which joined the Union prior to the Civil War, namely Minnesota (1858); Iowa (1846); Missouri (1821); Arkansas (1836); and Louisiana (1812). Not included were California (1850); Oregon (1859); and the territory of Washington, which

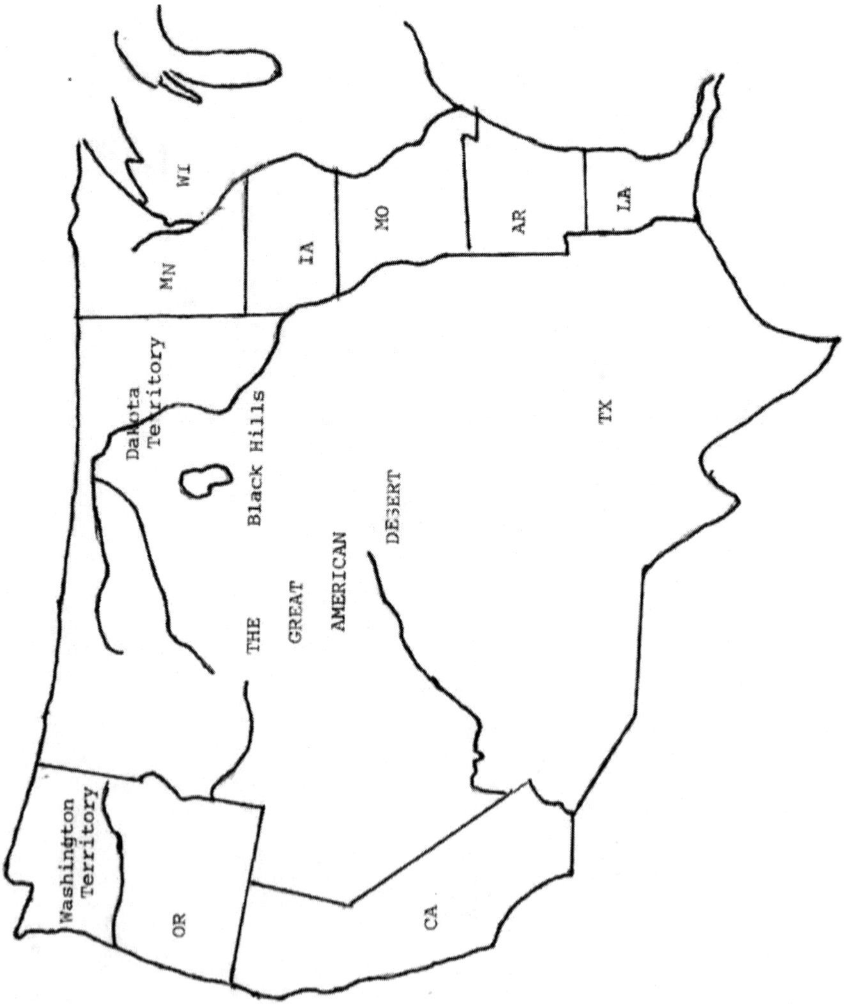

The Great American Desert.

didn't become a state until 1889. The Great American Desert specifically included "Indian Territory," (later Oklahoma), which became the depository of transplanted Eastern tribes, as well as a place for incarcerating hostile Indians from the Southwest and the Plains territories. Texas (although it became a state in 1845) and Kansas were also generally regarded as part of the Great American Desert. The enclosed map is perhaps a bit too precise. The boundaries of the Great American Desert were more vaguely defined than indicated which is only to be expected since the myth itself was only vaguely understood. The Oklahoma, Kansas, and Texas territories were the areas where Custer was first encamped after coming West. He was only later assigned to the Dakota, Wyoming, and Montana territories.

Custer's own account of the so-called "Great American Desert" goes as follows:

> It is but a few years ago that every schoolboy, supposed to possess the rudiments of a knowledge of the geography of the United States, could give the boundaries and a general description of the Great American Desert. As to the boundary the knowledge seemed to be quite explicit: on the north bounded by the Upper Missouri, on the east by the Lower Missouri and Mississippi, on the south by Texas, and on the west by the Rocky Mountains. The boundaries on the northwest and south remained undisturbed, while on the east civilization, propelled and directed by Yankee enterprise, adopted the motto: Westward the star of empire takes its way. Countless throngs of emigrants crossed the Mississippi and Missouri rivers, selecting homes in the rich and fertile territories lying beyond. Each year this tide of emigration, strengthened and increased by the flow from foreign shores, advanced toward the setting sun, slowly but surely narrowing the preconceived limit of the Great American Desert, and correspondingly enlarging the limits of civilization. At last the geographical myth was dispelled. It was gradually discerned that the Great American Desert did not exist . . . but that within its supposed limits . . . there existed the fairest and richest portion of the national domain, blessed with a climate pure, bracing, and healthful, while its undeveloped soil rivaled if it did not surpass the most productive portions of the eastern, middle, or southern states. (Custer, 3–4.)

In his book Custer points out what intrepid French trappers, missionaries, and explorers, with names such as Hennepin, Nicollet, Pierre (Chouteau), and Dupree, certain adventurous Englishmen, fur traders from the Hudson Bay Company, and Lewis and Clark already knew, namely, that the vast western territories were teeming with wildlife, plant life, beautiful mountains and valleys, and spectacular views. He whetted Eastern appetites for new lands and new fortunes more than any previous adventurers had. During the Civil War few persons could be persuaded to leave the safety of their eastern homes. Ohio, Custer's home state, was about as "western" a state in those days that they cared or dared to visit or inhabit. But after the War and after Custer's writings which he embellished on frequent trips to New York City in conversations with friends and politicians whose favor he sought, many thousands of "pioneers" were prepared to make the arduous but romantic trek from St. Louis, Missouri, to the West, determined to carve out a piece of it for themselves, come hell or high water, or starvation, or scalping by hostile Indians. After Custer's announcement to the world that he had found gold in the Black Hills, again something others knew about, many daring persons made the westward journey. It is significant and appropriate that the major museum at Rapid City, South Dakota, is called "The Journey Museum." And it is not surprising to learn, as Bob Lee says in his book, *The Black Hills After Custer*, that South Dakotans interested in the history of the area, usually do it in terms of B.C. or A. C., meaning "Before Custer" and "After Custer." That fact alone indicates just how influential Custer has become in creating the mystique of "The West," and bringing about the fulfillment of America's so-called "manifest destiny."

After his death, his wife, Elizabeth Bacon Custer, devoted her 57 years of widowhood (she lived until April 6, 1933, two days short of being 91 years old) to lionizing her husband and attempting to exonerate him of all charges of incompetence and arrogance associated with the Little Bighorn battle. She wrote three books, *Boots and Saddles, or, Life in Dakota with General Custer*; *Tenting on the Plains, or, General Custer in Kansas and Texas*; and *Following the Guidon into the Indian Wars with General Custer and the Seventh Cavalry,* --all of them defensive of her husband's reputation.

She took every opportunity to prevent the publication of negative criticism of his exploits. Although Major Marcus A. Reno requested a Court of Inquiry in 1870 to rebut charges of cowardice brought against him, and Captain Fred W. Benteen publicly denied that he had failed to follow Custer's orders, both were apparently somewhat intimidated by Mrs. Custer. They and others as well were inclined to withhold final comments until after her death. The trouble was that she outlived all the would-be critics.

A similar problem arose with respect to the question whether Custer had been scalped. Some accounts, including those of Indians, suggest that he wasn't scalped although most of the others, including Custer's brother, Tom, had not only been scalped, but had had their skulls crushed and bodies mutilated, and, as one might have expected, had most of their clothing taken. All that was left on that hilly battlefield were bloody, naked torsos, heads, arms, and legs, strewn about as if a tornado had struck. Generals Gibbon and Terry arrived at the site on June 27th, two days after the event, observed the scene, and arranged to have the dead, including Custer, buried where they had fallen. The graves were shallow and hurriedly dug, probably because there was evidence that many Indians were still within the vicinity. These persons were probably the ones in the best position to ascertain whether Custer had been scalped. The message sent out was that Custer—surprisingly—was not scalped although all of the others were. No one, it seems, wanted to affirm that he had been scalped or otherwise mutilated.

Some commentators have suggested that since Custer had had his hair cut short prior to the engagement and was wearing a buckskin jacket at the time, he wouldn't have been easily recognized as "Curley"—a nickname he shared incidentally with Crazy Horse (Ambrose, 38, 108). In times past Custer had let his blondish hair curl about his shoulders, making it a scalp well worth taking, one would think, but his short hair may have discouraged his Indian attackers, especially if he was somewhat balding, as has been suggested. There had in fact been cases in which bald men were killed but not scalped, primarily because of their baldness. However, this explanation is rather weak since Custer always wore a red cravat about his neck which would have easily distinguished him from all the other soldiers. Furthermore, it was standard practice for Sioux Indians to take scalps of their enemies, and those taken at this battle would have been regarded as premium.

A year later soldiers returned to give the fallen troops a proper burial. All they found were scattered bones from the shallow graves mixed with the bones of horses and mules. The animal bones were separated from the human bones which were then deposited in a common grave atop the hill, surrounded by a fence and designated by an obelisk giving the names of those who had died and were buried there. Custer's bones and perhaps those of certain other officers were disinterred and sent East. Custer's, or what they thought to be Custer's, were sent to West Point for burial. Again, it might be thought, here was another opportunity to determine whether Custer had been scalped. It would have been impossible, however, because (1) the identity of the bones had not been conclusively established; and (2) there were so few of them (in Custer's case, according to one Park Ranger, only enough to fill a hat); and (3) the graves had all been raided by wild animals in the region—coyotes, wolves, skunks, raccoons, rattlesnakes, and the like, making accurate identifications unlikely. Perhaps DNA testing could now solve that problem but I am sure that West Point is not about to open its Custer mausoleum for that purpose. The bones that are there enshrined may in fact not be Custer's but those of some lowly private or corporal, all because no one wanted to distress Libbie Custer, who, incidentally, according to the Park Rangers at the Battlefield Memorial, never during her lifetime chose to visit the site of her husband's "last stand."

One measure of a person's influence and/or popularity is the number of public places or institutions named for that person. In the Black Hills alone, the name, Custer, appears in the names of Custer State Park; Custer County; the city of Custer (near where his expeditionary force found gold); Custer Mountain (west of Custer Park); Custer Peak (north of the city of Custer); and Custer County Airport. It is interesting to note that the name of the city was decided by a vote of the residents who were asked to choose between "Custer" and "Stonewall." Since there were more Unionists in residence than Confederates, the name of Custer won out.

There are also counties in Colorado, Montana, Nebraska, and Oklahoma which are named after Custer; as are several townships in Minnesota and Michigan. There is a Custer, Michigan; a Custar, Ohio; and a Custer Wisconsin. There is an equestrian statue of Custer in Monroe, Michigan, his boyhood home, as well as a life-sized standing statue of him at his birthplace in New Rumley, Ohio. Camp Custer, or Fort Custer National Military Reservation, was established in 1917 and is still in use. A Fort Custer National Cemetery was established in 1943. The U.S. 85th Infantry Division is nicknamed "The Custer Division" And of course the 7th Cavalry has long claimed Custer as their founder and have adopted his favorite tune, "The Gerryowen," as their "Fight" song, and the name "Gerryowen" has become a way that fellow members of the 7th Cavalry greet each other, just as Marines often use the expression "Semper Fi."

The battlefield where Custer was killed was proclaimed the *National Cemetery of Custer's Battlefield Reservation* on December 7, 1886, ten and a half years after the actual battle. It was meant to include veterans of other campaigns and wars. The name was shortened to Custer National Cemetery. The Reno-Benteen Battlefield became a part of the National Monument and Cemetery on April 14, 1926, and the whole area including both battlefields and cemeteries was redesignated the *Custer Battlefield National Monument.*

Through the efforts of Senator Ben Nighthorse Campbell of Colorado (a member of the Northern Cheyenne tribe), legislation was passed and signed into law by President George H.W. Bush on Dec 10, 1991, renaming the site *The Little Bighorn Battlefield National Monument* (its present name), so as to give recognition to the Indian participants in the battle. The legislation also provided for an Indian Memorial to be constructed near the top of the hill on which rests the obelisk or pyramidal granite memorial which names the soldiers buried there in a common grave. The Indian Memorial has taken the form of a sunken low sand stone circle containing plaques naming the warriors by tribe who died there. Red granite markers are on the battlefield itself to designate where the Indians fell, just as the white marble markers indicate where the soldiers, including Custer, fell, or were presumed to have fallen. On one side, the open side, of the Indian memorial "grotto," if I may call it that, is a handsome wire sculpture depicting several Indian participants, presumably Crazy Horse and two companions riding into the fray.

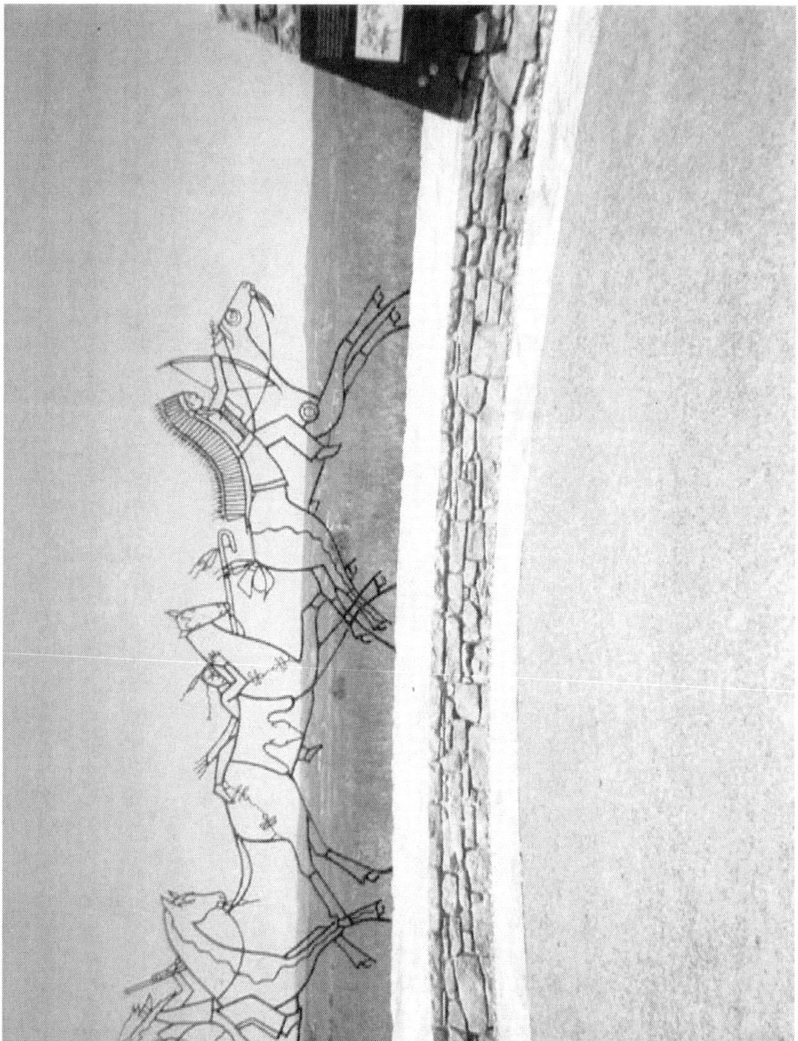

The Indian Little Big Horn Battlefield Memorial.

The Indian Little Big Horn Battlefield Memorial.

Was there something about Custer personally which would account for his tremendous posthumous fame? Was he, like Robert Gould Shaw, whom William James called "the blue-eyed child of fortune" who marched with his black compatriots "as warm-blooded champions of a better day for man," the epitome of self-less patriotism and sacrifice? Sadly that description does not fit George Armstrong Custer.

Although he fought fearlessly in practically every major battle of the Civil War, and had several horses shot out from under him, the casualty rate of the men under his command was higher than that of any other Union commander. (Ambrose, 196.) He was court-martialed in 1867 on charges of abandoning his command to visit his wife, and for having deserters hunted down and shot without a hearing. Three of the deserters were captured and wounded; one died because Custer would not let the regimental doctor give him prompt attention. Custer was convicted and sentenced to a year's suspension from rank and salary, although through the efforts of General Sheridan, his military mentor, he was reinstated ten months later. (Ambrose, 300–01.)

We have previously (in Chapter IV and V) indicated how Custer schemed to evade his superior commanders and their orders (General Stanley in the Yosemite River campaign and General Terry during the Little Bighorn Battle). In the first case, his insubordination would normally have involved another court martial, had it not been for General Stanley's alcoholism. And in the latter case Custer was to act in coordination with Gibbon and Terry's forces, but he deliberately sought to out-fight and out-flank them by needlessly pushing his men (31 officers and approximate 585 enlisted men) to near exhaustion in order to capture all the glory of victory over the Indians for himself.

Earlier, after the Battle of Washita, the battle which made Custer's reputation as an Indian fighter, Major Joel Elliott, a member of Custer's command, led a detachment of 19 men after fleeing Indians. His absence was noticed and several search parties were sent out to find him and his missing men. The found no trace of them near the Indian village and were afraid to pursue them further because of Indians in the near vicinity. Custer who was concerned about the safety of his supply train decided to withdraw without determining what had befallen Elliott. Later investigation discovered the entire group dead about two miles from the site of the Indian village.

Custer was severely criticized for his apparently callous abandonment of these men under his command. Captain Frederick W. Benteen was especially critical and even went so far as to write an anonymous letter the *St. Louis Democrat* criticizing Custer and belittling the regiment. Allegedly, when Custer read the letter he called all his officers together and demanded to know who the author was so he could "horsewhip" him. Captain Benteen, never a friend of Custer, stood up and said, "All right, General, start your horsewhipping now. I wrote it." Custer became dumbfounded, re-faced, and then walked out. (Monaghan, 322; Ambrose, 325.)

Custer was never particularly popular with his men. It is a bit astounding that he gave Benteen the command of one of three battalions of his regiment at the Battle of the Little Bighorn. At his Court of Inquiry Major Reno made known his dislike of Custer and that he had no confidence in his ability as a soldier. (Stewart, 168) The recurrent references to "Custer's Luck" during his career was intended by some to suggest that his achievements, such as becoming a brigadier general at the age of 23, were not the consequences of any particular merit or ability on his part. Two other junior officers were promoted to brigadier general at the same time Custer was, but both had had previous command experience and Custer had not. It was only natural that he should have been envied and disliked by his detractors, although he did have his admirers.

Most of those who spoke favorably of Custer and helped him to advance in his army career were members of the General Staff. During the first Battle of Bull Run General Winfield Scott picked him to carry messages to Major General Irvin McDowell. During the pursuit of Confederate General Joseph E. Johnson on May 24th, 1862, Custer persuaded a colonel to allow him to lead four companies of Michigan Infantry across the Chickahominy River to attack Johnson's forces. His attack was successful and none other than General George B. McCellan. then commander of the Army of the Potomac, called it "a very gallant affair," and made Custer his aide-de-camp. Later Custer served on Major General Alfred Pleasonton's staff and became his protégé. It was Pleasonton who promoted Custer to brevet brigadier general. (Monaghan, 135.)

The one general whom Custer seems never to have impressed was Ulysses S. Grant. During the War their paths must have crossed many times, especially during Grant's last campaigns against Lee around Richmond which ended at Appomattox, but it was General Sheridan, not Grant, who gave Custer one of the Confederate flags of surrender (there were several of them). It was during Grant's presidency that Custer had any personal relationship with Grant. In 1876 when Custer was called to testify regarding the acts of Secretary of War Belknap regarding kickbacks and other fraudulent acts relating to Indian annuities and supplies. He tried to excuse himself from testifying but was kept in Washington, D.C. up to the time scheduled for a major expedition against the Plains Indians. His testimony implicated Grant's brother Orville, which of course did not please the President. Custer, wanting to make up for any hard feelings he may have caused, and anxious to return to his post at Fort Abraham Lincoln in Dakota territory so he could rejoin his regiment and become part of the planned expedition, went so far as to request a personal interview with President Grant who kept him waiting for hours at a time in his outer office, not once but three times, and never granting him the interview. After the House committee before which he had testified dismissed him, he attempted to return to the west without the permission of either the War Department or the President. Grant had him arrested in Chicago. Finally, because of pleas on behalf of Custer by Generals Sheridan and Sherman, Grant allowed him to join the expedition on condition that he command only the 7th cavalry and not the entire campaign. After the Battle of the Little Bighorn, as previously indicated, Grant expressed the opinion that Custer had been rash in his attack and that the whole operation was entirely unnecessary.

It might also be mentioned in this connection that during his excursion into the Black Hills he saw to it that Grant's son, Colonel Fred D. Grant, was made a part of his staff. Just how this relationship was supposed to enhance Custer's reputation with the President is unclear, especially since while on the expedition Custer had Grant's son arrested for drunkenness. However, when Colonel Grant was called home for his grandfather's funeral, Custer, in one of his letters to his wife who was then in Monroe, Michigan, wrote the following:

> If he—Col. Grant—goes to Long Branch from Chicago by way of Monroe to see you, you will, of course, do all in your power to make his stay agreeable. If you know of his arrival in advance you should meet in at the depot with a carriage. Have his father's picture hung in the parlor . . . (Ambrose, 361)

Although Custer had his troubles relating to people, other than his wife and his officer-mentors such as Sheridan, he is often portrayed as one who loved horses and dogs. As far as horses were concerned he preferred thoroughbreds, partly because of their stamina in the long forced marches he often inflicted upon his cavalrymen who for the most part did not ride thoroughbred horses.

After the Battle of Washita, he found in his possession a herd of some 800 to 900 wild Indian ponies which he felt he could not take with him (since they would slow the regiment down) nor leave them for other Indians to recapture and use in battles against army posts and civilian wagon trains. So he had them all shot by four companies of his men who reluctantly obeyed his orders. Undoubtedly Custer himself regretted the slaughter, but from a purely military point of view perhaps he was justified. At least his immediate superiors, Generals Sheridan and Sherman, concurred. From a layman's perspective, however, the first alternative, despite the delay involved, would seem to have been the more humane action.

Whenever on the frontier, he always surrounded himself with large dogs, mostly staghounds and greyhounds. He slept with them (for their warmth) and took them along with him on any march with the 7th cavalry, as he did with his brass band at the head of the column. He also relied on them in times of need. For example, once while leading a column across deserted prairie country, he saw a group of antelope in the distance, and took off with a pack of his greyhounds after them, primarily to see whether they could match the speed of the antelope. He rode for several miles on his thoroughbred horse before giving up the chase and called back his dogs. He was miles from his column and was relying on his dogs to find their way to the column, but they were as mystified and lost as he was. Then he spied a large buffalo bull about a mile off. He raced after the buffalo. His thoroughbred caught up to the beast and Custer held his pistol next to the bull's head, and after a lengthy and purposely prolonged chase decided to end it all by shooting the animal when suddenly the bull suddenly wheeled in an attempt to gore the horse and rider, Custer inadvertently pulled the trigger, but instead of killing the buffalo he shot his own horse straight through the head. Without the vaguest idea of where he was, and with dogs worn out from the chase, he walked a few miles toward what he thought was the right direction, and then merely sat down in open Indian territory to await being discovered by men from his regiment who were sent out to find what had happened to their fearless but foolhardy leader.

Custer was often tempted to leave his command without notifying anyone of his intentions. Most commentators have attributed this tendency on his part to his "boyish" nature. Libbie, his wife, in later letters to him always urged him to stay close to the column. Custer himself seems never to have thought this behavior in any way strange or inconsistent with his stature as an army officer. In fact he describes this particular event in which he shot his own horse in his own book *My Life on the Plains* (79) without apology or expression of regret, except to say that it was "rashly imprudent."

During the war while on the staff of General McCellan, Custer overheard the General on the banks of the Chickahominy River ask, "I wish I knew how deep it is." When none of the closer officers could utter a reply, Custer, it is said, muttered "I'll damn soon show him," and lept into the river with his horse, crossed over and back, and called out, "That's how deep it is, General." (Monaghan, 80) There is some suspicion that the story is false, but it does at least tell something about Custer's impulsive personality.

Another episode in his life perhaps better than others demonstrates both his dramatic flair and his love of personal fame. On May 23, 1865 after the war, the Army of the Potomac held its Grand Review in Washington, D.C. Custer himself led the entire parade down Pennsylvania Avenue. As the 3rd Cavalry Division turned around the Treasury Building and started down toward the White House and the reviewing stand, some 300 girls all dressed in white threw flowers at Custer. As he leaned over to catch a bouquet his horse bolted and at full gallop took him down the parade route. As he reached the Presidential reviewing stand, he tried to give a saber salute but lost both his hat and his saber. Expert horseman that he was, he was able finally to restrain his horse—probably a thoroughbred—and received a gigantic ovation from the spectators and no doubt from President Johnson who had only assumed the office less than a month before because of President Lincoln's assassination.

Custer's hair at this time was very long, reddish blonde, and curly, and as he rode swiftly down the avenue without a hat to control it, it flowed out behind him in the breeze and made him without question the most conspicuous member of the parade. All the colorful incidents of his subsequent as well as his former life pale in comparison to this moment, but they all reveal the same thing about Custer, namely, his vanity, his love of fame, and his limitless desire to do whatever the situation required to achieve honor and glory.

Chapter Ten

Federal Indian Law and Self-Governance

The so-called "firewater" theory of Indian alcoholism has been around at least since the Indian Trade and Intercourse Act of 1832 which made it unlawful to sell liquor to Indians or for them to possess it in any form on or off reservations. The theory claims that Indians as a race are inordinately prone to crave alcoholic beverages and tend to lose control over their behavior when they drink. The term, "firewater," is of 19th century origin (Leland, 1) and may have been derived as a translation of a term used by Algonquinian speaking (Ojibway/Chippewa) Indians living in the United States and Canada around the Great Lakes region, the Ojibway expression being *iskotewabo.* (American Heritage Dictionary.)

Actually the general belief that Indians cannot "hold their liquor" has been around even before the 19th century, before the term, "firewater," was first employed, perhaps as far back as the 17th century. Joy Leland cites an observer at the time describing "the Ottawa as 'addicted' and 'passionately attached to brandy'" and who "noted with horror Bacchanalian excesses when they drank." (Leland, 1.) She comments that "the first Europeans naturally interpreted the Indians' response to alcohol as a constitutional or racial difference." Congress early on passed several "Indian Trade and Intercourse Acts," one in 1790 which was valid for only two years but regularly renewed to 1834. Most were concerned with just methods of dealing with Indians, e.g., land sales, etc. The 1832 Act specifically outlawed the sale of alcoholic beverages to Indians. The recommendation to Congress to pass these trade and prohibition acts came from President Washington himself and his Secretary of War, Henry Knox (Light and Rand, 27–8) and undoubtedly from one of the first "Offices of Indian Affairs," (later to become in 1824 the Bureau of Indian Affairs) whose initial membership included Benjamin Franklin and Patrick Henry. One other notable fact underlying these prohibitory laws is the assumption, which is still prevalent today, that the firewater theory applies not only to Algonquinian speaking Indians but to *all* tribes—from Eskinos in Alaska to Navajos in the Southwest and to Sioux and Cheyenne tribes in South Dakota, Montana and other Plains states.

In the twentieth century the firewater theory was labeled a myth, i.e., a false statement of the facts by numerous sociologists, social workers, and anthropologists whose views are succinctly documented by Joy Leland in her book, *Firewater Myths: North American Indian Drinking and Alcohol Addiction.* According to many social scientists and others who have studied the problem, there is no conclusive evidence that alcoholism, which all agree exists on the reservations, is caused by some genetic or hereditary condition peculiar to Indians. (Leland, 3; Medicine, 12). And according to the celebrated anthropologist, Beatrice Medicine, herself a Lakota Sioux, who died in 2005, "Though numerous theories have been applied to the drinking habits and subsequent behavior of any tribal group, no simple, yet cogent, explanation has been forthcoming." (7)

Nonetheless, since at least 1802 when Congress authorized the President "to take such measures . . . as to him may appear expedient to prevent or restrain the vending or distribution of spirituous liquors among all or any of the said Indian tribes . . ." (Medicine, 36) to the 1832 Trade and Intercourse Act, and to 1953 when President Eisenhower signed Public Law 277 which repealed all "discriminatory liquor laws as they pertain to Indians," all sales of liquor to Indians were prohibited by federal law—a period of over 150 years! The legal authority of all this so-called "discriminatory" legislation was, of course, Art. I, Sec. 8, of the U.S. Constitution, which explicitly gives Congress the power "to regulate commerce with foreign nations, and among the several States, and with the Indian tribes."

The motivation of the Eisenhower republican administration is somewhat difficult to fathom. By 1953, of course, all Indians in the United States were declared fully fledged citizens by the Indian Citizenship Act of 1924 (although even then some were not allowed to vote). Some Indians had acquired citizenship somewhat earlier as a result of their acceptance of the provisions of the Dawes Allotment or Severalty Act. So it may have been simply a desire on the part of President Eisenhower to eliminate any restrictions on their status as citizens and thus further integrate them into American society—a goal long sought for from Jefferson's day onward. But from a more negative, and somewhat more cynical, point of view, it may have been a desire to eliminate the "Indian Problem," and absolve the federal government from the burden of carrying on services agreed to by numerous treaties and administered by the BIA. There have always been persons such as Andrew Jackson who decried the legitimacy of all treaties with Indians, and states such as Georgia which initiated a wholesale ejection of Indians from their boundaries. The State of South Dakota has at various times sought to have the remaining reservations themselves eliminated. Put Indians on the same basis as whites and let them care for themselves as everyone else does.

The tribes have managed somehow to avoid entirely "going away" or giving up their treaty rights. What the 1953 repeal, in particular, did, was to (1) eliminate a major part of my father's occupation as an enforcer of federal laws, particularly those prohibiting the sale of intoxicants to Indians; and (2) make the problem of alcoholism on the reservations, and the myriad difficulties which that condition entails, all the more intransigent. The tribal councils of practically all of the largest reservations, e.g., the Navajo and Pine Ridge reservations, foresaw these difficulties and have enacted their own prohibition laws, which apply, however, and of necessity only to their reservation jurisdictions. Only about a third of the reservations now allow the sale of alcoholic beverages within their boundaries.

The basic idea among Indian leaders as well as among many white reformers was that if you deny the Indian access to liquor the alcoholism addiction will disappear along with all the other problems it generates. But of course as long as the adjoining States permit the sale of alcoholic beverages to Indians even though the Reservations don't, and there is no longer a federal control over such sales, the reservation Indian has little trouble obtaining his beer or liquor and getting stone-cold drunk.

The specific problem is well illustrated by the sale of alcoholic beverages to Pine Ridge Reservation Indians who have regularly traveled to White Clay, Nebraska, which is only two miles from the Agency, to purchase the previously forbidden drink. When the federal prohibition law was in effect (before 1953) Indians had more difficulty than they do now. I recall how my father would arrest many a white tavern owner or bar keeper there who greedily sold liquor to undercover Indian policemen. He conducted many such "sting" operations. Now of course white sellers violate no federal law, and as Nebraska has not passed its own prohibition law, nothing legally can be done about such harm producing acts. I believe the Tribal Council on the Pine Ridge Reservation has appealed to the Nebraska legislature to do something about the specific problem, but the only concession has been an agreement to allow the tribal police to enforce *Nebraska* laws in White Clay.

A somewhat similar situation exists in Gallup, New Mexico, only a short distance from the Navajo Reservation. The Navajo community has forbidden the sale of alcoholic beverages on the Reservation, but the Indian has only a few miles to go to obtain alcoholic beverages at local bars and restaurants. Yet, the situation at White Clay is somewhat unique. When the reservation was initially established in 1876, a four square mile area in Nebraska which included White Clay was within the boundaries of the reservation. In 1905 President Theodore Roosevelt by executive order removed those 4 square miles from the Pine Ridge Reservation. By that time, "executive order" as opposed to "treaty right" reservations were allowed, but his act was nonetheless legally challenged at the time. Why he sought fit to straighten out the northern border of Nebraska is unclear, unless it was simply a matter of cartographic aesthetics. There have of course been other questionable and incongruous state boundaries, such as those of Maine, West Virginia, and Minnesota. But perhaps because of his own land holdings in North Dakota, he was more concerned with this particular anomaly.

Would the cession of White Clay, a dreary, basically one-street town having according to the census of 2000 only 14 permanent residents and seemingly even today as having almost as many bars and liquor establishments, solve the alcoholism problem on the Pine Ridge reservation? Probably not. The Indians would simply have to travel a slightly longer distance (perhaps 20 miles) to other Nebraska towns such as Rushville. Is there then something wrong with the basic assumption that such problems can be solved simply by legally denying the Indians access to liquor? Perhaps other non-legal remedies should be tried, such as Alcoholics Anonymous. In fact that has been tried and failed because the public confession of one's guilt or shame, and membership in a support group are not effective means of discouraging Lakota drinkers, and do not coincide with other tribal traditions. (Medicine, 82, 120–21.) Should we then by appropriate legislation force arrested alcoholics to enroll in AA programs, despite their antagonism toward them on the assumption that somehow laws and constitutional revisions can solve all social problem?

Besides being in this particular case totally ineffective, such legalism has against it also the charge of being paternalistic. Such laws treat citizens regardless of their age or degree of maturity as though they were insufficiently responsible to provide for their own needs or welfare. Not all such laws are bad. A good example is the helmet law which many States, but not all, have passed which requires riders of motorcycles to wear protective headgear. It is not what most of the cyclists I have spoken with would prefer, since it restricts their freedom and denies them a certain kind of pleasure of riding without a helmet, but most, upon reflection, agree that such laws serve a good purpose.

On the other hand, many paternalistic "blue laws" of the past which regulated religious practices have been found to be too restrictive of the freedom of mature adults, and often in conflict with our Bill of Rights. Also, petty regulations of the BIA have too often treated adult Sioux Indians as if they were children. But is the prohibition of alcohol sales to Indians today—admittedly a paternalistic policy—one which on the whole benefits Indians or destroys their autonomy? The answer to that question is still out but it does raise another question which is connected with it and that concerns the role of Indian reservation police.

If one travels to the Rosebud Reservation today, one will discover none of the buildings I knew as a child, but what one will see is a rather large, prominently located, building on which are the words, *Rosebud Law Enforcement,* and nearby another identified as the *Rosebud Sioux Tribal Court.* A somewhat smaller structure houses the *Agency Headquarters.* It might be thought that the obvious presence of tribal police and tribal courts on Indian reservations is a sign of their increased autonomy and self-government, and correspondingly a decrease in the role of the federal government in Indian affairs. To an extent this is true. My father's role as a special agent of the BIA for the enforcement of federal laws affecting Indians has been eliminated; many paternalistic laws such as those relating to the sale of alcoholic beverages have been repealed; the forced enrollment of Indian children in off reservation boarding schools by Indian police has been stopped, as have attempts to prohibit the use of Indian languages, Sun dances, Ghost dances and other rituals of native American Indian religions. Many enforcement problems have been assumed by state and local agencies and others by the tribes themselves. In addition, many of the positions in BIA Agencies on reservations, such as that

Rosebud Law Enforcement Services

Rosebud Agency Headquarters.

of Superintendent, as well as others in the national office in the Department of the Interior in Washington, D. C. , such as the Commissioner of Indian Affairs, and the Director of the Smithsonian Museum of the American Indian, are now held by Indians, rather than held exclusively by white persons. Yet, as Wilcomb E. Washburn has rightly pointed out, when one considers the origins of Indian police and Indian courts, the impression one gets that there has been a substantial increase in self-government may be partly an illusion.

According to Washburn, "Indian police and courts were created in large measure for the purpose of controlling the Indian and breaking up tribal leadership and tribal government." (Washburn, 168) He cites the fact that in the 1860's and 1870's several agencies felt the need of Indian police. The agent for the Pawnee tribe took the lead and appointed 6 leading warriors of the tribe to assist with the enforcement of laws against horse stealing. In the 1870's an agent for the San Carlos Apaches, John P. Clum, consolidated five agencies into one and moved thousands of Indians hundreds of miles with the help of Indian police without either loss of life or property. The Commissioner of Indian Affairs in Washington, D. C., took note of these successful uses of Indians as policemen and ordered all agencies to organize police forces in so far as they were able to do so. Washburn also credits then Secretary of the Interior, H. M. Teller, in 1882 with setting up tribal courts, his aim being to suppress "heathen dances" such as the sundance, and to help attack

Rosebud Agency Headquarters.

the Indian institution of polygamy, the power of the medicine men, such as Sitting Bull, and other customs he regarded as offensive.

Despite low pay, and in some cases no pay for judicial responsibility, the Indian police performed their law and order duties better than the military troops that had earlier been assigned these tasks. The Wheeler-Howard Act of 1934, the so-called Indian Reorganization Act of the Franklin Delano Roosevelt administration, established some 51 newly formed "tribal courts" acting under regulations drawn up by the Department of Interior, thereby replacing some of the older somewhat less formal "courts of Indian offenses," which often used Indian customs and common sense rather than white man's law as the basis for deciding cases.

One cannot help wondering why so many Indians were so eager to serve as policemen and wear the blue uniforms and black hats which were issued to them, as were the metal badges they proudly wore upon their chests. Because of those badges they were known, at least among the Hunkpapa Sioux, as "Metal Breasts." (Vestal, 302.) So why would they so willingly assist white men who had been their mortal enemies (e.g., at Little Big Horn and Wounded Knee), who had tried in so many ways since conquering them to destroy their life style, their religions, and their culture, or what the Lakotas call their "tiyospaye."

It is perhaps understandable why such men as Custer always had Indian scouts. They were usually not members of the same tribe Custer at the time was attacking. The "Indian Wars" of the past were not always between white men and Indians. If frequently happened that it was Indian against Indian, e.g., Seneca versus Huron, Sioux versus Crow, or Navajo against Apache, et. al. In cases in which the Indian scout joined with white troops, often he was only siding with the white man against his own enemy. During the so-called French and Indian Wars many Indians sided with the French against the English, and similarly during the Revolutionary War, some Indians sided with the English and others sided with the Americans.

But these cases aside, why would Indians take jobs proffered by reservation officials (originally by Indian Reservation Agents whose positions were later abolished) to police their own people? An extreme example is the attempt by Indian police to arrest Sitting Bull at his home on the Standing Rock reservation. When General (*Bear Coat*) Miles, the Division Commander of the Department of Dakota located in St. Paul, Minnesota, became fearful that Sitting Bull might start another insurrection brought on by the Sioux acceptance of the newly introduced Ghost Dance, he issued an order for Sitting Bull's arrest. The Standing Rock reservation agent, Major James (*White Hair*) McLaughlin, could think of nothing to accuse him of until he learned that Sitting Bull was about to ask for a pass to go to Pine Ridge to investigate the new Ghost Dance religion.

Sitting Bull had made no secret of his plans and in fact had dictated a letter to the major in which he said in part,

> You should say nothing against our religion, for we said nothing against yours. You pray to God. So do all of us Indians, as well as the whites. We both pray to only one God, who made us al . . . . When you were here in my camp, you gave good words about my prayers, but today you take it all back again. And there is something else I want you to know. I am obliged to go to Pine Ridge Agency and investigate this Ghost Dance religion. So I write to let you know that. The policeman told me you intend to take all our ponies, and our guns too. So I wish you would let me know about that. Please answer soon. Sitting Bull (Vestal, 283–4)

McLaughlin's orders were not to make the arrest until further ordered, "unless it was discovered that Sitting Bull was preparing to leave the reservation." Learning that he was planning to leave gave the Agent his chance to send no less than 40 Indian policemen fully armed to arrest him. (Vestal, 288.) These policemen included Hunkpapa, Yantonais, and Blackfeet—all Sioux, many of whom had once been either his older former comrades or younger subordinates. They burst into his cabin just before dawn in the dark of night, rudely awakened him from his sleep, and forced clothing on him, evoking a joke, "You need not honor me like this." In Sioux culture being dressed by another was a sign of great respect and honor. At first he agreed to go as they demanded and ordered his old gray circus horse saddled, but as their insulting behavior persisted, Sitting Bull apparently changed his mind and resisted. At one point he appealed to his Hunkpapa followers to take action. One loyal companion shot policemen Bullhead in the leg. He in turn shot Sitting Bull in his left side, and Red Tomahawk, another policeman, shot him in the back. Both were fatal wounds. Had troops from the Agency not arrived about this time, there would have been no policemen left alive. As it was, when the troops arrived they began shooting the armed policemen who had to hold up a white flag to avoid being killed!

But the question still remains. Why would Hunkpapa policemen attack their old chief in this manner? It has been speculated by Washburn that

> It may well be that the chance to play a role of prestige and power, the right to bear arms among fellow warriors deprived of their arms, the privilege of wearing formal uniforms expressing that authority, and the frequent scouting and tracking missions against renegades, gave back to the Indian something he thought he had lost forever. Though he served as an agent of those who had destroyed the autonomy of his tribe his role demanded more individual physical courage, resourcefulness, and fidelity than did the role of chief of a people no longer able to make war or exercise an independent policy. Though the new role was provided by the conqueror, it served as a substitute for some of the values that the conqueror had destroyed. (Washburn, 171–2)

That may or may not be an adequate explanation, for it may be simply that the office of policeman was a job, and better that job than none at all (hunting buffalo was no longer a possible role nor was that of warrior). Or it may have been what Major McLaughlin himself has suggested, namely, that "people of their 'peaceable' faction (i.e., the Indian police) could not pass through the Ghost Dance settlement without being subjected to insults from Sitting Bull and his followers." (See Vestal, 286–7.) He cites the fact that Lieutenant Bullhead, the first policeman to wound Sitting Bull, as being "unable to brook with patience the indifference with which the magnanimity of the Government was regarded by Sitting Bull and his followers." Vestal adds, "And now the time had come; now they could get at him." In other words, it was simply a matter of personal resentment.

There may be some truth in the latter claim. Certainly the use of term "metal breasts" by Sitting Bull's followers to describe the policemen could only be taken as a term of derision, just as the term "bear coat" was previously used to characterize General Miles, and "white hair" to characterize McLaughlin. The Indians wearing the badges probably resented being called by their uncomplimentary nickname, much as I suppose Miles and McLaughlin also did.

But the despicable behavior we have described all happened in December of 1890. What of today's Indian police? Surely since that time more than a century later their roles and actions have changed and become more honorable and professional, perhaps, one would hope, like those of novelist Tony Hillerman's fictional characters, Navajo policemen, Sergeant Jim Chee and retired Lieutenant Joe Leaphorn. A personal not is perhaps here justified. During the 1930's, 40's, and 50's, my father often worked closely with Indian police and chiefs of police. Although I cannot now recall their names, I know that he trusted and respected them and became their friend. For example, when on the Red Lake reservation in Minnesota he would often visit them in their homes, and besides discussing and settling law enforcement problems, the Indians would share their knowledge of threshing wild rice, which grows only in a few parts of the world, Minnesota, Wisconsin, parts of Canada, and I believe also in China. Unsuccessful attempts have been made to grow it in Mexico. It is not biologically related to ordinary white rice. Being a former farmer, and at one time a Farm Agent, he was naturally interested in the process. Harvesting the rice involves beating the rise stalks as they grow up from the lake so that the kernels fall to the bottom of the rowboat, and are then gathered. My father would frequently come home with large packets of wild rice for which I am sure he paid much less than the commercial price. My mother took much pleasure serving the delicious food, when properly cleaned and hulled, to all of us.

The point of this aside is simply to suggest that in my father's opinion, his Indian co-workers were closer in character to Jim Chee and Joe Leaphorn than they ever were to former Indian policemen, Lieutenant Bullhead and Red Tomahawk.

But there have indeed been many landmark events during the twentieth century which have had profound effects on the self-esteem of Indians and their participation in self-government. From the purely political side, probably the most influential event was the passage of the Wheeler-Howard Act, or Indian Reorganization Act of 1934, during the administration of Franklin Delano Roosevelt when John Collier was Commissioner of Indian Affairs and Harold Ickes, Secretary of the Interior, both very pro-Indian. As indicated earlier modernized Indian courts were set up, loan funds were made available to assist entrepreneurial endeavors on the reservations, and preference was given to Indians applying for government positions.

During the Eisenhower administration during the 50's, however, the rights and welfare of Indians were again put in jeopardy. The questionable character of the 1953 repeal of the federal Indian prohibition law has already been commented on. It is also during this time that Congress passed the Termination Act of 1954 which sought to end federal subsidies to many Indian tribes; many Indian tribes—some 100 of them—were denied federal recognition; and many Indian lands were transferred to non-Indians.

Somewhat surprisingly, during the Richard Nixon administration the termination policy of the government was declared a disaster for the Indians.

In a campaign speech in 1960 entitled, "A Brighter Future for the American Indian," Nixon declared that "Termination of tribal recognition will not be a policy objective and in no case will it be imposed without Indian consent."

From a legislative point of view, one of the salient landmarks was the publication in 1942 of a *Handbook of Federal Indian Law* by Felix Cohen. It represented the first time all the disparate federal laws relating to American Indians had been codified, and its influence on behalf of Indians has been enormous. Cohen, son of legal philosopher and logician Morris Cohen, was at one time counsel for many Indian tribes and appeared on their behalf in the Federal Court of Claims. He was also a philosopher in his own right and published many articles and books in the field. His *Handbook* has been cited in hundreds of cases involving Indian rights. He died in 1953.

Another landmark in the attempt to increase the autonomy and self-government of Indians was the passage in 1968 of the Indian Constitutional Rights Act (82 Stat. 77), sometimes known as the "Indian Civil Rights Acts," or simply as the "Indian Bill of Rights." Excerpts are as follows:

> No Indian tribe in exercising powers of self-government shall—
>
> (1) make or enforce any law prohibiting the free exercise of religion, or abridging the freedom of speech, or of the press, or the right of the people peaceably to assemble and to petition for a redress of grievances;
>
> (2) violate the right of the people to be secure in their persons, houses, papers, and effects against unreasonable search and seizures, nor issue warrants, but upon probable cause, supported by oath or affirmation, and particularly describing the place to be searched and the person or thing to be seized;
>
> (3) subject any person for the same offense to be twice put in jeopardy;
>
> (4) compel any person in any criminal case to be a witness against himself;
>
> (5) take any private property for a public use without just compensation;
>
> (6) deny to any person in a criminal proceeding the right to a speedy and public trial, to be informed of the nature and cause of the accusation, to be confronted with the witnesses against him, to have compulsory process for obtaining witnesses in his favor, and at his own expense to have the assistance of counsel for his defense;
>
> (7) require excessive bail, impose excessive fines, inflict cruel and unusual punishment, and in no event impose for conviction of any one offense any penalty or punishment greater than imprisonment for a term of six months or a fine of $500, or both;
>
> (8) deny to any person within its jurisdiction the equal protection of its laws or deprive any person of liberty or property without due process of law;
>
> (9) pass any bill of attainder or ex post facto law; or
>
> (10) deny to any persons accused of an offense punishable by imprisonment the right, upon request, to a trial by jury of not less than six persons. 25 U.S.C.A. §1302

It might be wondered why the Indians who are all now citizens of the United States needed a separate Bill of Rights. The answer to that question is a bit complicated. It was discovered that in some tribal courts juries were not employed and legal representatives were not as professional as those in state and federal courts. Formal procedures differed in many respects. Furthermore, since the Bill of Rights of the U.S. Constitution was made to apply to state jurisdictions only because of the 14th Amendment, and was judged *not* to apply to Indian courts (*Talton v. Mayes,* 1896; *Colliflower v. Garland*, 1965; Washburn, 184), it was thought that in order to protect Indian defendants from unjust treatment, e.g., self-incrimination, in Indian courts, a separate Bill of Rights should be enacted, which at the same time accommodated some of the idiosyncrasies of typical tribal justice. For example, the ICRA (Indian Constitutional Rights Act) does not require trial by jury except in criminal cases and only if requested by the defendant. It was argued that tribal courts and councils are in their very nature set up as juries. There is an explicit provision stating that there be no law prohibiting the free exercise of religion, but none regarding the establishment of a religion. Native religions are so intertwined with Indian culture and traditions that the separation of the two would be practically impossible. Congress, in passing the ICRA, also did not require tribes to provide free counsel for the accused, citing limited tribal budgets. It requires that excessive bail, fines, and cruel and unusual punishment not be imposed, but restricts the punishment that tribal courts may impose to no more than six months in jail or a fine of $500, or both, thereby limiting tribal court jurisdiction more or less to misdemeanors.

The Congressional committee which formulated the Act after a period of seven years of hearings agreed that it should become law only if the majority of Indians consented to it, which they did, but only because it required Indian consent before allowing a state to assume jurisdiction over offenses committed on the reservation. (Washburn, 188)

The ICRA has done much to clarify the civil rights of Indians in the United States, but subsequent to its passage as federal legislation it has had both favorable and unfavorable receptions in the courts. From the standpoint of the landmark case of *Santa Clara Pueblo v. Martinez* (1978) which barred a tribal member from obtaining a federal judicial review of a tribal council decision concerning membership in a tribe, it was, as Wilkinson points out, "in some respects one of the modern decisions most favorable to the tribes." Among other things it "gave an expansive reading to tribal sovereign immunity." (Wilkinson, 113.) According to Canby, "it reduces the degree of federal interference in tribal self-government." (Canby, 362.)

The case involves a woman named Julia Martinez who brought suit under the equal protection and due process provisions of the ICRA against the Santa

Clara Pueblo. A tribal council had, by trial law, denied membership in the tribe to children of female tribal members who were married to non-members. Martinez was married to a Navajo. Children of marriages of male members to spouses outside the tribe were eligible for membership. She claimed discrimination against her daughter.

The U.S. Supreme Court in a decision written by Thurgood Marshall, a long time advocate for minority civil rights, held in favor of the Pueblo tribal council, arguing that the promotion of Indian self-determination and tribal sovereign immunity was more important than "promoting in wholesale fashion for the extension of constitutional requirements to tribal governments."

In effect, however, the case which also declared that habeas corpus proceedings were the only remedy a tribal member had against a tribal court or council action, i.e., one which required a showing that the detention of defendant was legally justified, had a chilling effect on most actions brought on the basis of the Indian Civil Rights Act. In *Martinez,* for example, there simply was no detention to bring an action for. Martinez was therefore totally without a remedy for her problem. The Supreme Court simply refused to require the tribe to observe the guarantee of equal protection, and there was nothing she could do about it.

The case, as Canby points out, eliminated "the jurisdictional basis upon which most decisional law under the Civil Rights Act had rested." (see Canby, 360–63, for relevant cases other than *Santa Clara Pueblo*). Bordewich (86) suggests that "the act [ICRA] became a virtual dead letter just ten years after its passage," although he does admit that "it was an important step in extending the principles of civil rights across Indian Country." *Dead letter* may be a somewhat extreme characterization in view of the fact that it intentionally promoted the independence and autonomy of tribal government. However, as even Canby and Wilkinson point out, it puts most of the burden of enforcing the civil rights of both Indians and non-Indians on the reservations on the tribal courts, and some of them are ill equipped to handle the task. (See Canby, 363; Wilkinson, 114–15.)

Bordewich cites another case, *Shortbull v. Looking Elk* (1982), decided in Federal Court of Appeals for the 8th Circuit, involving a former President of the Oglala Community College (1975–79) named Thomas Shortbull, who is currently and for the 17 or 18 years has been the President of Oglala Lakota College at Kyle, South Dakota. I find this case of particular interest because of my family's "accidental" relationship to several other Shortbulls (see above, Ch.2). Fortunately, I have been able to determine that Thomas Shortbull and the Chief Shortbull who was killed in the automobile accident are not related. However, that may be, it seems that Thomas Shortbull in 1980 entered he race for president of the Pine Ridge tribal council. No member of the tribal council denied that he was a Lakota Sioux or that his father had been an enrolled member of the tribe, or that his father had bequeathed him land on the reservation. Even his wife was an enrolled member. But because he had been born off-reservation and was opposed to the views of many on the council, he was classed by them as an NE, i.e., as a non-enrolled Indian. They refused to certify him as a legitimate candidate for the office he was seeking. Shortbull requested a ruling from the BIA and was told that because of *Santa Clara Pueblo v. Martinez* the criteria of tribal membership was wholly a matter to be decided by the tribal council. Lawyers for the Pine Ridge tribal council argued that *Martinez* established the tribe's sovereign immunity from lawsuits brought under the provisions of the ICRA. (Bordwich, 87–89.)

Many issues regarding Indian law which do not involve civil rights but are concerned with jurisdictional problems—tribal jurisdiction versus federal or state jurisdiction—or issues regarding the nature and extent of Indian sovereignty, were not settled or even directly dealt with by the ICRA. Questions specifically dealing with inherent tribal sovereignty, which Felix Cohen has maintained is "perhaps the basic principle of all Indian law" will be dealt with in the next chapter. Some of the cases dealing with jurisdictional problems will now be summarized to give at least a hint of the vagaries of federal Indian law.

Wilkinson claims that the first case, *Williams v. Lee*, decided in 1959, "opened the modern era of federal Indian law." (Wilkinson, 1.) Before this case, which of course precedes the ICRA of 1968, the courts decided few cases which established or expanded tribal powers. *Williams* sets the stage for far more controversial and important cases as far as affected interests are concerned, interests such as those mentioned in the following cases here summarized.

Williams v. Lee, 358 U.S. 217 (1959). Held: Tribal courts have exclusive jurisdiction over actions involving contracts entered into on an Indian reservation between a non-Indian and an Indian defendant. Comment: Establishes exclusive tribal jurisdiction in the type of contract case described.

Seymour v. Superintendent, 368 U.S. 351 (1962). Held: The U.S. has exclusive jurisdiction over prosecution for offenses covered by the Major Crimes Act that are committed by Indians on lands held in fee patent by a non-Indian within the boundaries of an Indian reservation. Comment: Establishes exclusive federal jurisdiction.

Arizona v. California, 373 U.S. 351 (1962). Held: Indian water rights were effectively reserved as of the time of creation of the reservation. Comment: Rejects state jurisdiction over Indian water rights.

Poafpybitty v. Skelly Oil Co., 390 U.S. 365 (1968). Held: An Indian landowner has standing to sue to enforce an oil and gas lease, approved by he

Secretary of the Interior, for use on land held by the Indian under a trust patent. Comment: Federal court jurisdiction provides Indians standing to sue.

Menominee Tribe of Indians v. United States, 391 U.S. 404 (1968). Held: The Menominee Tribe retains its treaty hunting and fishing rights despite the Termination Act of 1954. Comment: Tribal rights supercede federal legislation.

Tooahnippah v. Hickel, 397 U.S. 598 (1970). Held: Rejects authority of the Secretary of the Interior to disapprove an Indian's testamentary disposition of trust property on the subjective belief that the disposition was not "just and equitable." Comment: Rejects federal jurisdiction over an Indian's testamentary disposition of trust property.

Kennerly v. District Court, 400 U.S. 434 (1971). Held: State judicial jurisdiction does not extend to civil contract action brought by a non-Indian against an Indian concerning a transaction occurring on the reservation. Comment: Restricts state jurisdiction.

Mescalero Apache Tribe v. Jones, 411 U.S. 145 (1973). Held:Upholds the imposition of a state gross receipts tax on income earned from a tribal business conducted on off-reservation lands where the tax does not discriminate against Indians. Comment: Upholds state jurisdiction.

McClanahan v. Arizona State TaxCommission, 411 U.S. 164 (1973). Held: The imposition of a state tax on income earned on a reservation by a tribal member who resides on the reservation struck down. Comment: Restricts state jurisdiction.

Morton v. Ruiz, 415 U.S. 199 (1974). Held: Declared invalid a regulation of the BIA that denied general assistance to unassimilated Indians living in an Indian community near their native reservation. Comment: Invalidates federal (BIA) regulation denying federal assistance.

United State v. Mazurie, 419 U.S. 544 (1975). Held: Congress has authority to delegate to tribal governments the authority to regulate the distribution of alcoholic beverages on a reservation. Comment: Upholds authority of Congress to allow tribal jurisdiction over regulation of alcoholic beverages.

Moe v. Confederated Salish and Kootenai Tribes, 425 U.S. 463 (1976). Held: State has no right to impose a state cigarette tax on on-reservation sales by Indians to Indians; it does have authority to impose a state cigarette tax on on-reservation sales by Indians to non-Indians. Comment: Restricts state jurisdiction regarding sales by Indians to Indians; allows state jurisdiction regarding sales by Indians to non-Indians.

Oliphant v. Suquamish Indian Tribe, 435 U.S. 191 (1978). Held: There is no tribal jurisdiction over crimes committed by non-Indians on a reservation. Comment: Denies tribal jurisdiction over crimes committed by non-Indians.

United States v. Wheeler, 435 U.S. 313 (1978). Held: Successive tribal and federal prosecutions of an Indian for crimes arising out of the same offense committed on a reservation upheld. Comment: Uphold *both* tribal and federal jurisdiction over crimes arising out of same offense despite apparent double jeopardy.

Santa Clara Pueblo v. Martinez, 436 U.S. 49 (1978). Held: Writ of habeas corpus to be the exclusive remedy available for alleged violations of the Indian Civil Rights Act (ICRA). Comment: Restricts Indian legal remedies with respect to violations of ICRA.

Washington v. Confederated Tribes of Colville Reservation, 447 U.S. 134 (1980). Held: State may impose cigarette and sales taxes on on-reservation sales by a tribe to non-members of the tribe. Comment: State jurisdiction upheld against tribal jurisdiction.

Central Machinery Co. v. Arizona State Tax Commission, 448 U.S. 160 (1980). Held: State may not impose a state gross receipts tax on a non-Indian corporation constructing school facilities on reservation land. Comment: Restricts state jurisdiction.

New Mexico v. Mescalero Apache Tribe, 462 U.S. 324 (1983). Held: Tribe has exclusive regulatory jurisdiction over hunting and fishing by members and non-members within the reservation. Comment: Allows exclusive tribal regulatory jurisdiction.

Rice v. Rehner, 463 U.S. 713 (1983). Held: Court approves of concurrent tribal and state regulation of on-reservation sales of alcoholic beverages. Comment: Approved *both* tribal and state jurisdiction relating to on-reservation sales.

Solem v. Bartlett, 465 U.S. 463 (1984). Held: Cheyenne River Act construed to have opened a portion of the Cheyenne River Sioux Reservation to settlement by non-Indians, but as not having disestablished the open lands from the reservation. Comment: Upholds and in part restricts federal jurisdiction.

Montana v. Blackfeet Tribe of Indians, 471 U.S. 759 (1985). Held: State may not impose a state tax on tribal royalty interests in mineral leases on reservation land. Comment: Restricts state jurisdiction.

National Farmers Union Ind. Cos. v. Crow Tribe of Indians, 471 U.S. 845 (1985). Held: The Court construes 28 U.S.C. § 1331 as conferring jurisdiction on federal district courts to hear actions alleging that a tribal court has exceeded its jurisdiction after the appellant has exhausted tribal court remedies. Comment: Confers federal jurisdiction after tribal jurisdiction ends.

Three other cases deserve mention here, not because they concern the relationships between tribal, state, and federal governments, but because they express unequivocally the supreme sovereignty and plenary power of the United States Government. They are as follows:

United States v. Sioux Nation of Indians, 448 U.S. 371 (1980). Held: The U.S. Government is obligated to compensate the tribe for its illicit taking of the Black Hills in 1877.

United States v. Dann, 470 U.S. 39 (1985). Held: Shoshone Tribe's aboriginal title to lands in several western states was extinguished when, pursuant to a judgment awarded the tribe by the Indian Claims Commission, the United States placed $26 million in an interest-bearing trust account for the tribe.

United States v. Dion, 476 U.S. 734 (1986). Held: Congress, in the Eagle Protection Act, set out a clear and plain intent to abrogate the treaty rights of Indians to hunt eagles.

Other cases involving U.S. Supreme Court decisions relating to Indian affairs and relations with state and federal jurisdiction can be found in Charles F. Wilkinson's list of what he calls Indian law cases of the "modern era" from 1958 onward. (See the Appendix to his book, *American Indians, Time, and the Law).* His list includes cases through the 1985 term. Other later cases can be found discussedby William C. Canby, Jr., in the fourth edition of *American Indian Law in a Nutshell* (2004). Some of the cases in both Wilkinson and Canby more specifically concern the key issue of Indian sovereignty as such and will be discussed in the next chapter. But even at this point one can appreciate Wilkinson's own judgment that although branches of Indian law "have stabilized," it is "no perfect body of law." (122) and Canby, who emphasizes the point that by "Indian law" we are talking about federal law as it pertains and applies to Indians rather than the "internal" or indigenous laws and customs which different tribes apply to their own members, and which vary widely from tribe to tribe, also adds that Indian law, i.e., federal law relating to Indians, has always been dependent on national policy which has varied back and forth from *assimilationism* to *terminationism* to *separationism,* which is the current policy (my terms, by the way, not Canby's nor Wilkinson's although the latter does use the term "separatism"). Canby nonetheless speculates that "it is possible that contending forces in Indian affairs have reached some sort of final balance, and no further major changes of direction will occur." However, he qualifies that statement by saying "Nothing in the history of federal Indian policy . . . justifies confidence in such a conclusion." (33).

Chapter Eleven

Tribal Sovereignty and Casino Gaming

In a recent visit to the site of the Wounded Knee Massacre, I encountered several National Park Rangers, or possibly Pine Ridge Indian Police—all in uniform—who answered many of my questions. One of the rangers, or policemen, blurted out, quite spontaneously and not in response to anything I said, that he was not an Indian. He had never been to India, and he did not speak Hindi! Since he looked facially just about as close to the familiar image on the Indian head nickel as one can imagine (see Light and Rand, 109, quoting Richard Hayward of the Mashantucket Pequot tribe, "You gotta look like the guy on the nickel.") I was a bit dumbfounded, and so failed to ask him how then he identified himself. Since all American Indians are now citizens of the United States, he might have said, "American," or possibly "Native American," although that term can apply to anyone born here, so if not that, then "Sioux," but that is a French corruption of the Chippewa name for Lakota speakers, namely *Nadoweisiw-eg* (see Medicine, 3), or *Nadouessioux* (see Light and Rand, 212, n.46). Although many of the plains tribes have settled for the name "Sioux," he probably would have preferred either "Sicangu" or "Oglala," depending on which band of the tribe (e.g., Rosebud or Pine Ridge) he was a member of. In Rapid City I boldly asked one of the clerks at an Indian Arts and Clothing store whether she was Indian, and when she replied "Lakota" as opposed to Dakota or Nakota (different dialects), I then asked whether she was Oglala, and she responded "Sicangu," identifying her as associated with the Rosebud band. The same sort of response was typical of Sitting Bull when he was asked in an interview who (or what) he was. At first he answered rather philosophically, "I am a man." More specifically when asked, "Of what tribe are you?" he proudly said, "I am Hunkpapa." (See Graham, 66–67, who spells the Standing Rock Sioux band's name as "Uncpapa.")

The question, "Who is or is not an Indian?" is not as easily answered as one might suppose. Simply declaring that one is or is not an Indian is not sufficient to determine one's status, with one exception. The U.S. Census Bureau allows persons to be so classified if they choose to be. (See Bordewich, 66.) For all other governmental purposes, however, two major criteria must be met. Minimally, in addition to being accepted as a member of a tribe or Indian community, one must have some Indian blood. (See Felix Cohen, *Handbook of Federal Indian Law,* 2.) For the purposes of federal criminal jurisdiction, no one can be an Indian unless he or she belongs to a federally recognized tribe. However, for some other governmental purposes, e.g., receipt of the benefits of vested treaty rights, one may be an Indian even if not a member of a federally recognized tribe. (see Canby, 5, for relevant cases). Even a full blooded Indian, of which there are relatively few today, who terminates his or her tribal membership and has no allotments or other benefits or obligations relating to his tribe is, for legal purposes *not an Indian.* (Washburn, 163.)

The blood quantum requirement varies considerably from tribe to tribe. It can vary from ¼ in many Sioux and Alaskan tribes to as little as 1/256 in the Wyandotte tribe (Washburn, 163).

Increasingly, because of intermarriage, it is obvious that the biological requirement is becoming less important than the social and cultural ones.

Since, therefore, the requirement of belonging to a tribe is foremost, another question is of central and increasing importance in determining who is an Indian with rights to certain government benefits and tribal gaming profits. That question is "What is an Indian tribe?" and most importantly "Who has the final say in determining who is a member of the tribe?"

As Canby points out, there is no all-purpose definition of an Indian tribe, since "a group of Indians may qualify as an Indian tribe for the purpose of one statute or federal program but fail to qualify for others." (Canby, 3–4). The problem of definition is even more puzzling than that situation suggests. If we use membership in a tribe (or even more narrowly, membership in a federally recognized tribe) to define "Indian," and by a kind of circular reasoning use the meaning of Indian to define "Indian tribe," we will have obviously begged the whole question.

Lawyers and lawmakers, including judges, have ways to get around all such logical difficulties, often simply by ignoring them. For example, take the federal recognition legal requirement that the person claiming Indian status must have some quantum of Indian blood. The word some covers a great range of cases, namely, "black Indians," "white Indians," "yellow Indians," as well as "red Indians." These skin color differences have led many critics of the Mashantucket Pequot and their success with casino gaming to label them "imposters." (See Light and Rand, 109.) The BIA and the courts, however, have not yet deprived them of their status as members of an Indian tribe.

The second requirement that those claiming to be members of an Indian tribe must show, namely, that they belong to a political entity or community which has existed on a more or less continuous basis since Columbus discovered America, or at least since 1900, is difficult to establish in many cases, and is simply not insisted upon. Furthermore, since what counts ultimately in determining federal recognition may be one of many things, e.g., treaties, statutes, executive orders, decisions of the Secretary of the Interior, BIA decisions, etc., sometimes recognition is a purely arbitrary matter, and at least recently a painfully slow process. So perplexed was even Congress about which are and which are not recognized tribes in 1992 that they directed the Secretary of the Interior to publish an annual list of recognized tribes. The 2002 list includes 562 recognized tribes of which 225 are Alaska native entities. (Canby, 4, 8.)

It has apparently become very popular to be classed as an "Indian," even if one has only the most tenuous connection with a tribe, e.g., by having the slightest quantum of Indian blood. That makes about as much sense as classifying as German a person only one of whose great, great grandparents was German, and all the rest of his or her ancestors Czech. Mark Twain, in his novel, *Pudd'nhead Wilson* ridicules the notion that in ante-bellum years a person such as his character, Thomas á Becket Driscoll who was thirty one parts white and only one part black (1/32) and his mother, Roxy, described as being fifteen parts white and only one part black (1/16), were each "by a fiction of law and custom a negro." Nonetheless, many persons aspire to be identified with certain role models of recent years such as Will Rogers, Jim Thorpe, Cher Bono, and Ben Nighthorse Campbell, who served in the United States Senate from 1993–2005, won international judo championships, and has received numerous awards for jewelry design. All had or have some quantum of Indian blood, but none, as far as I know, can claim a quantum of more than ½ and perhaps in certain cases even less.

The census count of persons claiming to be Indian has more than doubled since 1970 (see Bordewich, 66). That figure of course includes persons who lack Indian blood or connection with any tribe, but who just like the idea of being Indian. A more legitimate and accurate figure might result if the petitions of some of the 150 or so political entities now in the appellate process of being officially recognized were granted. Their plight is well described by Fergus M. Bordewch in a chapter of his book, *Killing the White Man's Indian*, entitled "We Ain't Got Feathers and Beads."

He cites in particular the case of a group calling themselves "Lumbees," who live in North Carolina round the town of Pembroke on the Lumber River.

They are an industrious people who have been landowners since records have been kept, going back to the 18th century. They are jealous or their blood line, and like many southerners, including even my own grandfather, close to their own "blood kin." They have maintained their political identity over the years even during the Civil War. Physically, according to Bordewich, "they run the gamut from blonde hair and blue eyes to the nearly Negroid." (63).

Although they have long insisted upon their Indianness, the Department of the Interior has denied their petition for recognition of tribal status at least nine different times. Bordewich relates a conversation with Cynthia Hunt, a member of the group who has tried her best to convince not only the government but also other Indian tribes that she and her Lumbee tribe are as Indian as any of the recognized tribes. She has taken her case to the far west, e.g., to the Shoshone tribe in Idaho, thinking that they might be at least sympathetic to her cause, but their response was not what she expected. They refused to support her efforts, and when she pressed them for their reason all she received was "You can't be Indian—you've got no reservation," to which she replied, "Are you an Indian just because the feds gave you a reservation?" (Bordewich, 62.) In a fairly recent change of mind on the part of the Department of the Interior, the Lumbees, the ninth largest tribe, have been granted federal recognition, but remain ineligible for BIA services and are still without a reservation. (Getches, Wilkinson, Williams, *Federal Indian Law* (12).

Those questions, "Are you an Indian?" and "Do you have a reservation?" bring up the fact that most tribes, including most federally recognized tribes (FR) do not have reservations, and of course none of the non-federally recognized tribes (NFR) have them. For example, although there are 156 FR tribes in California (as of 2001. see Johnson and Hook, 292–94) there are only three reservations, namely, the Hupa Valley, Round Valley, and Tule River reservations. Besides these there are approximately 6400 persons claiming Indian status in the NFR tribes of Chumash, Costanoan, Esselen, Salianan, and other tribes. In addition, Johnson and Hook do not include in their lists about 100,000 Indians who live in but are not natives of California, mostly Cherokees from Oklahoma and Apaches from Arizona.

In contrast to California but still consistent with the federal government's federal recognition policy, South Dakota has nine reservations having a joint populatin in 2001 of 109,848. Johnson and Hook list the tribe at Lower Brule as FR but without a reservation, which it once had, but I believe this is in error. Furthermore, there are no NFR tribes in South Dakota. In other states, however, previously recognized tribes have had their recognition abrogated and much of their reservation homeland confiscated. Just as the federal government has the power to grant recognition, it also has the power to retract it. He who giveth can also taketh away. The most prominent and egregious case of this type concerns the Menominee Indians of Wisconsin, among whom my father worked enforcing federal Indian law.

Most of the 100 tribes "terminated" during the 1950's were small in population consisting of a few hundred members at most. (Canby, 58.) Two of them, on the other hand, the Menominee tribe of Wisconsin and the Klamath tribe of Oregon, had between 2000 and 3000 members each. Both reservations possessed large and valuable forests, supporting a lumber industry managed in each case by the BIA. The Menominees owned their own sawmill and worked it profitably with an annual budget of $450,000. They paid for all Bureau services, built a hospital and underwrote expenses of local schools. Unlike those tribes which were terminated because of their small populations, the Menominee reservation was terminated because of their financial success and their proven ability to govern their own affairs.

The result of termination under the Act of 1954 was loss of their tribal land in the sense that it passed out of the government trust and converted to private ownership. All federal benefits including aid to education, housing, and emergency welfare ceased, and the State of Wisconsin could now tax the land. As Canby, speaking generally, has pointed out, "the social and economic effects of termination were almost uniformly disastrous." (Canby, 61.) After termination of the Menominee Wisconsin tribe the logging and lumber industry there was at a standstill, resulting in widespread unemployment. (See Debo, 374.)

Finally the Menominees filed suit with the Court of Claims when termination threatened to deprive them of exclusive hunting and fishing rights which the Treaty of Wolf River of 1854 (10 Stat.1064) had granted them. The Supreme Court in *Menominee Tribe v. United States*, 391 U.S. 404 (1968) held that those treaty rights had not been abrogated by the Termination Act of 1954. Eventually the Menominees convinced Congress (in 1973) to restore the federal-tribal relationship and return their remaining land to the federal trust, thereby reestablishing to the extent possible their former reservation. (See Canby, 61; 25 USCA § 903f; Supp. 1980.) The Menominee Indian population, as of 2001, was 8,074. (Johnson and Hook, 301.)

But why, one might ask, all this concern for the exact status of Indians and their recognition as members of one tribe or another. Why not the same concern for other minority groups such as Black or Jewish Americans, or immigrant groups such as South Americans or Mexicans? Or Ellis Island immigrants such as the Poles, Czech, Italians, or Irish?

The answer to that question is pretty clear and simple even though it does raise some rather profound questions. The Indians predated the whites and all the others on this continent. Charles F. Wilkinson likes to put it in terms of the "preconstitutional and extraconstitutional" status of Indian tribes.

> Tribal authority was not created by the Constitution—tribal authority predated the formation of the United States and continued after it—but tribes were acknowledged by the Constitution in the affirmation of previously negotiated treaties (most of which were with Indian tribes), the two references to "Indians not taxed," and the Indian Commerce Clause. (Wilkinson, 117.)

None of the other minority or immigrant groups can claim such a relationship with the federal government.

The "extraconstitutional" status of Indian tribes is clearly illustrated by the fact that even after certain tribes, such as the Menominees, had lost their reservation status, they didn't cease to exist (i.e., lose their tribal status), as the State of Wisconsin tried to argue (Wilkinson, 75–76). Nor did the Klamath tribe. Both retained what Felix Cohen calls their "internal" or "inherent sovereignty."

Exactly what these terms and the more general term "sovereign" mean when applied to Indian tribes requires a backdrop of several early Supreme Court cases. The first to deal with the sovereignty issue head-on is the so-called "Marshall trilogy," namely, *Johnson v. McIntosh,* 21 U.S. (8 Wheat.) 543 (1823); *Cherokee Nation v. Georgia*, 30 U.S. (5 Pet.) 1 (1831); and *Worcester v. Georgia*, 31 U.S. (6 Pet.) 515 (1832). In the *Johnson* case involving a grant of land by Indian chiefs to private white individuals, Chief Justice Marshall enunciated and adopted the *European* doctrine of discovery which asserts the right of a discoverer/conqueror to extinguish the aboriginal title or "right of occupancy" which the native Indians held prior to the conquest or purchase of Indian lands by the invader. In *Cherokee Nation* the Court rejected the notion that the Cherokees qualified as a foreign state, and characterizes Indian tribes as "domestic, dependent nations" whose relationship to the United States "resembles that of a ward to his guardian." In *Worcester*, relating to several missionaries arrested by Georgia officials for failing to obtain a license from the state governor, the Court held that the Cherokee Nation was a distinct political entity, substantially independent of state jurisdiction. The Cherokees legally won their case, but President Jackson refused to enforce its findings against the state of Georgia, which was then in the process of acquiring all Indian lands within the state and forcing the Indians beyond its borders.

During the second half of the 19th century and the early part of the 20th century the Supreme Court swung away from Marshall's view and tended to deny the existence not only of limited sovereignty but of tribal sovereignty altogether. For example, in *United States v. Kagama,* 18 U.S. 375 (1886), the Court, distancing itself from the view expressed in *Cherokee Nation v. Georgia,* said:

> These Indians *are* wards of the nation. They are communities dependent on the United States—dependent largely for their daily food; dependent for their political rights. (Quoted in Canby, 37.)

This case was followed by a string of others up to at least *Lone Wolf v. Hitchcock*, 187 U.S. 553 (1903) adopting a generally hard line against the admission of tribal sovereignty. Wilkinson summarizes the thrust of these cases as implicitly conceptualizing "tribes as lost societies without power, as minions of the federal government." (see Wilkinson, 54 and 57 for a discussion of the relevant cases; see Washburn, 59–74, for the effect of treaties entered into up to 1871, when all treaty-making with Indians ceased.). The Peace Commission of 1868 adopted a set of resolutions which were sent to President Grant and Congress recommending that "the government should cease to recognize the tribes as domestic, dependent nations except where already provided for in existing treaties." (Wilkinson, 71.)

In the 1940's Felix Cohen undertook the task of reviving the Marshall thesis that tribes have a kind of sovereignty that is independent of the powers of the federal government. His argument is suggested in the following quotation.

> Perhaps the most basic principle of all Indian law, supported by a host of decisions hereinafter analyzed, is the principle that *those powers which are lawfully vested in an Indian tribe are not, in general delegated powers granted by express acts of Congress, but rather inherent powers of a limited sovereignty which has never been extinguished* . . . What is not expressly limited remains within the domain of tribal sovereignty. These powers are subject to qualification treaties and by express legislation of Congress, but, save as thus expressly qualified, full powers of internal sovereignty are vested in the Indian tribes and in their duly constituted organs of government. (Quoted in Wilkinson 58; emphasis in italics by Cohen).

This view which Wilkinson dubs the "Marshall-Cohen" formulation of the doctrine of tribal sovereignty might as well be called the "Marshall-Cohen-Wilkinson" formulation since he says quite unreservedly that "Cohen's conclusion that inherent tribal sovereignty is 'perhaps the most basic principle of all Indian law' is right." (Wilkinson, 62.)

Unfortunately all this talk of "limited sovereignty" and "dependent nations" fails to address some of the logical and moral questions relating to the status of Indian tribes. For example, how many sovereigns can exist within a given society? If we mean by sovereign a supreme plenary power, independent of all external authority and influence—the usual dictionary definition—then there cannot be more than one, any more than there can be many Supreme Beings. The existence of one would negate the claim of the other. The adjectival use of "limited" or "dependent" makes no sense of the idea of sovereignty. If the government has the ultimate and complete power, how can some subordinate part of the society claim to have a similar "supreme" power? That's like speaking of a power that is both unlimited and limited.

The doctrine of discovery may have been the rationale the English and other European nations used to claim sovereign control over New World lands, but when spelled out, the doctrine is indefensible and utterly absurd. Suppose that Sir Walter Drake was the first to sail along the coast of California. Is it to be concluded that because of his observations alone he thereby discovered and with good reason could claim it for the British crown? Justice Marshall seems to have concluded that if the claim of possession or "discovery" of the eastern coastal lands were sufficient to claim sovereignty over them, then their successors, the American revolutionaries, also could make that claim with the same rationale, which, when one thinks about it, is totally preposterous. And if one protests that discovery followed by conquest has always been the favored way of acquiring sovereignty, i.e., supreme and complete control over a territory, then it becomes apparent that sovereignty rests on nothing but the morally unacceptable principle that "Might makes Right," and does little to assuage the claim of Indians to unjust treatment.

The heart of the trouble lies in thinking of sovereignty too much in terms of power and too little in terms of fundamental rights. The founding fathers were on the right track when they declared in a 1787 ordinance passed under the Articles of Confederation that

> The utmost good faith shall always be observed toward Indians; their lands and property shall never be taken from them without their consent; and in their property, rights, and liberty, they shall never be invaded or disturbed, unless in just and lawful wars, authorized by Congress; but laws founded in justice and humanity, shall, from time to time, be made for preventing wrongs being done to them, and for preserving peace and friendship with them.

Washington himself in a six point program for dealing with Indians proposed an arrangement "for punishing those who infringed Indian rights, violated treaties, and thus endangered the peace of the nation." (See Prucha, *American Indian Treaties* (1994) 101.) As Secretary of State and in response to inquiries by President Washington, Jefferson put the whole matter of sovereignty in terms of a "right of pre-emption," which Wilcomb E. Washburn has called one of Jefferson's "most significant contributions to Indian law." He claims it stands "halfway between the preposterous or exaggerated European claims to title based on 'discovery' or observation of the shore line of a continent, and the indefensible, or rather undefendable claim to total sovereignty on the part of those (the Indians) who could not maintain it." (Washburn, 55–6.) Jefferson's own words are as follows:

> I consider our right of pre-emption of the Indian lands, not as amounting to any dominion, or jurisdiction, or paramountship whatever, but merely in the nature

> of a remainder after the extinguishment of a present right, which gave us no present right whatever, but preventing other nations from taking possession . . . that the Indians had the full, undivided and independent sovereignty as long as they choose to keep it, and that this might be forever. (Quoted in Prucha, 227.)

His words bear repeating (see Chapter VIII above) since they emphasize, as other theories of sovereignty do not, the fundamental right of Indians to their lands of first possession and occupancy rather than the Indians' inability to usefully enjoy and effectively exclude others from those lands. Like many of the founding fathers up to President Jackson, Jefferson favored contractual (or treaty) purchases as a way of acquiring Indian property, a method which was frequently ignored then and of course subsequently. This emphasis by Jefferson is difficult to explain in terms of the usual Lockean theory. There is no way that a Lockean advocate would agree that if the Indians decided not to sell their property, they might "rightfully" keep it forever. Immanuel Kant's theory of property might here seem to provide the rationale. If one should scoff at the notion that a German intellectual from Prussia should have been so relevant or influential, let him then make sense of the following statement of Justice Oliver Wendell Holmes:

> See how a hundred years after his death the abstract speculations of Descartes [have] become a practical force controlling the conduct of men. Read the works of the great German jurists, and see how much more the world is governed today by Kant than by Bonaparte. ("The Path of the Law." 1897.)

There is no evidence that Jefferson ever met Kant or even read his books, although they were contemporaries. But Kant's ideas were well known in France during the time that Jefferson was our ambassador there, and he had a flair for absorbing ideas however remotely received. In any case, genius that he was, it remains possible that he came by his "right of pre-emption" quite independently.

The basic notion that Kant entertained, and that Jefferson expresses, is that neither the inability to use vast acreages of land profitably, nor defend it against all intruders is sufficient to deny title to the land. Kant even rejects the human need of the produce of the land for subsistence as a basis of entitlement either for the holders or the takers of the land. Instead he cites the "innate right of freedom which humans of every stripe possess. There is no need here to repeat all the implications of Kant's (and Jefferson's) theory. (see Ch.VII, above), except to say that when applied to what we have been calling "tribal sovereignty" what we really mean to say is that the Indian's innate right to freedom (and as a corollary to equality) entails his right to be autonomous, self-determining, self-legislating, and self-governing (terms all meaning pretty much the same thing). And if because of historical and geographical circumstances the United States is now divided into three jurisdictions—federal, state, and tribal—then the contemporary Indian, being a member of all three, has every right and legitimate expectation to be treated fairly in all of those jurisdictions. In our final chapter we shall discuss various proposals for rectifying some of the injustices to Indians which have occurred in the past and others which are on-going.

One current and widely publicized attempt by various tribes to assert their "sovereignty," or more precisely, their inherent right to be self-determining, is their attempt to overcome economic disadvantage by means of *gaming* casinos, the term preferred over *gambling* casinos, even in Las Vegas. They have at last found a way to transform the white man's vices into advantages for themselves. The bare fact of the matter is that except for the states of Utah and Hawaii, every state in the Union allows gaming of one type or another. Surprisingly, there is at present no *national* betting sponsored by the federal government, nor anything resembling the Irish Sweepstakes or national lotteries. But it is easy to show that most Americans love gambling or "gaming." All one has to do is to notice the recent upsurge in poker tournaments on television, or state-wide betting parlors, or the record attendance at the more than 350 tribal gaming establishments across the country from Connecticut to California.

There are indeed various tribes who, for moral or cultural reasons, do not allow gambling on their reservations, e.g., the Navajos and the Hopi (a recent exception: a casino called *Fire Rocks*, east of Gallup, N.M., approved by the Navajo Tribal Council, November, 2008). But the majority of North American Indian tribes not only approve of it but regard it as part of their own culture. Class I gaming as defined by the Indian Gaming Regulatory Act (IGRA) of 1988 includes games of chance "connected with tribal ceremonies or celebrations." (Canby, 306.) In Johnson and Hook's *Encyclopedia* (116), there is a photograph of a group of Sioux Indians gambling at an unidentified game. It was taken in 1909; the caption says "probably at a Wild West touring show," which allows for the speculation that it was taught to them by white men. But historically there is no doubt that the Indians themselves had their own games of chance resembling dice and shell games, and games of dexterity such as archery and horse and foot races, etc., on which the Indians could and did wager. (see Light and Rand, 39). Regarding such Class I types of gaming the federal government has not attempted any regulation, and has left such matters up to the tribal councils.

When I was living on the Rosebud and Pine Ridge reservations, the game of bingo was frequently played. The local churches often sponsored such entertainment. At the Protestant churches the games were played simply "for fun," and usually without payment of any fee.No money passed hands and the winner received an inexpensive prize. At the Catholic church they were more serious (or perhaps I should say more enterprising), and money was involved, although the stakes were very low. Nonetheless, the idea of winning there was a definite attraction to Indians as well as to members of the agency personnel. The Protestants of the community continued to regard gambling for money as somehow wrongful if not totally evil.

In the 1970's and 80's, a few tribes in California and Florida, followed by tribes in many other states in the 1990's, including Oklahoma and New Mexico (see Mason, 178–9), opened high-stakes bingo halls or parlors. This type of gambling falls under Class II gaming according to the IGRA and includes bingo whether electronic, computerized, or not, and other games such as lotto, but excludes games such as baccarat, chemin de fer, and blackjack. Class II gaming falls within the jurisdiction of the tribes, but is subject to restrictions such as the requirement that it be authorized by a tribal ordinance. It is also subject to oversight by a National Indian Gaming Commission, and requires the approval of the Secretary of the Interior for any plan to distribute per capita payments to tribal members.

Class III gaming which includes all other sorts of gaming, especially slot machines and poker, is the big money maker for the tribes which have casinos. Before the passage of the Indian Gaming Regulatory Act (IGRA) in 1988, many tribes were emboldened by their success with high stakes bingo and began offering other games of chance such as poker. In California the manner in which these games were played and the lack of a $250 limit on pots did not always conform to California law, even though they were supported by tribal ordinances and approved by the Secretary of the Interior, who was under Congressional pressure to promote economic development on the reservations. A suit was brought against one of the errant tribes, *California v. Cabazon Band of Mission Indians* in 1987.

California had been one of six states to which Congress in 1953 had extended state criminal jurisdiction by Public Law 280 (67 Stat. 588), thereby reducing the jurisdiction of the Indian tribes in those states and their "inherent sovereignty," or right to self-governance. States had already been declared to possess jurisdiction over wholly non-Indian crimes within Indian country, but PL 280 was intended to cover all the other cases. PL 280 was and still is in many respects a peculiar law in that it allows multiple exceptions, e.g., in California all Indian country within the state is covered, but in Minnesota all Indian country is covered except the Red Lake Reservation; in Oregon, all Indian country except the Warm Springs Reservation. The legislation also allows other states the option of being covered by PL 280 either totally or partially, and without the consent of the tribes. The states of Arizona, Florida,

Idaho, Iowa, Montana, Nevada, North Dakota, Utah, and Washington all opted for such various extensions of state jurisdiction. Arizona opted only for the purposes of regulating air pollution. (Canby, 250.) The total result is a maze of distinctions which only an expert in federal Indian law can totally comprehend.

California as a designated PL 280 state sought by the *Cabazon* lawsuit to exercise its authority over tribal gaming. The issue in the case turned on whether California's restrictive laws regarding bingo games (to be conducted only by charitable organizations) and its prohibition against all poker games were "criminal/ prohibitory" or "civil/regulatory." The Court held that since California allows various kinds of gambling including pari-mutuel betting on horse racing, subject only to regulation, then their laws are "civil/regulatory" and the state's authority does not extend to Indian reservations or other "Indian country."

The decision with respect to the California case boosted the tribal jurisdiction with respect to gaming throughout the United States. However, Congress sought in the 1988 Indian Gaming Regulatory Act (ICRA) to set its own limits. In order for a tribe to participate in type III gaming, it must meet two conditions. First it must have an approved authorizing ordinance and be located in a state which permits gaming (thereby excluding the two states which don't, Utah and Hawaii). Second, it must be "conducted in accordance with a Tribal-State Compact." And incidentally the IGRA provides for gaming only "on Indian lands," including reservations and individual or tribal trust lands over which the tribe "exercises governmental power."

The IGRA also specifies that a State which refuses to negotiate a "compact" in good faith can be sued by the tribe in federal court. This article was challenged in the case of *Seminole Tribe v. Florida*, 517 U.S. 44 (1996). The Supreme Court held that Congress lacked the power to abrogate state Eleventh Amendment immunity to prosecution under either the Indian or the Interstate Commerce Clause. (Canby, 314.) A kind of impasse or stalemate seemed to result because without tribal/state compacts, there could be no legal Class III gaming.

But this is where politics comes into the picture. Most Indian tribes, of course, want the income from gaming casinos (billions at the Foxwood Resort and Casino run by the Mashantucket Pequot tribe in Connecticut; millions at Minnesota and Wisconsin casinos; lesser profits elsewhere, and in some casinos in the plains states of North and South Dakota little or nothing except jobs for Indian employees and a heightened sense of well-being. (See Light and Rand, 91–3.) Generally speaking, however, all the tribes which have casino gaming maintain that they have been assisted economically. (Light and Rand, 83, 98–9; Mason, 147–8.) Most states want to allow casino gaming because since they have no taxing jurisdiction over Indian lands, they think they can reasonably expect some share of the revenues received by the gaming tribes because local neighborhoods are affected by the presence of casinos (increased crime, traffic congestion, etc.) and they are required by PL 280 (in California, although not in all states) to provide criminal law enforcement without any federal government appropriation to cover the costs. The Tribal-State compact is the obvious way to *compromise* (Light and Rand's preferred expression) or *accommodate* these distinct and at times competitive interests.

A recent example of this attempt to reconcile interests is the primary election held February 5, 2008, in California. Voters were asked to vote on several referenda or *Propositions*, as they are called in California, aimed at ratifying four laws passed by the legislature which amended existing gaming compacts with four southern California tribes. Those tribes, the Aqua Caliente, Morongo, Pechanga, and Sycuan, are among the wealthiest in the state because of their successful gaming casinos. What they were seeking was the permission of the state to allow several new casinos and up to 17,000 additional slot machines. In return for such approval Governor Schwarzenegger persuaded them to agree to give more of their profits to the state—amounting to around $9 billion over two decades to help reduce the state's budgetary deficit; share tens of millions of dollars with 70 other California tribes, including *all* non-gaming tribes and tribes with small casinos; enter into binding mitigation agreements with neighboring cities and counties, and provide compensation for law enforcement, fire protection, and other services. The Indians were also pledged to allow inspections and audits conducted by the California Department of Justice and the California Gambling Control Commission. They also agreed to address the environmental impacts of the casinos, including provisions that reflect the California Environmental Quality Act.

Among the arguments against ratification were the claims that not one penny of the Indian's financial contribution to the state was earmarked for education; promotion of the fortunes of these four tribes would only increase the poverty of the smaller tribes without their political clout; no dollar amounts were given with respect to how much each of the lesser tribes will receive; and no guarantee is given that these casinos won't increase criminal activity which California police will be required to control. One worry expressed by San Jose Mercury news reporter, Dan Walters, was that California police might be implicated in the banishment of members of the tribes "disenrolled" because of disagreements with dictatorial tribal councils and casino operators. Yet, as he said, "The state has no power to enforce democracy and non-discrimination in tribes since they claim the status of' 'sovereign nations.'" (San Jose Mercury News, 3–13–08. More on this topic in Chapter XII.

But by far the biggest objection—which many Indians themselves fear—is that by entering into such revised and complex compacts the tribes will have surrendered to the state authorities an increasingly large share of their "inherent sovereignty" or right to be self-governing. The propositions, incidentally, passed overwhelmingly in favor of the Indian tribes and increased gambling in the State of California.

Chapter Twelve

Justice

Madeline Colliflower, a member of the Gros Ventre tribe living on a part of the Fort Belknap Reservation in Blaine County, Montana, was arrested by the Chief of Police of the Reservation for failing to obey a lawful order of the Court of Indian Offenses to remove her cattle from land leased to another person. She was found guilty on June 25, 1963, exactly eighty seven (87) years to the day of Custer's demise at the Battle of the Little Bighorn on June 25, 1876, which incidentally but significantly is also celebrated on the 2008 calendar of the Red Cloud Indian School on the Pine Ridge, South Dakota Reservation as the day "Custer Defeated at Little Big Horn."

It is also significant that her "landmark" case was first adjudicated in 1963 just five years *before* Congress passed the Indian Civil Rights Act of 1968 (82 Stat. 77), and became one of the main reasons, among others, a Congressional Committee chaired by Senator Sam J. Ervin, Jr. of North Carolina spent some seven years of hearings and discussions regarding the constitutional, moral, and religious issues it raised either directly or tangentially.

Surprisingly, the facts of the case as well as all the legal maneuvers which were involved are relatively simple to understand. Colliflower was sentenced to a fine of $25.00 or five days in jail. She chose the five days in jail, and proceeded to bring a habeas corpus proceedings in federal district court, claiming that under the due process clause of the Fifth Amendment of the *Constitution of the United States* and the Fourteenth Amendment her confinement was illegal and a violation of her civil rights, because she was not provided with counsel, nor given any trial, nor confronted with any witnesses against her, and because the action of the tribal court was taken summarily and arbitrarily. The District Court decided it did not have jurisdiction over the matter and could not issue a writ of habeas corpus because the defendant/appellant was committed by a tribal court. This decision was appealed to the federal Court of Appeals (9th cir.) which on February 4, 1965, reversed the order of the District Court and remanded the case for further proceedings, claiming that the federal judiciary did have jurisdiction to order a writ of habeas corpus. Recall that this case was brought before the ICRA was enacted, an act which specifically allows the defendant to bring a habeas corpus proceeding.

The case of *Madeline Colliflower v. John Garland, Sheriff of County of Blaine, Montana* (342 F.2d 369, 9th Cir., 1968) is particularly interesting not only because it concerns an injustice—albeit a relatively minor one—against an Indian, but also because the appellate court in announcing its decision had to review the whole legal history from Justice John Marshall's early decision in *Worcester v. Georgia* (1832) to the 20th century regarding the peculiar status tribal entities are thought to have in our society, from being "Nations," "dependent nations," or "wards of the Nation," to *not* being Foreign States, nor States, but having a status "higher than that of states," to being merely "wards" or "dependent communities."

The Court doubted the view expressed in *Native American Church of North America v. Navajo Tribal Council* (272 F.2d 131, 10th Cir. 1959), in *Talton v. Mayes* (163 U.S. 376, 1896), and by Felix Cohen, *Handbook of Federal Indian Law,* 124, 181 (1942) that the *U.S. Constitution* applies to Indians only when it expressly binds them, or is made binding by treaty or act of Congress. The Court, however, disclaimed any intention of requiring tribal courts to comply with every constitutional restriction which is applicable to federal or state courts, and the Court specifically denied that the Fourteenth Amendment requiring due process applied to or "bound" tribal courts. Despite these apparently conflicting statements the Court of Appeals concluded that

> In spite of the theory that for some purposes an Indian tribe is an independent sovereignty, we think that, in the light of their history it is pure fiction to say that the Indian courts functioning in the Fort Belknap Indian community are not in part, at least, arms of the federal government. . . . Under these circumstances, we think that these courts function in part as a federal agency and in part as a tribal agency, and that consequently it is competent for a federal court in a habeas corpus proceeding to inquire into the legality of the detention of an Indian pursuant to an order of an Indian court. (Washburn. 183–85; Deloria, 1971, 194.)

Obviously the judge's, and the Court's, decision appears to be a *non-sequitur*, a conclusion which does not follow from the given premises, except in the logic of material implication where any statement follows from a false one or a pair of contradictory statements. I doubt that that degree of sophistication is involved in this case. The other alternative is that the conclusion follows but only if some missing or unstated premise is provided or made known by inference. Unfortunately in *Colliflower* it is not made explicit, nor is there even a hint except that we are told that it is "pure fiction" to suppose that Indian courts are not in part arms of the federal government.

Perhaps a look at other similar cases, some cited in this case and others occurring later, will provide the missing assumption. The justice cites, for example, *Talton v. Mayes* (163 U.S. 376) which was decided in 1896, some sixty seven years earlier. In that case a Cherokee Indian was tried in a special court of the Cherokee Nation, convicted of the murder of another Cherokee Indian within Cherokee Territory, and sentenced to be hanged. He appealed in a Federal District Court seeking a writ of habeas corpus, alleging that he was deprived of his liberty without due process of law and was in confinement in contravention of both the *Constitution of the United States* and the laws and constitution of the Cherokee Nation. The indictment under which he was tried was returned by a jury of only five grand jurors which was an insufficient number under the Constitution and laws of the United States and inadequate according to the laws of the Cherokee Nation which required a grand jury of thirteen.

The Court recognized that the Cherokee tribe had a system of law which predated the *U. S. Constitution*, and that although not a State was nonetheless a separate people with the power of regulating their own internal social relations in a way that was not inconsistent with the values set forth in the *U.S. Constitution*. It decided, therefore that the Bill of Rights and in particular the Fifth Amendment did not apply to decisions of Cherokee tribal courts.

Of course this decision involved a much more serious offense than occurred in *Colliflower*, and occurred long before later cases which have given increased state jurisdiction over crimes committed on reservations and the passage of federal statutes such as Public Law 280 which grants to certain states both criminal and civil jurisdiction over acts committed within specific Indian territories. However, like the court in *Colliflower* the court seemed to think that self-government and tribal autonomy were values worth supporting particularly if, as in this case, the Indian court was, in terms of its own values and customs, fair and just in its treatment of Indian wrongdoers.

In the case of *Native American Church of North America v. Navajo Tribal Council* (272 F.2d 131, 10th Cir. 1959) also mentioned in *Colliflower*, the Native American Church brought suit in Federal District Court against the Navajo Tribal Council. The officers of the Church sought to enjoin the enforcement of an ordinance adopted by the Tribal Council making it an offense to sell, use, or possess within Navajo country the bean known as peyote and imposing both imprisonment and a fine for its violation. It was alleged that the Church's right to use the substance which has a narcotic effect violated the Church's rights under the First, Fourth, and Fifth Amendments of the *U.S. Constitution*.

In deciding this case which involves quite obviously serious questions regarding the religious freedom of individual Indians in relation to their tribal government, the Court adopted the following position:

> The First Amendment applies only to Congress. It limits the powers of Congress to interfere with religious freedom or religious worship. It is made applicable to the States only by the Fourteenth Amendment. Thus construed, the First Amendment places limitations upon the action of Congress and of the States. But as declared in the decisions hereinbefore discussed, Indian tribes are not states. They have a status higher than that of states. They are subordinate and dependent nations possessed of all powers as such only to the extent that they have expressly been required to surrender them by the supreme law of the land, but it is nonetheless a part of the laws of the United States. Under the philosophy of the decisions, it, as any other law, is binding upon Indian nations only where it expressly binds them, or is made binding by treaty or some act of Congress. No provision in the Constitution makes the First Amendment applicable to Indian nations nor is there any law of Congress doing so. It follows that neither, under the Constitution or the laws of Congress, do the Federal courts have jurisdiction of tribal laws or regulations, even though they may have an impact to some extent on forms of religious worship. (Deloria, 1971, 120–121.)

One might wonder why the Amendments in the Bill of Rights do not apply to cases involving Indian tribes or tribal members as they do to state jurisdictions. An examination of the following portion of the Fourteenth Amendment makes it clear that they do not.

> No State shall make or enforce any law which shall abridge the privileges or immunities of citizens of the United States; nor shall any State deprive any person of life, liberty, or property, without due process of law; nor deny to any person within its jurisdiction the equal protection of the law. Amendment XIV (1868)

No mention is made of Indians or Indian jurisdictions. At the time of its passage in 1868 Indians had not been regarded in the law as citizens of the United States. That change of status came officially and for all Indians in 1924 by the passage of the Indian Citizenship Act. Given that history and the flood of cases such as the ones just recounted involving issues of individual deprivations of liberties the *Constitution of the United States* was enacted to prevent, it becomes clear why Senator Erwin's Committee thought it necessary to fill the gap and pass the Indian Civil Rights Act in 1968, one century after Amendment XIV was adopted. It was the clearly perceived, although unspoken, view in the *Colliflower* case that no rational system of justice could allow the kind of injustice which Mrs. Colliflower suffered. It would be, as the judge said, a "pure fiction" to assume that our judicial system was not empowered to deal with such an obviously wrongful treatment of an American citizen. In short, although the judge hesitated to put it this way, the missing ingredient in his reasoning was the moral aspect of the case. Washburn puts the matter quite correctly when he says that "Cases such as the Colliflower case indicate the degree to which courts will condition their decisions on the basis of non-legal assumptions. . ." although he seems to regret this aspect of judicial reasoning when he admits that "That the attitude can dominate court decisions as it has too often dominated legislative halls and executive agencies, and that it can be phrased in terms of a moral duty, constitutes another of the tragic elements in American Indian policy." (Wilkinson, 185) Many another student of American Indian legal history would perhaps not regret this fact, but rejoice in the admission that besides mere precedent and arbitrary legislation, some acknowledgement of moral factors are in fact ingredients of many a legal decision.

Whatever the motivation for the passage of the ICRA, it did attempt to extend the protections of human liberty to the Indian population which the Bill of Rights of the *U.S. Constitution* has done for all other citizens. Unfortunately, the total effect was less than it could have been because of the case of *Santa Clara Pueblo v. Martinez* (1978) which was previously discussed. (See Chapter X.) Bordevich, it might be recalled, said that *Martinez* made the ICRA in effect a "dead letter," and quotes Ramon Roubideaux, who was the first Indian certified to practice law in South Dakota, as saying "*Martinez* set Indian law back thirty years." (Bordewich, 89.) Wilkinson, commenting on the case, says that the ICRA "imposes free exercise [of religion], due process, and equal protection constraints on tribes but *Santa Clara [Pueblo v. Martinez]* refused to imply any federal remedies . . . Thus *Santa Clara* results in the anomaly of a federal civil rights act that provides only very limited federal remedies to enforce it," (Wilkinson, 114).

The solution of this quagmire of legal decision making and an almost total frustration of civil rights for Indians is pretty obvious. Either repeal the holding in *Martinez* or make the U. S. Bill of Rights directly applicable to tribal courts as it now is applicable to the state courts by means of the Fourteenth Amendment. Instead of "No State shall make . . ." perhaps it could be made to read "No State or Tribal Council shall make . . ." An amendment of the Fourteenth Amendment or to the Constitution itself might be necessary although the politics of that approach might cause more difficulties than simply new legislation or judicial action to that effect. But how else can Indians be assured of their rights as American citizens?

Consider another type of injustice which American Indians have suffered. When Lieutenant Colonel Custer in 1874 invaded the Black Hills in contravention of the Fort Laramie Treaty of 1868, and arrogantly ordered his band to play the Seventh Cavalry's fight song, *Garryowen*, he acquired, besides "Curley" and "Long Hair," another nickname by the Sioux Indians residing there. They called him "Chief of all the thieves" and his route "the Thieves Trail." (Debo, 236.) Announcing to the whole world that gold was to be found there, he was directly responsible for such an influx of mining prospectors and entrepreneurs, who by the Treaty were required first to obtain permission from the Indians to enter, that President Grant had to rescind his order to the Army to prevent any non-Indians from entering Paha Sapa. Grant then authorized a Commission to offer to buy the lands from the Sioux for $6 million, an offer which the Indians rejected. According to the version of the event given by Stephen E. Ambrose (394–95), the Indians represented by Chiefs Spotted Tail and Red Cloud (Sitting Bull and Crazy Horse refused even to come to the meeting) offered to sell the Black Hills for $7 million. The interpreter misunderstood or misstated the amount as $70 million, which the white commissioners promptly rejected as impossible. They in turn offered $6 million for the outright purchase of the land or $400,000 annually for the mineral rights, and subsequently offered a mere $50,000 for the unceded Powder River hunting grounds. Even Red Cloud who desperately wanted his people to accommodate the white conquerors was appalled by the offer. In 1876 Congress, embarrassed by the Grant Administrations failure to buy the Black Hills, passed a resolution not to provide treaty guaranteed rations to the Sioux until they agreed to sell Paha Sapa—the so-called "sell or starve" option. The Sioux response: *Paha Sapa kin Wiyopeya Unkiyapi kte sni yelo!* or "We will not sell the Black Hills!" In 1877 the United State Government passed the Black Hills Act, without tribal consent or vote, which transferred sole ownership of the Black Hills to the United States.

Before the U.S assumed ownership, George Hearst in 1877 purchased a prospecting claim (from whom is unclear, but presumably from Fred and Moses Manuel and their partner Hank Harvey who filed their Homestake claim April 9, 1876) for $70,000 which he had borrowed from his mother. He established the Homestake Gold Mine from which until its closure in 2002 produced many billions of dollars of gold bullion. Much of the land in what has sometimes been labeled "Custer Country" was opened to homesteaders, although after 1916 all mineral rights to homesteaded land were retained by the government. In 1951 uranium was found near Edgemont. In 1971 Homestake Mining Company obtained a license to remove minerals including uranium from 1,040 acres of state land in Custer and Fall River counties. In 1977 Union Carbide announced that it had discovered a deposit of uranium in Craven Canyon, Black Hills National Forest. In 1978 it was reported that there exist more than 8 million pounds of uranium, worth $800 billion in

South Dakota, mostly in the Black Hills.(source: The Crazy Horse Advocate Martin, SD; http://www.geocities.com/ crazyoglala/pahasapa. html?20069).

The Black Hills Claims case brought in 1942 was dismissed by the U. S. Court of Claims. In 1946, however, the Indian Claims Commission Act passed allowing monetary compensation for lands taken illicitly from Indians. In 1977 the United States offered the Sioux Nation $17.5 million, the value of the land in 1876, plus $450,000 in damages and 5% interest on the value of land, making a grand total of $106 million. Offer rejected. In 1980 in a Supreme Court decision written by Justice Blackmun, the Lakota Indians were awarded $105 million for the Black Hills. The settlement is refused by all the Sioux Tribal Councils, but the money is deposited and collecting interest annually. It is estimated that the amount by 1996 had reached to more than $350 million. (Bordewich, 230.) Now with the recent discoveries of uranium in the Black Hills their financial value should run into the billions.

But besides the purely financial or material value of the Black Hills, the Sioux attribute a certain spiritual value to the place. Some even suppose that the Sioux Nation sprung into life in the Black Hills, perhaps out of Wind Cave. It would take an extremely credulous person to believe such a claim. Most historians of America Indian history and Indian migrations within the continent of North America are firmly of the belief that the Lakota/Dakota speaking tribes were forced by Chippewa/Ojibwa tribes of Minnesota, Wisconsin, and Canada to seek food (mainly buffalo) and shelter in the plains states of North and South Dakota, Nebraska, Wyoming, and Montana.

Setting apart the superstitious belief regarding primeval origins, it remains an indubitable fact that the Sioux and the Cheyenne who preceded them in the Black Hills, as well as other tribes, think of it as a holy place not to be disturbed by miners, railroads, white settlers, or soldiers of Custer's 7th Cavalry. Given that emphasis on the spirituality of Paha Sapa, it is surprising that the Indians allowed or in any way encouraged either the sculpture on Mt. Rushmore or that of Crazy Horse. In the first case, Congress and President Coolidge gave the Indians no choice whatsoever in the matter, not even in deciding whose faces should be enshrined there. In the latter case, however, some ten Indian chiefs approved the Crazy Horse Monument even though the defacing of the mountain and the obliteration of the natural environment there when completed will be of even greater magnitude than the damage created by the Rushmore Memorial. It is really incredible, almost inexplicable, and totally unjustified given the Sioux reverence for the entire area. I am sure this comparison has been made before but I cannot help thinking that what happened to the Black Hills is comparable, in thought at least, to the leveling of the ancient city of Jerusalem. It would be regarded as a calamity not only by Jews and Muslims, but also by Christians. The spiritual values which many persons regard the Black Hills and Jerusalem to have cannot be quantified in terms of dollars and cents. So how can Indians be compensated not only for their material but also for their spiritual loss of Paha Sapa?

My first thought on the subject is to give back to the Indians all the properties in the Black Hills associated with the name of Custer. On further reflection I realize how practically impossible that would be. The long time residents of Custer City would be outraged, although they perhaps would need to be reminded that the land on which they reside, in the opinion of the United States Supreme Court, was stolen from the Indians in 1877. However, I fail to see why deeding over the Black Hills Forest, a federal possession, or Custer State Park, a South Dakota property, would be very difficult. The now private homesteaded property is the main obstacle.

Other options have to be considered. One would be to make the entire Black Hills subject to tribal jurisdiction and give to the tribes all tax revenues collected. Or if that option is again found intolerable, perhaps an arrangement to share jurisdiction and tax revenues with the State of South Dakota would be more equitable. As earlier federal Indian legal cases have shown, concurrent jurisdiction, e.g., with respect to liquor sales on reservations, has proved to be feasible. So why not with respect to the entire scalplock of the Black Hills?

Another option would be to give the Indians the millions (or billions as the case may be) of dollars which the Supreme Court has already granted them (which so far has not by itself alone been deemed sufficient), but also return to them all public (state and federal) properties for their exclusive use and legal control. And just as the Honeywell Corporation has generously given 1200 acres of Black Hills land back to the Oglala Sioux (see *The Crazy Horse Advocate,* op.cit), perhaps public pressure could be put on other corporate interests such as those of Westinghouse and Union Carbide to do the same.

The Hearst Homestake Mining Company has a special obligation to make reparations. Its acquisition of the Black Hills mining properties which occurred prior to the transference of the entire Black Hills to the ownership of the United States would appear to be as much a theft as the Supreme Court declared the entire Congressional Act of 1877 to be, and the aesthetic damage to the Black Hills was and continues to be enormous. See the picture of one of the great holes they left, some of which extended some 8000 feet below the city of Lead, South Dakota. The motivation of the Hearst Corporation appears to have been nothing short of pure greed, evincing an indifference to Indian sensibilities that is unmatched by the practices of other corporations. After George Hearst's death in 1891, his widow, Phoebe, made substantial contributions to the educational and cultural life of Lead, establishing the first kindergarten in the West, and constructing a Opera House and Recre-

Hearst Homestake Gold Mine. Lead, South Dakota.

ation Building. Use of the swimming pool, bowling alley, meeting rooms, and library are free. (Homestake Visitor Center, http://www.homestaketour.com/history.html.) Unfortunately these contributions, though notable, pale when compared to the billions of dollars worth of gold extracted from the Hills in contravention of the Treaty of 1868 and taken from their true owners, the American Indians.

The position of the Sioux Nation, however, cannot be "all or nothing." Not even Red Cloud was willing to go that far (although perhaps Sitting Bull was). But times have radically changed and the legal doctrine of adverse possession (i.e. if you claim another's land long enough and pay taxes on it, it's yours) may now become a serious legal ploy against the interests of the Indians. A compromise of some sort is inevitable, unless the United States public is prepared to see further onslaughts like the AIM protests and armed conflicts which occurred in the 1970's on the Pine Ridge Reservation and at Wounded Knee.

Another injustice besides the denial of basic civil rights and the theft of the Black Hills is related to the General (Dawes) Allotment Act of 1877, which was integral to the scalping of the Great Sioux Nation. It aimed to give individual Indians their own private property, while breaking up tribally owned land and making more land available to settlers and miners in the Black Hills and elsewhere in the Great Sioux Reservation of 1868, which consisted of half of what is now South Dakota.

A string was attached to the grant of individual parcels of land. The lands were held in trust by the U.S. Government for a period of 25 years. During that time the Indians could use but could not sell their property. As a consequence many Indian allottees, who had no interest in farming, leased out their land to non-Indians. The money received from these leases was to be placed in an Individual Indian Money (IIM) Trust to be managed by the Government, namely, the Department of the Interior and the Treasury Department, and annual checks were to be sent to the individual Indian landowners.

For over 100 years now the IIM Trust has been woefully mismanaged. In some memoirs my mother wrote regarding her first job at the Rosebud Agency Office, she describes the "terrible mess" her predecessors had left behind in the Individual Indian Money Department as early as 1920.

> On the desk I took over, we found letters with currency and checks, lease money on Indian land, that had not been taken up in the accounts. The Washington office sent two auditors out to audit the books. . . They were there at least three months checking over the books. Consequently the halls were jammed with Indians waiting for their checks. When Mr. Buntin [the Superintendent] was in Washington, they purchased loose ledgers and bookkeeping machines. . . They had 6 or 7 ledgers of individual Indian accounts which were about 8 or 9 inches thick, written in long hand. This all had to be transferred to the new loose leaf system. . . . This took long hours of work; I often went to work after supper. Well, in three months we were able to take care of the Indians' needs and everything was running smoothly.

She does not mention that for all her after-hours work (from 5 or 6 p.m. to 9 p.m.) she was not paid an extra red cent! She managed to straighten out the books on one reservation, but think of all the others who were not fortunate enough to have such a conscientious employee. And of course the situation regarding the IIM accounts in Washington, D.C. must have been many times as bad as that at Rosebud. The Native American Rights Fund reports more recently on the IIM trusts, which are still in a "terrible mess," in its Spring 2002 publication entitled "Justice" as follows:

> Accurate account balances cannot be provided to Native Americans who are legally entitled to this money and count on it for basic necessities .In fiscal 1995, there were 15,599 duplicate accounts with the same number. Innumerable accounts are routinely and arbitrarily closed. More than 54,000 accounts containing more than $46 million were for individuals without accurate addresses or names.

In June, 1996, NARF (Native American Rights Fund) filed a class action suit on behalf of all present and past individual trust beneficiaries. Judge Royce C. Lamberth ordered the federal government to produce all records pertaining to the plaintiffs representing the class. The government agreed to do so but failed to produce the document. Judge Lamberth then held the then Secretary of Interior, Bruce Babbitt, Secretary of Treasury, Robert Rubin, and Kevin Gover, Assistant Secretary of Indian Affairs, in civil contempt of court. During this first phase of the trial which then ensued, from June 10 to July 21, 1999, the government admitted that it had failed in its fiduciary responsibilities. The court ordered a full accounting of the money belonging to the individual Indian plaintiffs. No action was brought at this time regarding tribal interests. The government appealed the decision to the U.S. Court of Appeals for the District of Columbia Circuit which unanimously upheld the lower court ruling. However, it wasn't until mid-February of 2002 that the government started sending checks to the beneficiaries of the IIM Trust. The second phase of the case, which will involve an accounting to the individual Indian trust beneficiaries, has yet to be scheduled for trial. The government currently has some $500 million in approximately 500,000 accounts, in addition to the more than $400,000 which flows through these accounts each year. Justice requires that the entitled beneficiaries get what is theirs, by law and by moral right.

Two other problems involving issues of justice facing contemporary Indians, concern the status of the reservation system and the advisability of basing the future welfare of the American Indian on an economy propelled, in part at least, by a reliance on gaming revenues. The problems can be dealt with together since in many respects they are related. Indian gaming, as now established by federal law, cannot exist except on Indian lands, either federally recognized reservations or other lands held in trust for Indians. On the other hand, reservations and other trust properties can hardly be sustained without some economic stimulus or activity, and the one that is now most promising of success is casino gaming. But are either of these two institutions—reservations and casino gambling—really in the long run beneficial to the tribes or detrimental to their interests, since both appear to rest, historically and morally, on the white man's inordinate greed for land and money?

Reservations didn't just happen. They grew out of early nineteenth century attempts to move all eastern tribes to west of the Mississippi. As Francis P. Prucha reports, "But generally the tribes were unwilling to remove entirely . . . It was necessary to allow reduced tracts of land to be retained by the tribes and in addition to set aside reserves for special individuals." (Prucha, 136.) Larger reserves were included in treaties with the Wyandots, Shawnees, Seneca, and Ottawas. The term "reserves," it is interesting to note, was used in this connection much as the Canadians today use it to refer to their "reservations." After the War of 1812, during which many Indians sided with the British, there were increased demands by white settlers for cessions of Indian lands either by brute force or by means of treaties, which was the method preferred by the politicians. The idea, first suggested by Jefferson, was that the removal of Indians to west of the Mississippi be an *exchange* of lands. (Prucha, 146.) During the 1820's and 1830's many tribes, the Choctaws and the Creeks initially, were given the opportunity to look over the lands reserved for them in Indian Territory, and to decide whether they approved of the exchange. Many did, but others such as the Cherokees were unwilling to move, and as we all know, that led to a forced evacuation and march to the reserves or reservations within Indian Territory where later western tribes such as the Nez Percé and the Apaches were exiled and in effect held prisoner.

After the Civil War, President Grant initiated a "Peace Policy" toward Indians, with the intent of preventing the total extermination of Indians by Generals Sherman, Sheridan, and Custer. He instituted a wholly revamped system of reservations, better organized than before, aimed at "civilizing." "educating," and "Christianizing" the western bands of Indians. The policy effectively failed to achieve these goals, but at least Grant is to be credited with the attempt to assure Indian survival.

The Dawes Allotment Act of 1887, as we have already seen, did its best to destroy the Great Sioux Reservation by breaking it up into six smaller reservations and granting allotments to individual Indians. During the 1950's a "termination" policy was adopted and about 100 small reservations were liquidated. The motivation during the Eisenhower years was not so much the attempt to acquire more Indian lands for white settlers, but to absolve the U.S. Government of its obligations under past signed treaties. The termination effort was itself terminated during the Nixon administration. As we have observed in Chapter X there has been an increase of self-governance on the reservations, but at the same time there has arisen rampant alcoholism on practically all reservations and other domestic calamities such as ill-health, poor housing, underemployment, school drop outs, etc. Only the relatively few tribes who have been able to profit from gaming casinos have escaped these tragic circumstances.

So the question is still relevant: Are reservations on the whole beneficial or detrimental to the tribes who live on them. It has been estimated that about one-half of the enrolled members of the tribes live on or adjacent to a reservation (Getches, Wilkinson, and Williams, 15); the others seek employment and well being in urban centers. Yet that number is considerable, and should there be a return to the reservations by those now absent as a result of improved conditions, it would constitute a major population increase.

One argument which has frequently been used to justify the abolition of reservations is that reservations, at least during the Grant administration, were never intended to become permanent institutions but only temporary arrangements to prevent the extinction of the Indian race. Since the threat of extinction no longer exists, reservations have lost their purpose and so should be eliminated. An added bonus would be that the U. S. Government would save a great deal of money in annuity and other payments.

Another argument is that reservations now serve only to create mal-contents, foster the "loafing habit," to use one of my high school principal's expressions, and encourage "time wasters," to cite another of my teacher's expressions. Indians living on the reservation, it is claimed, have become "dependents," and not in the sense used in early documents such as the Delaware Treaty of 1778 of being merely the recipients of traded goods from the U.S. Government, but merely as servile creatures waiting for a handout. As Vine DeLoria, Jr. has pointed out, "Dependency, as the term is used today, implies a group of lazy, dirty Indians loafing the day away at the agency." (DeLoria, 2461969, 39.) The implication is that no one, and especially no tribe of Indians, has the right to be so unemployed at the expense of the federal government. Presumably, the elimination of reservations status would provide incentives to action and industry which do not now exist.

A third argument is that the treaties by which many of the reservations were created, including the 1868 Fort Laramie Treaty, which created the Great Sioux Reservation, are no longer valid. Promises then made can be broken because times have changed so radically that it is no longer obligatory or practical for U.S. Government to keep its word. The bottom line is that reservations no longer serve the interests of either Indians or the Government.

Arguments in favor of keeping reservations range from moral to legal to economic ones. The chief moral argument for retaining reservations is that their creation occurred because of promises made by the U.S. Government, and even as children are aware promises should be kept. Many of the current reservations came into existence by executive order rather than by explicit treaty, but underlying the dissection of the Great Sioux Reservation was the Fort Laramie Treaty of 1868 which was sworn to by both representatives of the U.S. and by numerous Indian tribes. And as Justice Hugo Black has put it, "Great nations, like great men, should keep their word." (Getches, Wilkinson, and Williams, 29.) Or as Charles F. Wilkinson has expressed it,

> These old laws emanate a kind of morality profoundly rare in our jurisprudence. It is far more complicated than a sense of guilt or obligation, emotions frequently associated with Indian policy. Somehow, those old negotiations—typically conducted in but a few days on hot, dry plains between midlevel federal bureaucrats

> and seemingly ragtag Indian leaders—are tremendously evocative. Real promises were made on those plains, and the Senate of the United States approved them, making them real laws. My sense is that most judges cannot shake that. Their training, experience, and, finally, their humanity—all the things that blend into the rule of law—brought them up short when it came to signing opinions that would have obliterated those promises. (Getches, Wilkinson, and Williams, 32); Wilkinson, 121–22.)

If the motive for dismantling reservations is simply the desire to reduce governmental cost, then the only consistent behavior on the part of the government would be to give back to the Indians all that has *illicitly* been taken from them. Some land transactions between white persons and Indians, as far back as the beginning of this country were, as Jefferson himself attests (Jefferson, 96), perfectly legal, but others were not, the prime example of which is the Black Hills which Congress itself acquired for the U.S., but which the Supreme Court has declared was wholly unwarranted and contrary to existing law.

Although the threat of annihilation may have been the primary purpose for establishing reservations during the Grant administration, it was also thought of as a means of achieving peace for the nation as a whole, and for educating Indians for a life in the greater society of which they were a part. Making citizens of all Indians born in this country in 1924 only increased the need for such education and although that task has been bedeviled by controversy and many wrong-headed ideas about Indian education, nonetheless Red Cloud, Spotted Tail, and other chiefs were well within their legal and moral rights to condone and promote attempts, on as well as off reservations, to improve the education of their young, and so give them the tools with which to deal successfully with white society.

The supposed laziness of Indians should not be confused with either lethargy or incompetence. If the reservations assigned to the Indians had not been in such desolate and hardly inhabitable regions, successful farming could have become their means of livelihood. As Councilman Crawford White, referred to earlier (above, Ch. I), said, "The white man placed us here and told us to survive . . . but he took away much of our water so white settlers could feed their crops." How can one be expected to farm or even survive if the government siphons off the water? The whole point of BIA policy now is supposedly to promote economic development on reservations, not retard it, and the advent of casino gaming appear to provide a measure of hope for the future survival of the tribes. Of course not all reservations are well situated, i.e., near enough to large population centers, to conduct large scale, high stakes, gaming. Fortunately there are other industries which certain tribes, if not all, can pursue on reservation lands to enhance their economic well-being.

The Klamath, Menominee, and Red Lake Chippewas have developed timber industries on their reservations; some tribes have discovered minerals on their lands; other tribes have gone into the production of energy, either by means of wind or hydro-electric turbines; the Choctaw of Mississippi have started a greeting card company; the Blackfeet of Montana manufacture writing instruments. The Sycuan band of Kumeyaay Indians now owns the Ulysses S. Grant Hotel in San Diego.

All these and other industrial efforts on the part of reservation Indians are noteworthy and laudable, but the raw fact remains that with a few exceptions Indians on reservations on average live below or near the poverty level; health conditions have improved in recent years and yet, except for cardiovascular disease, the mortality rates of the following diseases are higher than the national average: tuberculosis, alcoholism, diabetes, pneumonia, and influenza. In addition, the mortality rates are higher for accidents, homicide, and suicide. (Getches, Wilkinson, and Williams, 17.)

Coupled with all the other reasons not to live on a reservation why would any Indian want to do so? Justice Hugo Black considered precisely this question and his answer is as relevant today as it was in 1960.

> It may be hard for us to understand why these Indians cling so tenaciously to their lands and traditional tribal way of life. The record does not leave the impression that the lands of their reservation are the most fertile, the landscape the most beautiful or their homes the most splendid specimens of architecture. But this is their home—their ancestral home. There, they, children, and their forebears were born. They, too, have their memories and their loves. Some things are worth more than money and the costs of a new enterprise. (*Federal Power Comm'n v. Tuscarora Indian Nation*, 362, U.S. 99, 142. 1960.)

Casino gaming offers a hope that the situation on reservations will change for the better. At least that is what the promoters of Indian casinos are claiming. Yet some tribes do not have reservations or lands near large population centers where successful casinos might be built. But the latest California compacts with four southern California tribes may suggest that that particular problem might be surmounted. Future state-federal compacts might all be required to offer a percentage of earnings to tribes not so privileged.

Whether such a change in state-tribal compacts would be sufficient to solve all the problems of living on a reservation, however, is very problematic. Many critics of casinos, including the Navajo who, until very recently did not tolerate on-reservation gaming, point to the possibility that non-Indian casinos may by their sheer numbers put Indian casinos out of business. Or the public may grow tired of them. Given the penchant for gambling that most Americans seem to have, the latter seems unlikely. And the growth in numbers of casinos may not pose a problem either. All one has to do is to drive through or stay over in a town in Nevada, say Winnemucca, which is named for the Paiute Indian Chief, and note not only that the large Casino/Hotels have plenty of customers, but so also do the smaller casinos to be found in practically every restaurant, bar, and motel in town. The desire to gamble is apparently so pervasive of the local and traveling public that no amount of competition will ever put the Indian casinos out of business.

The casinos, however, may have within themselves the seeds of their own destruction. Alcoholics, of which there are many on practically every reservation, tend also to be gambling addicts (see article by Candi Cushman, http:// www.gamblingwithgoodlife. com/ candi.html, who quotes various sociological studies). On reservations where alcoholism as well as poverty is the norm, the addition of an addiction to gambling can devastate not only family income, but also family unity and the welfare of children. It can also be the direct cause of automobile and other accidents, as well as profound depression leading to suicide.

Milton Shirleson, a one-time Navajo medicine man, now Christian pastor, who has counseled roughly 150 Indian families hurt by gambling addiction, is quoted by Candi Cushman as saying:

> Long before the advent of casinos . . . ancient Navajo folklore warned of this new monster. Elderly Navajos still tell stories about a mysterious character called The Gambler who tricked Navajo people out of everything they owned and made them slaves until the people over-came him and shot him to heaven on a rocket. To this day, the story goes, The Gambler bides his time in heaven, waiting for an opportune moment to exact revenge.

In the same article Cushman also quotes Edison Wauneka, chairman of the Navajo Public Safety Committee, who in reference to The Gambler says:

> The prophecy was he'll be back. So a lot of people say, "What's the use of trying to go against it? . . . But I look at it differently If we fight against it, if we unite to oppose gaming, I don't care if this [is] prophecy or legend. The People can prevail.

There will always be fatalists who think that nothing can alter the future course of affairs, but hopefully there will also be persons such as Wauneka, Shirleson, and Cushman who retain a stalwart belief in the freedom of the human will. The advice they all give, however, not only to Navajos but to all American Indians is *Beware the Gambler!*

Beware the Gambler!

Table of Cases

Arizona v. California, 373 U.S. 546 (1963) 127

California v. Cabazon Band of Mission Indians, 490 U.S. 202 (1987) 141–142

Central Machinery Co. v. Arizona State Tax Commission, 448 U.S. 160 (1980) 129

Cherokee Nation v. Georgia, 30 U.S. (5 Pet.) 1 (1831) 136

Colliflower v. Garland, 343 F.2d. 369 (1968) 125, 145–148

Federal Power Cmm'n v. Tuscarora Indian Nation, 362 U.S. 99 (1960) 159

Johnson v. McIntosh, 21 U.S. (8 Wheaton 592) 543 (1823) 89, 136

Kennerly v. District Court, 400 U.S. 434 (1971) 128

Lone Wolf v. Hitchcock, 187 U.S. 553 (1903) 137

McClanahan v. Arizona State Tax Commission, 411 U.S. 164 (1973) 128

Menominee Tribe of Indians v. United States, 391 U.S. 404 (1968) 128, 135

Mescalero Apache Tribe v. Jones, 411 U.S. 145 (1973) 128

Mitchell v. United States, 9 Peters 746, 9 L.Ed. 283 (1835) 89

Moe v. Confederated Salish and Kootenai Tribes, 425 U.S. 463 (1976) 128

Montana v. Blackfeet Tribe of Indians, 471 U.S. 759 (1985) 129

Morton v. Ruiz, 415 U.S. 199 (1974) 128

National Farmers Union Ins. Cos. v. Crow Tribe of Indians, 471 U.S. 845 (1985) 129
Native American Church of North America v. Navajo Tribal Council, 272 F.2d.131 (1959) 147
New Mexico v. Mescalero Apache Tribe, 462 U.S. 324 (1983) 129
Oliphant v. Suquamish Indian Tribe, 435 U.S. 191 (1978) 128
Poafpybitty v. Skelly Oil Co., 390 U.S. 365 (1968) 127
Rice v. Rehner, 463 U.S. 713 (1983) 129
Santa Clara Pueblo v. Martinez, 436 U.S. 49 (1978) 125–127, 129, 149
Seminole Tribe v. Florida, 517 U.S. 44 (1996) 142
Seymour v. Superintendent, 368 U.S. 351 (1962) 127
Shortbull v. Looking Elk, 677 F.2d. 645 (1982) 126
Salem v. Bartlett, 465 U.S. 463 (1984) 129
Talton v. Mayes, 163 U.S. 376 (1896) 125, 147
Tooahnippah v. Hickel, 397 U.S. 598 (1970) 128
United States v. Dann, 470 U.S. 39 (1985) 130
United States v. Dion, 476 U.S. 734 (1986) 130
United States v. Kagama, 18 U.S. 375 (1886) 136
United States v. Mazurie, 419 U.S. 544 (1975) 128
United States v. Sioux Nation of Indians, 448 U.S. 371 (1980) 130
United States v. Wheeler, 435 U.S. 313 (1978) 129
Washington v. Confederated Tribes of Colville Reservation, 447 U.S. 134 (1980) 129
Williams v. Lee, 358 U.S. 217 (1959) 127
Worcester v. Georgia, 31 U.S. (6 Peters) 515 (1832) 136

References

Adams, David Wallace, *Education for Extinction: American Indians and the Boarding School Experience, 1875–1928.* Lawrence, Kansas: U. Press of Kansas, 1995.

Ambrose, Stephen E., *Crazy Horse and Custer: The Parallel Lives of Two American Warriors.* N.Y.: Anchor Books, 1996.

Bordewich, Fergus M., *Killing the White Man's Indian: Reinventing Native Americans at the End of the Twentieth Century.* N.Y.: Doubleday, 1996.

Brown, Dee, *Bury My Heart at Wounded Knee: An Indian History of the American West.* N.Y.: Bantam, 1972.

Canby, William C., Jr., *American Indian Law in a Nutshell,* 4th ed. St. Paul: West, 2004.

Cohen, Felix, *Handbook of Federal Indian Law.* Washington, DC: Government Printing Office, 1942.

Custer, George Armstrong, *My Life on the Plains,* ed. by Milo Milton Quaife. Lincoln: U. of Nebraska Press, 1966.

Debo, Angie, *A History of the Indians of the United States.* Norman: U. of Oklahoma, 1970.

DeLoria, Vine, Jr., *Custer Died for Your Sins: An Indian Manifesto.* N.Y.: Avon, 1969.

——. ed. *Of Utmost Good Faith.* San Francisco: Bantam, 1971.

Getches, David H., Wilkinson, Charles F., and Williams, Robert A. Jr., *Cases and Materials on Federal Indian Law,* 3rd ed. St. Paul: West, 1993

Graham, W. A., *The Custer Myth: A Source Book of Custeriana.* N.Y. Bonanza Books, 1993.

Hagan, William T., *Theodore Roosevelt and Six Friends of the Indians.* Norman: U. of Oklahoma Press, 1997.

Hobbes, Thomas, *Leviathan.* N.Y.: Liberal Arts, 1958.

Holmes, O.W., Jr., "Path of the Law," in *The Essential Holmes*, ed. Richard A. Posner. Chicago: U. of Chicago Press, 1992.

Jefferson, Thomas, *Notes on the State of Virginia*, ed. William Peden. N.Y.: Norton, 1954.

——. *Writings of Thomas Jefferson,* ed. Merrill D. Peterson. N.Y.: Library of America, 1984.

Johnson, Michael G. and Hook, Richard, *Encyclopedia of Native Tribes of North America* Buffalo, NY: Firefly Books, 2007.

Jones, W.T., *A History of Western Philosophy: Hobbes to Hume, 2nd ed.* N.Y.: Harcourt, Brace, and World, 1969

Kant, Immanuel, *Groundwork of the Metaphysics of Morals*, tr. H.J. Paton. N.Y.: Harper, 1964.

——. *Critique of Practical Reason*, tr. T.K. Abbott. London: Longman's, 1873, reprinted 1968.

——. *The Metaphysics of Morals, Part I: Metaphysical First Principles of the Doctrine of Right* in Immanuel Kant, *Practical Philosophy,* tr. & ed. Mary J. Gregor, *The Cambridge Edition of the Works of Immanuel Kant*. Cambridge U. Press, 1996. Herein referred to as Kant's *Philosophy of Law* or *Rechtslehre*.

——. "Of the Motives of Pure Practical Reason," in the *Critique of Practical Reason,* tr. T.K. Abbott. London: Longmans, 1873.

Lee, Bob, *The Black Hills After Custer*. Virginia Beach, VA: The Donning Company Publishers, 1997.

Leland, Joy, *Firewater Myths: North American Indian Drinking and Alcohol Addiction.* New Brunswick, NJ: Rutgers Center of Alcohol Studies, 1976.

Light, Steven Andrew and Rand, Kathryn R. L., *Indian Gaming and Tribal Sovereignty: The Casino Compromise.* Lawrence, KS: U. Press of Kansas, 2005.

Locke, John, *Second Treatise of Civil Government: An Essay Concerning the True Original, Extent, and End of Civil Government* in *Two Treatises of Government.* N.Y.: Hafner, 1947.

Mason, W. Dale, *Indian Gaming: Tribal Sovereignty and American Politics.* Norman: U. of Oklahoma Press, 2000.

McGregor, James H., *The Wounded Knee Massacre: From the Viewpoint of the Sioux.* Minneapolis: Lund Press, 1940.

Medicine, Beatrice, *Drinking and Sobriety Among the Lakota Sioux.* Lanham, MD: Altamira Press, 2007.

Monaghan, Jay, *The Life of General George Armstrong Custer.* Lincoln: U. of Nebraska Press, 1959.

Mulholland, Arthur, *Kant's System of Rights.* N.Y.: Columbia U. Press, 1990.

Nerburn, Kent, *Chief Joseph and the Flight of the Nez Percé.* San Francisco: Harper Collins, 2005.

Peterson, Merrill D., ed. *Writings of Thomas Jefferson.* N.Y.: Library of America, 1984.

Powers, William K., *Oglala Religion.* Lincoln: U. of Nebraska Press, 1977.

Prucha, Francis Paul, *American Indian Treaties: A History of a Political Anomaly.* Berkeley: U. of California, 1994.

Quaife, Milo Milton, Historical Introduction, Custer, *My Life on the Plains.* Lincoln: U. of Nebraska Press, 1966

Roosevelt, Theodore, *The Winning of the West*. (New York, 1889–96), I-III.
Sheehan, Bernard W., *Seeds of Extinction: Jeffersonian Philanthropy and the American Indian.* N.Y.: Norton, 1974.
Sprague, Donovin Arleigh, *Images of America: Pine Ridge Reservation.* Charleston, SC: Arcadia Publishing, 2004.
——. *Images of America: Rosebud Sioux.* Charleston, SC: Arcadia Publishing, 2005.
Stange, Mary Zeiss, "Living with the Ghosts of the Indian Wars," http://www.hcn.org. Vol.38, No.2, Feb.6, 2006.
Stewart, Edgar I., *Custer's Luck.* Norman: U. of Oklahoma Press, 1955.
Vestal, Stanley, *Sitting Bull: Champion of the Sioux.* Norman: U. of Oklahoma Press, 1932.
Washburn, Wilcomb E., "The Moral and Legal Justification for Dispossessing the Indians," in *Seventeenth Century America: Essays in Colonial History*, ed. James Morton Smith. Chapel Hill: U. of North Carolina Press, 1959.
——. *Red Man's Land/ White Man's Law: A Study of the Past and Present Status of the American Indian.* N.Y.: Charles Scribner's Sons, 1971.
Welch, James, with Stekler, Paul, *Killing Custer: The Battle of the Little Bighorn and the Fate of the Plains Indians.* N.Y.: Norton, 1994.
Whittaker, Frederick, *A Complete Life of General George A. Custer*, vol.2: *From Appomattox to the Little Big Horn.* Lincoln: U. of Nebraska Press, 1993.
Wilkinson, Charles F., *American Indians, Time, and the Law: Native Societies in a Modern Constitutional* Democracy. New Haven: Yale U. Press, 1987.
Yenne, Bill, *Sitting Bull.* Yardley, PA: Westholme Publishing, 2008.

Index

Adams, David Wallace, 67
Adams, John, 37, 88
Adams, John Quincy, 37
alcoholism, firewater theory, 114–15
Ambrose, Stephen, 84, 105
American Indian Movement (AIM), 43
Anthony, Susan B., 36
Appomattox, viii, 99
arithmetic, 28, 68–69
Articles of Confederation, 37

Babbitt, Bruce, 155
Battle of the Little Big Horn, 33, 55–58, 79, 98
Battle of the Washita, 44, 57, 109
Beard, Dewey (Wasu Maza), 62
Belknap, W.W., 55, 79
Benteen, Frederick W., 56, 109
Big Foot, Chief, 59–60
Bill of Rights, U.S. Constitution, not applicable to decisions of Cherokee Tribal Court, 147; not applicable to Indian courts, 125, 149; *Indian Bill of Rights,* 124
bingo, church sponsored, 140–41; high stakes, 141
Black Hills (Paha Sapa), 34; sale of, 51–52; claims case, 151
Black Hills Act of 1877, 57, 80
Black, Justice Hugo, 159
Black Kettle, Chief, 44
blood quantum, 132
Bono, Cher, vii, 133
Borglum, Gutzon, 28, 36, 56
Borglum, Lincoln, 28
Bordewich, Fergus M., 126, 133–34
Bozeman Trail, 44, 48
buffalo slaughter, viii, ix, 48
Buntin, Superintendent, 10
Bureau of Indian Affairs (BIA), 12
Bush, George W., 71
Bush, George H.W., 106
Butterbrodt, Dr. Mark, 17–18, 30

California: Public Law 280, 144; proposition to expand casinos, 143–44
Campbell, Ben Nighthorse, 106, 133
Canadian Indian Schools, 70–71
Cantrell, Fay, 25, 28
Carlisle Indian Industrial School, 64, 73–74; football teams, 75
Carrington, Henry B.,44
Carson, Kit, 84
casino gaming, 140–44
casinos, Indian, *Fire Rock,* 140; *Foxwood Resort & Casino*, 142; *Mystic Lake*, 31; *Little Six,* 31

Chandler, Zachariah, 79
Chivington (Sand Creek) Massacre, 43–44
Civil War, viii-ix, 3–4, 36
Clark, William, 4, 37
Clemens, Samuel L. *See* Mark Twain
Cleveland, Grover, 80
Clymer, Heister, 54
Cody, William F. (Buffalo Bill), 4, 83
Cohen, Felix, 124, 127, 136–37
Cohen, Morris, 124
Collier, John, 86, 123
Constitution, U.S., pre-dated by Cherokee system of law, 136, 147
Coolidge, Calvin, 21, 36
Cornwallis, General Charles, 3
Crazy Horse, 39–40, 46, 65, 79
Crazy Horse Memorial, 39–40, 151
Crook, George, 54, 57, 81
Cushman, Candi, 160
Custer, Elizabeth, 56, 104, 111
Custer, George Armstrong, viii-ix, 36, 41; compared to TheodoreRoosevelt, 39; musical entry to Black Hills, 50; deception of Cheyenne Chiefs, 45; discovery of gold, 51; return to Fort Abraham Lincoln, 53; dress compared to George C. Patton's, 53; arrested, 111; gets command free from General Terry, 56; attitude towards Blacks and Indians, 57, 101; Carlisle beats Army (& Custer), 75; compared to Pickett, 98–99; court-martialed, 109; evades Stanley and Terry, 109; displeases Grant, 110; orders slaughter of 900 ponies, 57; shoots own horse, 112

Dakota, dialect, 17–18, 131
Davis, Alonzo Grant, 3–4, 83, 87
Davis, Herbert C., 14
Davis, Herbert P., 3, 4–8
Davis, John, 3
Davis, Laura Bradshaw, 3
Davis, Nellie Mae (Post), 4, 8–12, 15, 32, 35, 154
Dawes General Allotment Act of 1887, 80, 85
DeLoria, Vine, Jr., 16–20, 30, 42–43, 80, 91
DeLoria, Vine, Sr., 17, 67
deportment, 25, 28
Descartes, Rene, 139
Drake, Walter Sir, 138

education, English, 47; moral, 28, 68; Pratt's theory of, 70
Eisenhower, Dwight, 123
Evans, Beverly, 24
Evans, Helen, 24
Evans Plunge, 35

federal Indian Law, political policies regarding, 130
Fetterman Massacre, 44
Fifth Amendment, 145, 147
First Amendment, 147–48
Fort Abraham Lincoln, 49, 53, 55
Forsyth, James W., 61
Fourth Amendment, 147
Fourteenth Amendment, 145; due process not applicable to tribal courts, 148
Franklin, Benjamin, 114

Gallup, New Mexico, 116
gaming, term preferred over gambling, 140
Garryowen, 50, 150
Geronimo, Chief, 39
Gibbon, John, 54–55, 104
gold, discoveries of in CA, CO, MT, 49–50; in Black Hills, 51; Custer's report of, 51
Gover, Kevin, 155
Grant, Fred D. (son of president), 50
Grant, Orville (or Orvil), brother of President), 54, 110

Grant, Ulysses S., viii, 3, 15, 41; visited by Red Cloud, 64; peace policy of, 57, 66; treatment of Custer, 110–11; orders Indians to return to reservations, 54, 79
Great American Desert, The, 101–3
Great Sioux Agreement of 1889, 81, 83
Great Sioux Reservation, 46; map, 47
Guantanamo, inmates compared to Pratt's at St. Augustine, 71

Hampton Virginia Normal and Industrial School, 73
Hancock, Winfield Scott, 44
Harrison, Benjamin, 83
Harrison, William Henry, 92
Hawkins, Benjamin, 41
Hayes, Rutherford B., 20
Hayward, Richard, 131
health, Indian, 14, 17, 115–16, 156, 160
Hearst, George, 150
Hearst, Phoebe, 152
Henry, Patrick, 114
Hillerman, Tony, 123
Holmes, Justice Oliver W., 139
Homestake Gold Mine, 150, 152

Ickes, Harold L., 86, 123
Indian Citizenship Act, 22, 115
Indian Constitutional Rights Act, (ICRA), 124–27
Indian Gaming Regulatory Act, (IGRA), 140; Classes I, II, III, 140–41; compacts with states, 142
Indian Reorganization Act of 1934, 86, 123
Individual Indian Money Trust (IIM), 154–55
injustices, habeas corpus restriction, 145–47; land theft, 81, 85–86, 123, 153; of Black Hills, 51, 80, 151–52; denial of due process, 148; IIM accounts, 154–55; breakup of GSR, 83; forced removals, 92
innate right to freedom, 95
Iron Horn, Chief, 53

Jackson, Andrew, 37, 87, 115, 139
James, William, 90, 100, 109
Jefferson, Thomas, 4–5, 37, 57, 64–65, 88–91, 138–39
Joseph, Chief, 40–41
Joyner, Reverend, 15

Kant, Immanuel, 92, 94–97, 139; theory of property, 95–97
Knox, Henry, 114

Lakota, 30–31, 64, 70, 131
Lamberth, Judge Royce C., 155
Lame Deer Cheyenne Indian Reservation, 8, 10
Lemen, Mary R., 28
Lee, Robert E., 98
Lewis, Meriwether, 4, 377, 41, 87
Lincoln, Abraham, 37–38, 113
Lieutenant Bullhead, 122
Little Big Horn Battlefield National Monument, 106
Locke, John, 92; theory of property, 93–94
Lone Wolf, Chief, 44

Man-Afraid-of-His-Horses, 43
Marshall, Chief Justice John, 89, 136
Marshall, Justice Thurgood, 126
McCellan, George B., 112
McGregor, James H., 59, 65
McLaughlin, James, 81, 121–22
Means, Russell, 43
Menominee Tribe, 135
Miles, Nelson A., 58–59, 65
Monroe, James, 79
Morgan, Thomas J., 69
mumblety-peg, vii
Mount Rushmore Memorial, 36; pictured on report card, 27–28

Native American Rights Fund (NARF), 154–55
New Ulm Minnesota Massacre, 38
Nineteenth Amendment, 22–23

Oglala, Sioux, 131

paternalism, 117–18
Pickett, George, 98–99
Pine Ridge Reservation, 6, 17, 21, 24
Pinkerton, R. S., 31, 33
Pipe-on-Head, Norman, 32
Pocahontas, 37, 76
Post, Nellie. *See* Nellie M. Davis
Pratt, Richard H., 65, 68, 70–76, 88
prohibition, of liquor to Indians, 7, 114, 117; repeal of law, 115, 123
property, Locke's theory of, 93–94; Kant's, 95–97; Jefferson's, 92–93, 94, 97

Quaife, Milo Milton, viii

Rain-in-the-Face, 53
Ramsey, Alexander, 85
Red Cloud, Chief, 43, 48, 59, 64, 67, 69, 89
Red Tomahawk, 122
Reifel, Benjamin, 23–24, 30
religion, Indian, 16, 18; Sitting Bull's view of, 121
Reno, Marcus, 56, 104, 110
reservations, federally recognized, 134; terminated, 135; history of, 155; arguments for abolition of, 157; arguments in favor of, 157–58
right of pre-emption, 89, 138–39
Rogers, Will, vii, 133
Roosevelt, Franklin Delano, 86, 123
Roosevelt, Theodore, 19, 38–39, 49, 68, 87; compared to Custer, 39; *The Winning of the West,* 38, 49, 88
Rosebud Reservation, 5, 13, 24
Rubin, Robert, 155
Rushmore, Charles E., 36

Sacagawea, 41
St. Francis Indian School, 20
St. Francis Mission, 20
Santana, Chief, 44
Scabby Face, Alex, 32
scalping, viii; defined, 84; European practice, 84; Navajos non-scalpers, 84; Sioux custom, 84–85; Crazy Horse an exception, 54; whether Custer scalped, 104–5
schools, Indian boarding, 20; Canadian, 70–71; county, 24–25, 42; compared, 28, 67; blessed by Red Cloud, 64; teachers, 67
Shakopee, Chief, 31; town of, 31
Shannon County *Course of Study,* 28, 42
Shaw, Robert Gould, 98, 100, 109
Sheehan, Bernard W., 92
Sheridan, Philip H., 41, 44, 49–50, 66, 74, 110
Sherman, William T., 41, 43, 57, 66, 74
Shirleson, Milton, 160
Short Bull, Chief, 31, 60
Shortbull, Thomas, 126
shivaree, 14
Sicangu Sioux (Rosebud), 131
Sibley, Henry H., 85
Sinte Gleska. *See* Spotted Tail
Sioux, origin of name, 131
Sitting Bull, 40–41, 46, 48, 61, 65, 79, 120–21, 131
Skinner, B.F., 74
sovereignty, tribal, 136; limited, 137; power versus rights, 138
Spotted Tail, Chief, 20, 64–65, 69
Stanley, D.S., 49
Stange, Mary Zeiss, 62–63
Stewart, Edgar I., 40
Stowe, Harriet Beecher, 72

Taylor, E. B., 43
Temple, Shirley, 21
termination policy, 123–24
Terry, General, 56, 104

Thorpe, James, 75, 133
Thorpes, Pine Ridge High School, 76
tribes, federally recognized (FR) and not federally recognized (NFR), 134
Twain, Mark, ix, 133

voting rights, 22–23

Wakantanka (God, Great Spirit), 19
Warren, G. H., 50
Washburn, Wilcomb E., 119, 122
Washington, Booker T., 73
Washington, George, 36–37, 88
Washita. *See* Battle of the Washita
Wauneke, Edison, 160
Wheeler-Howard Act, 86. *See also* Indian Reorganization Act
Whipple, Henry Benjamin, 38, 72–73
White Clay, Nebraska, 116
White, Crawford, 5, 158
Whitside, Samuel, 60–61
Wilkinson, Charles F., 135–36
Winnemucca, Chief, 31, 160
Winnemucca, Nevada, 153, 160
Wounded Knee Massacre, 33, 65
Wovoka, Medicine Man (religious leader), 60

Ziolkowski, Korczak, 39

About the Author

Philip E. Davis is Professor of Philosophy, Emeritus, at San Jose State University. He and his wife, Laura, split their time between San Jose, California and Charlottesville, Virginia. He has written or edited books and articles on Ethics, Philosophy of Law, and the History of Modern Philosophy. His special interests, besides the plight of the American Indian, lie in the thought of the philosopher, William James; the jurist, Oliver Wendell Holmes, Jr.; America's greatest novelist and a philosopher in his own right, Mark Twain; and Thomas Jefferson, the author of our *Declaration of Independence*.